Basic IBM Mainframe Assembly Language Programming

Kevin C. Ó Kane, Ph.D.
Professor Emeritus
Department of Computer Science
The University of Northern Iowa
Cedar Falls, Iowa 50614-0507

The author can be reached at
kc.okane@gmail.com
www.cs.uni.edu/~okane

Other books by this author on Amazon & Kindle

The Mumps Programming Language
Omaha
The Constitutional Convention of 2022

Front cover: Beach Point, Barnstable, MA

Cut & Paste text copies of the examples used in this book may be
downloaded from:

http://threadsafebooks.com/

Table of Contents

List of Tables

List of Figures

1. Preface

1.1 Goals

The goals of this book are to give the reader a basic understanding of the IBM mainframe architecture from the perspective of the instruction set and to serve as an assembly language text for introductory college courses in computer organization. The text originally began as a set of class notes for an undergraduate computer science course on Computer Organization. Over the years it has been expanded and enlarged to the text you see here.

Many computer architectures have come and gone in the past 50 years and only a relatively few designs remain in production today. In the early 90s, the rapid rise of new computer manufacturers such as Sun, Apollo, Silicon Graphics, MIPS, Digital Equipment Corporation (DEC), Tandem, Prime, Data General, SDS (also knows as XDS) and many more seemed to point to a world without the mainframes. All these, however, are now gone along with several legacy mainframe manufacturers such as NCR, Burroughs, Control Data Corporation, General Electric, Honeywell, RCA and UNIVAC (UNIVAC and Burroughs merged to form UNISYS which still manufactures a limited line of mainframes).

In the not too distant past it was assumed that the rise of microprocessors and server centric computing would bring an end to the age of *big iron* as mainframes were referred to.

But the IBM mainframe architecture has endured and, rather than declining, is growing in popularity and becoming the platform of choice for such rapidly emerging technologies as cloud computing and virtualization. As the world chokes in an energy and space intensive microprocessor based server sprawl, a single mainframe system can deliver thousands of virtual Linux platforms for a fraction of the cost in dollars, energy and space.

While most computer users are familiar with the ubiquitous Intel x86 microprocessor line, few have had any experience with another widely used architecture, the IBM mainframe.

As the baby-boom generation programmers who wrote the billions of lines of mainframe assembly language code since the introduction of the IBM 360 in 1964 are beginning to retire, the demand for replacement programmers to maintain, support and extend these applications as well as develop new ones is growing rapidly. To those looking to meet this need, this text will serve as a basic road map and introduction to the fundamentals of the architecture.

The other purpose of this book is to provide an alternative assembly language platform for introductory college level courses in computer organization. From an academic perspective, the question of which architecture to use when teaching assembly language poses several challenges. Once, the answer was simple: the Intel x86 assembly language. However, as the Intel x86 architecture has grown into an intricate and unwieldy collection of exceptions and special cases, its value as a viable pedagogical platform in an introductory course has diminished.

So, in many cases, the choice defaults to an assembly language based on a simulator for a non-existent, abstract RISC based architecture. Although this gives students a taste of a machine level architecture, it provides little real experience that can actually be used to further their careers and is often regarded by students themselves as an exercise in futility.

For most, the basic impediment to teaching mainframe assembly language is actual access to a mainframe. While many colleges and universities use mainframes, students seldom have access.

This text, however, is designed to be used in combination with a free, portable, open sourced, GPL licensed, Java based z390 mainframe emulator and macro assembler which permits a student to assemble and execute IBM mainframe programs on a Windows, Linux or Apple based computer (see: http://www.z390.org/). Other options also exist including the Hercules System/370, ESA/390, and z/Architecture Emulator (http://www.hercules-390.eu/).

For the most part, this text mainly concentrates on the basic architecture in order to keep to a manageable size suitable for a section in a college course in computer organization. While there are a number of instructions and features not discussed here, these are, for the most part, logically intuitive extensions of the basic architecture or of a substantially more application or operating system specific nature.

1.2 History and Background

The current series of IBM mainframes (System z13) had its roots in 1964 with the introduction of the IBM 360 Series. This was conceived as a family of computers designed to meet a wide range of applications both scientific and commercial. The system was intended to be a collection of compatible computers ranging from small, basic machines to large, enterprise level configurations. Originally the architecture was based on a 24 bit address space (16 MB, massive at the time) and a basic 32 bit word size. This has evolved in the latest models that support for 64 bit addressing and data.

Prior to the introduction of the 360 Series, IBM, as was the case with other vendors, sold machines with differing architectures and computing power to different markets. There was the IBM 1620, a small machine often used for scientific calculations, the IBM 1400 series designed to replace unit record devices in commercial settings, and the high end 7000 series for large commercial and scientific applications.

These architectures were mainly incompatible with one another and used widely varying primitive operating systems. They were based on six bit characters with either fixed or variable word sizes. Some had hardware supported binary and floating point instructions while others did calculations on varying length binary coded decimals. Some had multiply and divide instructions while others did not. The 1620 did arithmetic by means of lookup tables! This chaos extended across all manufacturers at the time. The concept of software portability was just that. A concept.

So, in the 1960s the idea of a single architecture that would meet the needs of all users, both business and scientific, was new and daring. The design and implementation effort was considerable. It required a completely new architecture with many new features and a massive programming effort to create a totally new operating system and related software. Basically, IBM bet the company on the project.

But the experiment proved wildly successful and IBM quickly became the dominant player in the mainframe market. Even to this day, all models of the IBM mainframe, even the most recent, are backwards compatible with the earliest of the 360 series. That is, a program written for the oldest and smallest 360 Model 20 will run on the largest system made today.

With each new generation, additional facilities and instructions were added. These are referred to as *architecture levels*. At present, there are three architecture levels named: *ARCHLVL1* (ESA 390 systems), *ARCHLVL2* (zSeries and System z9 machines), and *ARCHLVL3* (System z10 machines). These reflect additions to the original design which are, for the most part, consistent with the original design.

The z/Architecture was introduced in 2000 and is represented by machines in the z9 through z13 families. It is a 64 bit CISC (complex instruction set computer) architecture with sixteen 64/32 bit general purpose registers, sixteen 64 bit floating point registers, sixteen access registers, and sixteen 64/32 bit control registers. The access registers permit multiple address spaces to be utilized by a program and, due to their complexity, are not discussed in this text. In some models, the high order 32 bits of the 64 bit registers can be used as a second set of 32 bit registers.

Memory addressing is implemented as either 24, 31 or 64 bits and all modes can be used concurrently depending upon the application program's needs. Much legacy programming is still operates in 24 bit mode. This book will deal mainly with 31 bit addressing as this is the primary mode supported by the z390 emulator and assembler.

As of this writing, the z390 emulator corresponds to the system definition as found in the *IBM z/Architecture Principles of Operation,* Document Number: SA22-7832-03 (05/04/04) which is available online from IBM.

The initial models in the 360 series were known as models 20, 30, 40, 44, 50, 65, 67, 75 and 91, 95 and 195. These systems, depending on model, featured multiple independent input/output channels, multiple processors, dynamic address translation (more commonly known as MMU now), cache memory and varying memory bandwidths. Memory was originally made from ferrite cores and limited to a maximum of 1 megabyte. Some models were hardwired and some were microcoded. Operating systems ranged from a simple disk based operating system for low end hardware to the resident O/S 360 that supported multiple concurrent tasks. All input output was centralized through the operating system. By means of memory protect keys and supervisor/problem states, programs were isolated from one another. The operating systems were mainly priority event driven. The use of a spooling subsystem permitted unit record input/output queues to be managed by the operating system rather than by separate computers as had been the case in previous systems. The original 360 series supported hardware binary, floating point (optional depending on model) and decimal arithmetic (optional depending on model).

In 1970, the 360 series was supplanted by the 370 series which expanded on the original base to include enhanced support for virtual memory, additional instructions and larger memory. The 80s and 90s saw the architecture continue to evolve with the System 390 (September 1990) and the Z series (in 2000 for models z900 and z990) followed by the System Z moniker in 2006.

Typical of a CISC (Complex Instruction Set Computer) architecture, the IBM mainframe has several addressing modes and instruction lengths. In a RISC (Reduced Instruction Set Computer), on the other hand, instructions are generally of one size and nearly all operations are done register to register. On the IBM mainframe, however, operations may be performed register to register, register to memory, or memory to memory.

The IBM mainframe architecture normally uses the EBCDIC (Extended Binary Coded Decimal Interchange Code - see chapter 25) to represent characters rather than the more common ASCII-7 (American Standard Code for Information Interchange, 7 bit). Note, however, that EBCDIC has changed over the years and there are likely to be differences between this table and others you may find online.

2. Quick Overview of Numbering Systems

2.1 Binary

The IBM mainframe, as is the case with all modern digital computers, internally codes all numbers, characters, instructions, pointers and so forth in binary. Binary is based on only two digits: 0 and 1.

When writing a number, each position, reading from right to left, represents a higher power of two as shown in Table 1. This table shows the equivalence between the first 16 binary, decimal, hexadecimal numbers (base 16, see next section). The value of a number in binary is, for each position in the binary number consisting of a 1, the sum of the values of the powers of 2 corresponding to those positions.

Binary	Decimal	Hexadecimal	Power of 2
0000	0	0	
0001	1	1	2^0
0010	2	2	2^1
0011	3	3	2^1+2^0
0100	4	4	2^2
0101	5	5	2^2+2^0
0110	6	6	2^2+2^1
0111	7	7	$2^2+2^1+2^0$
1000	8	8	2^3
1001	9	9	2^3+2^0
1010	10	A	2^3+2^1
1011	11	B	$2^3+2^1+2^0$
1100	12	C	2^3+2^2
1101	13	D	$2^3+2^2+2^0$
1110	14	E	$2^3+2^2+2^1$
1111	15	F	$2^3+2^2+2^1+2^0$

Table 1 Numbering Systems

Any decimal integer can be represented exactly by a corresponding binary number. For example, the binary series which is equivalent to the decimal number 10 is:

$$1*2^3 \ (8_{10}) \ + \ 0*2^2 \ (4_{10}) \ + \ 1*2^1 \ (2_{10}) \ + \ 0*2^0 \ (1_{10})$$

or, stated as a single number: 1010_2

2.2 Hexadecimal

Internally, most modern computer memories are organized as a collection of 8 bit bytes grouped into words of 4 or 8 bytes each. However, when printing the contents of memory, representing bytes and words in binary digits yields inconveniently long sequences of 1s and 0s. To avoid this we use hexadecimal, that is, base 16 numbers.

Note that a byte consists of two 4 bit fields and that in 4 bits you can count from 0 to 15 (16 values). A single digit hexadecimal number also ranges from 0 to 15. Thus, you can represent the contents of any byte with exactly 2 hexadecimal digits, one digit for the first 4 bits and a second digit for the second 4 bits. Since 16 is itself a power of two, conversion between a digit in base 16 and the corresponding value in base 2 and back is a trivial substitution as can be seen in Table 1.

In order to use base 16 we need 16 symbols to represent the digits of the numbering system (the equivalent of 0_{10} through 15_{10}). For the first 10 digits, we use the same symbols as the decimal numbering system (0 through 9). For digits above nine, representing the values 10_{10} through 15_{10}, we use the upper (or lower) case letters A, B, C, D, E, and F (see Table 1).

When we have a binary numbers longer than 4 bits, we group the bits, from right to left, into groups of 4 bits each and then substitute the equivalent hexadecimal code. Thus, if you have a binary number such as:

```
0000 0001 1010 1011 0010 0011 0111 1000
```

Using the values from Table 1, it can be represented in hexadecimal as:

0000	0001	1010	1011	0010	0011	0111	1000	bin
0	1	A	B	2	3	7	8	hex

Conversion from a hexadecimal number (also referred to as *hex*) to its equivalent decimal notation, however, requires more work because there is a fundamental change in base. When you want the decimal equivalent of a hex number, you need to sum, in decimal, the contributions of each hex digit. To do this, a table such as that in Table 2 is useful. It gives, for each hex digit position (up to an eight digit hex number), the contribution of that digit expressed in decimal.

Thus, if you have the hexadecimal number such as: 01 AB 23 78, it can be converted to decimal by adding the positional decimal equivalent contributions of each of the hex digits as shown in Table 3.

Conversion from decimal to hex can be done in several ways. The easiest, if you have Table 2, is to successively find the largest decimal value in the table and subtract it from the decimal number until the remainder is zero. Each corresponding hex digit from each step is retained as part of the final answer. If you skip a hex position in the process, insert a zero in the skipped position. For example, if you have the decimal number: 123456789, this can be rendered in hex as shown in Table 4.

Hex			Decimal Equivalent by	Digit Position				
0	0	0	0	0	0	0	0	0
1	268435456	16777216	1048576	65536	4096	256	16	1
2	536870912	33554432	2097152	131072	8192	512	32	2
3	805306368	50331648	3145728	196608	12288	768	48	3
4	1073741824	67108864	4194304	262144	16384	1024	64	4
5	1342177280	83886080	5242880	327680	20480	1280	80	5
6	1610612736	100663296	6291456	393216	24576	1536	96	6
7	1879048192	117440512	7340032	458752	28672	1792	112	7
8	2147483648	134217728	8388608	524288	32768	2048	128	8
9	2415919104	150994944	9437184	589824	36864	2304	144	9
A	2684354560	167772160	10485760	655360	40960	2560	160	10
B	2952790016	184549376	11534336	720896	45056	2816	176	11
C	3221225472	201326592	12582912	786432	49152	3072	192	12
D	3489660928	218103808	13631488	851968	53248	3328	208	13
E	3758096384	234881024	14680064	917504	57344	3584	224	14
F	4026531840	251658240	15728640	983040	61440	3840	240	15
Col	8	7	6	5	4	3	2	1

Table 2 Hex to Decimal Conversion Chart

Of course, another method to convert between binary, decimal and hexadecimal is to use the programming mode of a calculator such as that which comes with many Linux distributions.

from table col 8 corresponding to	0	add	0	(0)
from table col 7 corresponding to	1	add	16777216	(1)
from table col 6 corresponding to	A	add	10485760	(A)
from table col 5 corresponding to	B	add	720896	(B)
from table col 4 corresponding to	2	add	8192	(2)
from table col 3 corresponding to	3	add	768	(3)
from table col 2 corresponding to	7	add	112	(7)
from table col 1 corresponding to	8	add	8	(8)
		sum	27,992,952	

Table 3 Conversion from Hex to Decimal

The above discussion concerns positive integers only. Negative integers and numbers with fractional parts (floating point numbers) and binary coded decimals (BCD) numbers will be discussed later.

from 123456789   subtract   117440512 7_{16} (col 7)   leaving   6016277
from 6016277   subtract   5242880 5_{16} (col 6)   leaving   773397
from 773397   subtract   720896 B_{16} (col 5)   leaving   52501
from 52501   subtract   49152 C_{16} (col 4)   leaving   3349
from 3349   subtract   3328 D_{16} (col 3)   leaving   21
from 21   subtract   16 1_{16} (col 2)   leaving   5
from 5   subtract   5 5_{16} (col 1)   leaving   0

Result: 07 5B CD 15_{16}

Table 4 Decimal 123456789 to Hex Conversion

3. Data Types

Modern computers use a variety of data types to represent and manipulate information. These include character and bit strings, addresses, signed and unsigned binary integers, signed floating point numbers, binary coded decimals and so forth. For each of these, there are hardware instructions to operate on instances of the data.

In this section, we review the basic data types and how they are represented in the IBM mainframe. Some of these data types are used on all computers, from cell phones to mainframes, while others are peculiar only to larger systems.

3.1 Arithmetic Data

The IBM mainframe architecture supports three basic arithmetic data types: integer binary, floating point and packed decimal. When we say *supports*, we mean that there are specific hardware instructions to perform arithmetic on these data types. The details of each data type are:

Signed binary integers of either 2, 4, or 8 bytes in length. Negative numbers are coded in *2s complement* notation (see section 3.1.2).

Unsigned binary integers of either 4 or 8 bytes in length. The unsigned data type treats each binary value as a positive entity. It can never be negative.

Binary coded decimals up to 16 bytes (31 digits) long. In this data type, calculations are done in decimal rather than binary. It is used mainly in financial calculations. This data type is also referred to variously as BCD, Packed, Packed Decimal or Decimal.

Floating point numbers of either 4, 8 or 16 bytes length with either binary, hexadecimal or decimal radices. A floating point number, as opposed to a fixed point number (binary integers and BCD numbers are fixed point numbers), has a varying number of significant digits part and an exponent. It is subject to round off error but is useful for scientific calculations.

3.1.1 Packed and Zoned Decimal Format Data

Printable numbers are represented in what is called *zoned format*, often referred to simply as *zoned*, which is a close cousin to *packed decimal* format. In zoned format, the high order 4 bits of each byte are always ones (F_{16}) and the low order 4 bits are the digit portion. The high order 4 bits of a byte are called the *zone* and the low order 4 bits are called the *digit*.

When text digits are read from a keyboard or other input device, each digit is encoded in zoned format. Thus, if you type 1234 into an EBCDIC (See Chapter 25) terminal, internally this will be coded as the four bytes: F1 F2 F3 F4 (Note: in the z390 emulator, ASCII PC keyboard input is automatically converted to EBCDIC). Likewise, if you send F1 F2 F3 F4 to a display device or printer, the decimal number 1234 will appear.

Zoned decimal format is a character string data type and you cannot perform arithmetic on it directly. To perform arithmetic, a zoned format number must be converted to packed decimal (BCD), binary or floating point format. Conversion to packed format is the easiest and quickest and you can perform arithmetic directly on packed decimal numbers.

On an IBM mainframe, packed format decimal numbers are represented as strings of from 1 to 16 bytes. Each byte contains two binary coded decimal digits except for the final byte which consists of a 4 bit digit (high order bits) and a 4 bit sign (low order bits). Thus, on an IBM mainframe, in BCD you can represent numbers up to 31 digits in length (the sign must always be present). The shortest BCD number is one byte (one digit) and the longest is 31 digits. The decimal numbers 0 through 9 are represented in packed format by their binary equivalents 000_2 through 1001_2 (hex codes 0 through 9).

In a BCD number, the codes 1100_2, 1010_2, 1111_2 and 1110_2 (hex digits C, A, F, and E) are legal only in the sign position and indicate that the number is *positive* while the codes 1101_2 and 1011_2 (hex digits D and B), also only legal in the sign position, indicate a *negative* number. These are easy to remember: the positive codes are CAFE and the negative are DB (as in debit). Any code is equally valid but C and D are the defaults for positive and negative, respectively, used by the system.

You convert from zoned decimal to packed decimal by removing the zones and packing two digits into each byte except for the last which gets one digit and a sign code. There is an instruction for this called, not surprisingly, the PACK instruction.

Table 5 gives several examples of zoned and packed numbers (in this table, $4E_{16}$ is the hex code for a printable plus sign and 60_{16} is the code for a printable minus sign). As you can see, packed decimal numbers are merely an encoding of the original decimal number with a sign appended to the end.

Zoned Decimal	Packed Decimal	Packed Decimal Size
4E F1 F2 F3 F4 F5	12 34 5C	3 bytes
60 F1 F2 F3 F4 F5	12 34 5D	3 bytes
4E F1	1C	1 byte

Table 5 Example packed decimal numbers

One advantage of packed decimal is that it allows for numbers with many digits of precision. Another advantage is that character versions of numbers (such a user might type on a terminal) can be converted very quickly to packed decimal and, likewise, packed decimal can be quickly converted back to printable numeric text.

The main disadvantage of packed format is that arithmetic operations themselves are relatively slow and thus they are not suitable for procedures which require many mathematical steps. Furthermore, while BCD numbers have a great number of digits of precision, they do not have the large range of magnitude often required for scientific calculations.

To convert a zoned decimal number to signed or unsigned integer binary, you must first convert the zoned number to packed. Conversion between packed and binary is handled by the CVB (converts packed to binary) and CVD (converts binary to decimal) instructions.

Conversion from packed decimal to printable zoned decimal is handled mainly by the ED (edit) instruction and, to a lesser extent, by the UNPK (unpack) instruction. Additional details are described in Chapter 17.

Conversion to floating point is considerably more complex and is done by software with some hardware assistance.

3.1.2 Binary Integers and 2s Complement

While packed decimal is mainly used in financial transactions, for more common programming arithmetic, signed binary numbers are the data type of choice.

The value of a decimal number is the sum of the values of each decimal position in the number (1, 10, 100, 1000 ...) times the value at the position (0 through 9). Thus, the number 123 is 1*100 + 2*10 + 3*1.

Similarly, positive binary integers are strings of zeros and ones whose overall value is the sum of the values of the positions times the value at the position (0 or 1). The value of the positions of a binary number, expressed in decimal, are the powers of two: 1, 2, 4, 8, 16, 32 and so forth. Table 6 gives the powers of two from 0 to 31 (32 altogether), the corresponding bit pattern, and the decimal equivalent.

	1	2^0	0000 0000 0000 0000 0000 0000 0000 0001
	2	2^1	0000 0000 0000 0000 0000 0000 0000 0010

4	2^2	0000 0000 0000 0000 0000 0000 0000 0100
8	2^3	0000 0000 0000 0000 0000 0000 0000 1000
16	2^4	0000 0000 0000 0000 0000 0000 0001 0000
32	2^5	0000 0000 0000 0000 0000 0000 0010 0000
64	2^6	0000 0000 0000 0000 0000 0000 0100 0000
128	2^7	0000 0000 0000 0000 0000 0000 1000 0000
256	2^8	0000 0000 0000 0000 0000 0001 0000 0000
512	2^9	0000 0000 0000 0000 0000 0010 0000 0000
1024	2^{10}	0000 0000 0000 0000 0000 0100 0000 0000
2048	2^{11}	0000 0000 0000 0000 0001 1000 0000 0000
4192	2^{12}	0000 0000 0000 0000 0001 0000 0000 0000
8 192	2^{13}	0000 0000 0000 0000 0010 0000 0000 0000
16 384	2^{14}	0000 0000 0000 0000 0100 0000 0000 0000
32 768	2^{15}	0000 0000 0000 0000 1000 0000 0000 0000
65 536	2^{16}	0000 0000 0000 0001 0000 0000 0000 0000
131 072	2^{17}	0000 0000 0000 0010 0000 0000 0000 0000
262 144	2^{18}	0000 0000 0000 0100 0000 0000 0000 0000
524 288	2^{19}	0000 0000 0000 1000 0000 0000 0000 0000
1 048 576	2^{20}	0000 0000 0001 0000 0000 0000 0000 0000
2 097 152	2^{21}	0000 0000 0010 0000 0000 0000 0000 0000
4 194 304	2^{22}	0000 0000 0100 0000 0000 0000 0000 0000
8 388 608	2^{23}	0000 0000 1000 0000 0000 0000 0000 0000
16 777 216	2^{24}	0000 0001 0000 0000 0000 0000 0000 0000
33 554 432	2^{25}	0000 0010 0000 0000 0000 0000 0000 0000
67 108 864	2^{26}	0000 0100 0000 0000 0000 0000 0000 0000
134 217 728	2^{27}	0000 1000 0000 0000 0000 0000 0000 0000
268 435 456	2^{20}	0001 0000 0000 0000 0000 0000 0000 0000
536 870 912	2^{29}	0010 0000 0000 0000 0000 0000 0000 0000
1 073 741 824	2^{30}	0100 0000 0000 0000 0000 0000 0000 0000
2 147 483 648	2^{31}	1000 0000 0000 0000 0000 0000 0000 0000
4 294 967 295	$2^{32}-1$	1111 1111 1111 1111 1111 1111 1111 1111

Table 6 Powers of two

The last row shows the largest value you can store in an
unsigned 32 bit binary integer: 2^{32}-1. Similarly, the largest
number you can store in an unsigned 8 bit field is 2^8-1 or 255 (0
through 255 are 256 values, however).

The binary number:

```
0001 0000 1001 0000 1000 0000 1011 1001
```

can be converted to its decimal equivalent as shown in Table 7 as the sum of the decimal equivalents of the binary components.

268 435 456	1 0000 0000 0000 0000 0000 0000 0000
8 388 608	0 0000 1000 0000 0000 0000 0000 0000
1 048 576	0 0000 0001 0000 0000 0000 0000 0000
32 768	0 0000 0000 0000 1000 0000 0000 0000
128	0 0000 0000 0000 0000 0000 1000 0000
32	0 0000 0000 0000 0000 0000 0010 0000
16	0 0000 0000 0000 0000 0000 0001 0000
8	0 0000 0000 0000 0000 0000 0000 1000
+ 1	0 0000 0000 0000 0000 0000 0000 0001
277 905 593	1 0000 1001 0000 1000 0000 1011 1001

Table 7 Conversion of a binary number to decimal

However, not all numbers are positive. Then how can you represent negative numbers? There are several possibilities.

The first is to use what is referred to as *sign and magnitude*. In this technique, one of the bits, usually the leftmost bit, becomes a sign bit. If it is zero, the number is positive and if it is one, the number is negative. For example, in an 8 bit computer, the positive number 109 is: 0110 1101 and -109 would simply be: 1110 1101

Sign and magnitude notation, however, has several problems. The first of these is there are two ways of expressing zero:

```
0000 0000
1000 0000
```

The first is a positive zero and the second is a negative zero. Both, however, are zero. This sort of thing confuses the hardware. If you compare two values you need to take into account that they could both be positive, both negative, or mixed. This adds complexity and reduces speed.

Also, you can't do arithmetic directly on a number in sign and magnitude notation. If you add the value of 109 and -109, you should get zero but you don't:

```
  0110 1101
+ 1110 1101
```

```
        1 0101 1010
```

The extra bit on the left is an overflow. The answer is not zero and this is a problem. To do arithmetic on sign and magnitude you need even more specialized hardware to take into account all the possible combinations of positive and negative operands.

A second possible solution is called 1s complement. In 1s complement we form the negative of a number by inverting (complementing) the bits. This, 109 and -109 appear as:

```
0110 1101      109
1001 0010     -109
```

As it turns out, in this format all negative numbers have a leading one bit so that position is still called the sign but the remainder of the number is quite different. Does this work? It solves the arithmetic problem when we add +109 to -109:

```
      0110 1101
    + 1001 0010
      1111 1111
```

And the answer is zero. Yes, 1111 1111 is zero because 1s complement also has two zeros:

```
0000 0000     positive zero
1111 1111     negative zero
```

So, we still have the problem of two zero values but there is a solution: *2s complement*.

A 2s complement number is formed by adding one to the 1s complement. Thus 109 becomes negative in the following way:

```
0110 1101     +109
1001 0010     1s complement
1001 0011     2s complement
```

How does this solve the two zeros problem:

```
0000 0000     zero
1111 1111     1s complement
0000 0000     2s complement (overflow ignored)
```

In other words, if you try to create a negative zero, you get the original zero again. There is only one zero!

Can we do arithmetic? Yes. Here we add +109 and -109:

```
0110 1101       109
1001 0011      -109
0000 0000         0
```

Note: there are special rules for handling overflows which won't be covered here.

A consequence of this, however, is that, basically, one bit is lost to sign representation. So, in the case of a 32 bit number, the range is -2,147,483,648 to + 2,147,483,647. Also note that in 2s complement notation, there is always one more negative number than positive numbers (that extra zero had to go some place).

Unsigned 32 bit numbers, however, range from 0 to 4,294,967,295. The mainframe architecture supports both unsigned binary integers as well as signed binary integers up to 64 bits in length.

3.1.3 Nomenclature

Table 8 gives the decimal values of several powers of two along with the terms by which we refer to them. Terms such as *kilobytes, megabytes* and *gigabytes* derive from these thresholds. Thus, 1 gigabyte of memory actually has 2^{30} or 1,073,741,824 bytes if expressed in decimal.

However, it is currently fashionable among disk drive manufacturers to call 1,000,000,000 bytes a gigabyte - note the small print on the package. This lets them claim what appears to be a higher capacity for their offerings. In fact, however, they are shorting you more than 73 million bytes per "gigabyte."

Clock rates are normally expressed in base 10 so 1 gHz is 1,000,000,000 Hz. Memory manufacturers, however, are stuck with the higher binary values due to manufacturing issues.

3.1.4 Threshold Binary Values

In many cases, it is very useful to know the maximum number that can be stored in an unsigned binary number of a particular number of bits. For example, the largest binary number in 4 bits is 1111_2 which corresponds to 15 decimal. The minimum number, of course, is 0000_2 or zero. The range 0 to 15 has 16 values. Thus, 4 bits are needed to specify one of the 16 general purpose registers in an IBM mainframe. Hence, the instruction formats all have a 4 bit field whenever a register is designated.

With 8 bits you can have numbers between 0 and 255, a total of 256 values. Similarly, if your unsigned binary number has 12 bits, the size of an original assembly displacement, it can have 4096 values between 0 and 4095. Thus, the maximum displacement from a base register used in addressing is 4095. In 16 bits you can count from 0 to 65,535. At 24 bits your numeric range is 0 to 16,777,215.

The number 16,777,215 is significant as it was the upper limit of memory size on the original 360 Series. As it takes 3 bytes to hold a 24 bit number, and since addresses were almost always stored in 4 byte full words, one byte (the high order or leftmost) was not actually part of the address. Many programs and operating system conventions used (and still do) that high-order byte to communicate information.

1 024	2^{10}	1 K (kilo)
2 048	2^{11}	2 K
4 096	2^{12}	4 K
8 192	2^{13}	8 K
16 384	2^{14}	16 K
32 768	2^{15}	32 K
65 536	2^{16}	64 K
131 072	2^{17}	128 K
262 144	2^{18}	256 K
524 288	2^{19}	512 K
1 048 576	2^{20}	1024 K or 1 M "meg"
2 097 152	2^{21}	2 M
4 194 304	2^{22}	4 M
8 388 608	2^{23}	8 M
16 777 216	2^{24}	16 M
33 554 432	2^{25}	32 M
67 108 864	2^{26}	64 M
134 217 728	2^{27}	128 M
268 435 456	2^{28}	256 M
536 870 912	2^{29}	512 M
1 073 741 824	2^{30}	1024 M or 1 G "gig"
2 147 483 648	2^{31}	2 G
4 294 967 296	2^{32}	4 G
Table 8 Binary Nomenclature		

Thus, many older, legacy programs still run in 24 bit addressing mode to this day because, if they were executed in 31 bit addressing mode, the high order byte would be considered part of the address and lead to erroneous results. However, modern mainframes can execute programs in 24 bit, 31 bit and 64 bit addressing modes simultaneously so this is not really an issue.

4. Assembly Language Overview

4.1 Basic Instruction Set Overview

In the original IBM 360 architecture, there were six basic instruction formats and these are still the basis of many of the instructions in use today as well as the model for newer formats.

Assembly language programs are comprised of sequences of instructions that the assembler translates to binary machine language. Each instruction consists of an operation code (opcode), which identifies which instruction to execute. This is followed by one or more operands that tell the assembler the location of the data on which the instruction is to work. Optionally, there may be additional information qualifying the opcode.

All instructions when coded in binary are either two, four or six bytes long. In the original architecture, the first byte was always the opcode. An opcode is a numeric value that indicates which instruction is to be executed. As a result, since there are 8 bits in a byte, the maximum number of unique opcodes represented by one byte is 256 (2 raised to the eighth power). Originally, most, but not all, possible eight bit codes were used. However, in newer versions of the architecture, some of these unused codes are used to indicate that additional bits elsewhere in the instruction are also part of the opcode. Consequently, the total number of permissible opcodes is now very much larger than the original maximum of 256.

Following the opcode is one or more (usually two) operand specifications. The opcode determines the number and nature of the operands. That is, whether the operand is in memory, in a register, a constant or something else.

Registers are very high speed memory located in the CPU. There are two classes of registers: *general purpose registers* and *floating point registers.*

The floating point registers are used to perform calculations on are approximate representations of a real numbers. As this is very specialized programming seldom done in assembly language, floating point calculations will not be discussed here.

There are also 16 general purpose registers (GPR). These are used for manipulating binary data, integer calculations and addressing. Originally, they were all 32 bits in length but on more recent machines they are 64 bits long. Some instructions work only on the lower 32 bits of these while others work on all 64. For the most part, we will work mainly with the lower 32 bits in this text.

The general purpose registers are addressed by a number between 0 and 15. These are the binary codes between 0000_2 (0_{10}) and 1111_2 (15_{10}). Thus, in all machine language coded instructions, a general purpose register operand is specified by a field of four bits.

If an operand is in a register, the register number will be given. If an operand is in memory, the architecture mainly uses an addressing scheme known as *base/displacement* addressing (Some newer instruction formats permit relative addressing as well). In base/displacement addressing, the address of the operand is calculated by adding the contents of a base register with a constant called a *displacement*. A base register is a register selected by the programmer from general purpose registers 1 through 15 (register zero is not normally used) but certain registers are more commonly used than others.

Originally, displacements were always 12 bit unsigned integer numbers although in newer systems, 20 bit signed displacements are possible in some instructions. Twelve bit displacements are always treated as positive integers and, consequently, can range from 0_{10} ($0000\ 0000\ 0000_2$ or 000_{16}) to 4095_{10} ($1111\ 1111\ 1111_2$ or FFF_{16}).

The purpose of the base/displacement addressing scheme is to achieve program *relocatability*, that is, the ability to place a program anywhere in memory. Consider that if a program used actual memory address constants to specify operand addresses, the program image would always need to be located in same place in memory. This would make it very difficult for a computer to run multiple programs at the same time because programs might compete for the same memory locations. In machines designed prior to the S360, this was often the case.

Base/displacement addressing makes it possible to load a program anywhere in memory as the memory addresses of operands are calculated relative to the contents of a base register. Thus, when a program is loaded into memory, the base register is loaded with a memory address whose value is usually points to a byte near or at the starting point of the program. Since operand addresses are specified as positive offsets from the address in the base register, they will be correct if the base register is correct. Should the program be placed somewhere else in memory, a different value would be loaded into the base register and operand addresses will be likewise relocated.

For example, if an assembly language program has a label located 1000 bytes from the start of the program and if the base register (let us say R15) is presumed to point to the start of the program, the base/displacement address for the label is written as 1000(R15) or, the sum of the value in R15 and 1000. If you load the program into memory such that the program begins, for example, at location 100,000, the label will be at location 101,000 (contents of R15 will be 100,000). If you load the program beginning at location 500,000, the label will be at location 501,000 (R15 contains 500,000). Any register can be used as a base register however, if register zero is used it means no register. That is, regardless of the actual contents of register zero, its contribution to the calculated address will be zero.

In addition to base and displacement, some instructions have what is called an *index register*. In these instructions, the contents of the index register are added with the contents of the base register and the displacement to calculate an operand address. Index registers are useful for array manipulation where the base / displacement combination points to the start of an array and the index register is used to give an offset from this point into the array. In those instructions where an index register is permitted, if register zero is specified as the index register, it means there is no index register (contributes nothing to the calculation). Register zero never contributes to address arithmetic.

4.2 Macro Assemblers

It is technically possible (although very tedious) to write programs directly in binary or hexadecimal. In the very earliest days of computing, this was normally the case. To improve productivity, however, people soon developed a class of programs known as *assemblers* whose purpose it was to allow programmers to write in symbolic code and leave the job of translating it into binary to the assembler.

Thus, when we write a program in *assembly language*, we use symbols for the instructions and operands. Instead of coding an *Add* instruction with its hex opcode $5A_{16}$, we use the *mnemonic* symbol A. The assembler translates our symbolic representation into binary. Instead of coding a base and displacement to address memory, we place labels on data areas in our program and, in instructions, use the labels as operands. The assembler calculates their correct base and displacement. The end result is still a binary program but with a lot less effort on our part.

When we write in assembly language, each line of code normally generates a single executable machine instruction. Compare this to a line of code written in a language such as C++ where a single line of code may result in the generation of many instructions. Languages where the ratio between the number of programmer written lines of code and the number of instructions generated is near 1 are said to be *low level* languages while languages where the ratio is a fraction of 1 are said to be *high level* languages (one to one *versus* one to many).

When we write in a high level language, a compiler translates each line of code into one or more (usually more) machine instructions. However, the instructions generated by the compiler might not always be optimal: there may be faster and shorter ways to accomplish the same task. In many cases, in assembly language we are able to write a program more efficiently. Generally speaking, high level languages increase programmer productivity but low level languages can increase program efficiency.

The output of the assembler (or a compiler, for that matter) is a binary *object module* which is a memory image of the program's instructions and data. While this module is nearly executable, it usually still needs subroutines to be included from as well as resolution of subroutine addresses. To build a final, executable module we employ a program known as the *link editor* or linking *loader* which adds needed library routines and fills in any subroutine addresses. The result is then either written to disk as an executable module or loaded it directly into memory for immediate execution subject to some final adjustments.

A *macro assembler* is an assembler where the assembly language source code is initially read by a macro pre-processor. Entries in the source code cause the pre-processor to insert source code modules from a disk library of macros (not to be confused with binary object modules included by the link editor). The pre-processor may also modify and generate source code based on macro language commands. The modified source code is then passed to the assembler. The IBM macro pre-processor, as is the case with most others, has a language of its own and is briefly touched upon in this text. Macros allow us to create small code packages for frequently done tasks and store them for reuse.

4.3 Overview of Assembly Language Statements

Assembly language statements break down into four classes:

1. **Instruction statements** These are statements, one per line, which are to be translated into machine language for execution at run time. Each specifies an operation to be executed and the data to be used. All instructions have one or more operands. All instruction statements result in binary code being added to the program image.
2. **Data Definition Instructions** (DS/DC). These are statements that tell the assembler to reserve memory in the run time program image for data. The data area may be uninitialized (DS statements - declare storage) or initialized (DC statements - declare constant).
3. **Assembler directives** These are statements that inform the assembler of some situation or direct the assembler to take some action. While these statements may affect the way in

which your machine language program is generated, they do not themselves directly result the generation of code or data. The main assembler directives we will use are shown in Table 9

4. ***Macro statements*** Macros are small, library resident code modules that contain segments of frequently used code. Rather than re-write the code new each time, we direct the pre-processor to insert macros into our programs. From the program level, macros look very much like instructions. Internally, macros may contain instructions, data allocation statements and assembler directives as well as statements in the macro language itself. Before your program is seen by the assembler, it is first processed by the macro pre-processor.

CSECT	start or continue control section.
CNOP	align to a boundary.
DSECT	start or continuation of a dummy section.
ENTRY	define an entry point.
EJECT	skip to top of next page in listing.
END	end of the source module.
EQU	define one symbol to be the equivalent of another.
EXTERN	identify symbols defined in other modules.
LTORG	placement of literal pool.
ORG	adjust location counter.
PRINT	assembler print options.
SPACE	insert line feed in listing output.
START	initiate first or only control section.
TITLE	set title to appear at top of listing page.
USING/DROP	designate/undesignate a base register.

Table 9 Assembler Directives

4.4 Line Format and Naming Conventions

Historically, assembly language programs were punched on 80 column cards and followed a format consistent with that media. Although there has been some relaxation of the format in recent years, most assembly programmers follow the original format to this day:

1. Labels begin in column one and are from one to eight upper case characters in length.

2. The first character of a label is either a letter in the range A through Z, $, # or @.

3. Characters after the first character of a label may be any of the above as well as digits in the range 0 through 9.

4. The mnemonic (short abbreviation) for the operation code or assembly directive begins in column ten.

5. Operands, if any, begin in column sixteen and may *not* include embedded blanks except within quoted strings.

6. After the operands and one blank, comments may be written.

7. Comments and operands may not extend beyond column 71.

8. If column 1 one is an asterisk, the remainder of the line is a comment.

9. If an operand is so long that it would extend beyond column 71, place a character (usually an X) in column 72 and continue the operand on column sixteen of the next line. There may be at most two continuation lines.

10. Blank lines are ignored.

11. Quoted strings use the single quote character, not the double quote. If you want a quoted string to contain single quote, it should be represented in the string as two immediately adjacent single quotes such as: `'Mike''s computer'`

12. If you use an ampersand as a character in a quoted string, you must use two immediately adjacent ampersands such as: `'computers && technology'`

5. Hello World

5.1 The z390 Portable Mainframe Project

The examples in this book were developed using the z390 Portable Mainframe Assembler and Emulator. This is a Java based, GPL licensed project to "...*Enable z390 and zcobol users to compile, assemble, link, and execute mainframe COBOL and assembler problem state programs with minimum source code changes using Windows, Linux, and other platforms supporting the J2SE runtime....*" from the web site:

> http://www.z390.org/

The emulator can be run either in a graphical user window or from a command prompt.

5.2 Hello World

Now it's time to write the customary *Hello World* program as shown in Figure 1.

The first few lines of every assembly program deal with assembler directives and linkage. Linkage refers to the process of connecting your program to the program that called it. It involves saving the calling program's registers so they can be restored at exit, establishing a base register for your program, and creating a save area in your program. These will each be discussed later in this book. Normally these actions are done with macros (macros are small, pre-written, disk resident, code modules) as they seldom differ from one program to the next.

The z390 emulator has a macro named SUBENTRY that establishes your program's linkage, its save area, and sets register 13 as your base register.

When you assemble a program, the assembler will generate a file showing your program and its translation to machine language along with other information. This is often referred to as the *listing* and, in the z390 emulator, will appear as a file with the same name as your program but with the *.PRN* file extension.

The directive PRINT NOGEN is a directive to the assembler that tells it to display the names of the macros but not show the macro expansion (code) itself in the listing. If PRINT NOGEN is omitted, the assembler will display the contents of the of the macro expansion which are usually not very interesting after you see them once.

The label on SUBENTRY is HELLO. The SUBENTRY macro uses this label to establish the external linkage name of your program. This is the name other programs would use if they were calling your program. The SUBENTRY macro also does the other program entry housekeeping tasks: saving the contents of the calling program's registers, setting up a local save area , and establishing a base register.

Labels	Op-codes	Operands
	PRINT	NOGEN
HELLO	SUB-ENTRY	
	EQUREGS	
XPRNT		MSG,L'MSG
	SUBEXIT	
MSG		DC C'Hello World!'
	END	

Figure 1 Hello World

The next macro, EQUREGS doesn't actually generate any code but it tells the assembler to accept notation such as R1, R2, R3 as the equivalent of 1, 2, 3. To make their programs more readable, many programmers prefer to refer to the sixteen general purpose registers as a number preceded by the letter R however this notation is not accepted by the assembler. So, we use EQUREGS to tell the assembler that codes such as R1 are equivalent of their numeric part.

The program in Figure 1 Hello World writes the phrase *Hello World* then returns to the operating system. Return is accomplished by the macro SUBEXIT. The program's output is performed by XPRNT, part of the Assist package of macros originally developed by Dr. John R. Mashey at the Computer Science Department of The Pennsylvania State University. We will use several of these so-called X-macros in the examples in this text. They provide simplified access to common tasks and are useful for novice programmers. Normally, the Assist package consists of a library of macros each of which contains multiple lines of assembly language code. In many emulators, however, including z390, these macros are implemented as pseudo-instructions. That is, they appear to be real machine instructions so as to simplify debugging and program development.

XPRNT prints data to the default output device (the screen for most users). It takes two arguments: the address of the data field to be printed and its length. In Figure 1, the address of the field to be printed is given by the label MSG and the length as L'MSG. The assembler calculates the base and displacement necessary to address MSG. L'MSG is assembler shorthand which evaluates to the value of the length attribute of the label MSG which, in this case, is 12. Note that the assembler uses *single quote* marks rather than double quote marks.

5.3 Running Hello World

Once you have typed and saved the program, assemble and execute it by typing the command:

>   assist hello

to the command prompt. The *assist* command runs the z390 emulator with the Assist macro support feature enabled and then executes the result if the assembly step was successful *(i.e.,* error free).

The result on your screen should be several messages and the line *Hello World!* as shown in Figure 2 (longer lines have been truncated). In Figure 2 you see each of the steps: assembly (MZ390), linking (LZ390) and execution by the emulator (EZ390). Each step can have errors. The assembly step can have syntax errors, the linking step may discover missing subroutines and the execution step can encounter many mishaps. You need to look for error messages after each step.

The assembler creates several files in your directory each with the file name *hello* but with different extensions. The file *hello.PRN* (examined below) is the main assembler listing of your program. It contains syntax error messages (if any) and a description of the machine language program created.

```
C:\user>rem assemble, link, and exec ASSIST prgram hello.mlc.MLC
C:\user>echo off
18:13:22 hello MZ390 START USING z390 V1.5.01b ON J2SE 1.6.0_18
18:13:22 hello MZ390 ENDED   RC= 0 SEC= 0 MEM(MB)= 42 IO=681
18:13:22 hello LZ390 START USING z390 V1.5.01b ON J2SE 1.6.0_18
18:13:22 hello LZ390 ENDED   RC= 0 SEC= 0 MEM(MB)= 15 IO=32
18:13:22 hello EZ390 START USING z390 V1.5.01b ON J2SE 1.6.0_18
Hello World!
18:13:22 hello EZ390 ENDED   RC= 0 SEC= 0 MEM(MB)= 19 IO=21
```

Figure 2 Assemble and Run Hello World

5.4 Examining hello.PRN

Now we'll examine the file *HELLO.PRN*. You can do this several ways including printing it or, more likely, opening it with an editor.

The *.PRN* file is one of the output files from the assembler. It shows many things but for now we want to examine the area in the center of the page that looks something like Figure 3. In this figure, text to the left part of each line has been removed and we have also removed the PRINT NOGEN directive from the program thus causing the macro expansions to be visible. The PRINT NOGEN directive suppresses [rinting of the contents of macros. What remains is the assembler's listing of your code with macros shown. For each macro, you see its invocation followed by its expansion. Code generated as a result of macro expansion is preceded by plus signs.

Label	Op-code	Operands
1 HELLO	SUBENTRY	
2+HELLO	CSECT	
3	STM	14,12,12(13)
4	BAL	15,104(15)
5	DC	18F'0'
6	DC	CL8'HELLO'
7	DC	CL8'09/06/10'
8	DC	CL8'19.02'
9	ST	15,8(13)
10	ST	13,4(15)
11	LR	13,15
12	USING	HELLO+8,13
14	EQUREGS	
15+R0	EQU	0
16+R1	EQU	1
17+R2	EQU	2
18+R3	EQU	3
19+R4	EQU	4
20+R5	EQU	5
21+R6	EQU	6
22+R7	EQU	7
23+R8	EQU	8
24+R9	EQU	9
25+R10	EQU	10
26+R11	EQU	11
27+R12	EQU	12
28+R13	EQU	13
29+R14	EQU	14
30+R15	EQU	15
33	XPRNT	MSG,L'MSG
34	SUBEXIT	
35	LA	15,0
36	L	13,4(,13)
37	L	14,12(,13)
38	LM	2,12,28(13)
39	BR	14
41 MSG	DC	C'Hello World!'
42	END	

Figure 3 Macro Expansion

Lines 2 through 12 are the expansion of the SUBENTRY macro and, except for lines 2 and 12, are machine instructions and data allocations. Lines 15 through 30 are the result of the EQUREGS macro and are assembler directives (*i.e.* not machine instructions or data declarations). Lines 35 through 39 are the result of the SUBEXIT macro and are machine instructions. Further details on the meaning of this code will be covered later. Lines 1, 14 and 34 are the macro invocations themselves that were originally present in the source code module. They are shown for reference purposes.

The left hand portion of the *.PRN* file (not shown) contains the translation of the program into hexadecimal and other information about the executable module. The left hand side is entirely in hexadecimal. The right hand side is text and numbers are normally in decimal notation with some exceptions. We will examine the left hand side of the page shortly.

5.5 Quick Overview of Assembly Language Programming

As we have seen, assembly language programs consist of sequences instructions that operate on data. In a program, an instruction is written as one or more letters that are an abbreviation or other indicator of the instruction's name or function. These are referred to as mnemonics.

Each instruction in a program has one or more operands which designate the data on which the instructions operate. The operands specify the location of the data which can be in constants, registers, memory or all three.

Typical instructions involve mathematical operations (add subtract, multiply, divide), logical operations on bits (AND, OR, Exclusive OR, *etc.*), data movement, and comparisons (is A greater than B?), and branch instructions (GOTOs).

In the IBM architecture, most instructions have two operands and the result of an operation is usually placed in the first operand. The second operand, in most cases, is unchanged.

In some instructions, both operands are in registers, in others the first operand is a register and the second is in memory and, in a few instructions, both operands are in memory. While most instructions have two operands, some have more. In some instructions, one or more operands are constants contained in the instruction itself.

Also, there are instructions to initiate and control input/output. These are normally only executed by operating system.

Programmers invoke operating system routines to perform input/output.

With this in mind, Table 10 is a quick overview of several common groups of instructions that we will use in subsequent examples. For the most part, registers will be designated with a leading R such as R0, R1, R2 *etc.* although this is only valid if the EQUREGS macro, shown earlier, has been invoked. Each of the instructions in Table 10 operates on 32 bits (4 bytes). There are also similar instructions that operate longer data fields that will be introduced later.

Instruction	Purpose
Load Store	Load instructions load data from memory into one or more registers and Store instructions store data from one or more registers to memory. As many operations require that one of the operands be in a register, Load/Store instructions are quite common. For example, a Load instruction that loads 32 bits (4 bytes) from memory into a register: L R5,LABEL The four bytes beginning at the address associated with the label LABEL are loaded into register 5. The store instruction is similar except the data movement is from the register to memory.
Add Subtract Multiply Divide Shift And Or Exclusive Or Complement *Etc.*	There is a wide assortment of instructions that operate on and manipulate data. Some computer architectures have more than others (for example, RISC machines normally do not support multiply and divide instructions, among others). The Add instruction is illustrative of the class. The basic Add instruction adds a 32 bit fixed point binary number stored in memory to the contents of a register. The register is specified as the first operand and the result is stored in the first operand register replacing its previous contents. The second operand points to the 4 bytes in memory. The memory value is not changed. Example: A R7,VAR The 4 bytes located in memory beginning at label VAR are added to the 4 bytes in R7 and the result is left in R7. There is also a version where both operands are registers such as: AR R3,R8 The 4 bytes in R8 are added to R3. In some instructions both operands are in memory but in most, at least one operand is a register.
Compare	Compare instructions compare values. The result of a Compare instruction (first operand is: equal, less than, or greater than the second operand) is reflected in the value of what is called the Condition Code (see section 7.3). The value in the Condition Code is used by Conditional Branch instructions to determine if they should branch or not. For

	example: C R4,LABEL The 4 byte signed binary value in R4 is compared with the 4 byte signed binary value in memory at the location designated by LABEL. Both operands are treated as signed, binary, fixed point values. There is also a version where both operands are in registers.
XPRNT XREAD XDECO XDECI	The XPRNT (note the spelling), XREAD, XDECI, and XDECO macros are used in connection with input/output. XPRNT writes data, XREAD reads data, and XDECO and XDECI convert data from internal binary to printable decimal and vide versa. These are normally macros, that is, short segments of code loaded into your program from a library, but, in the *z390* emulator, they appear to be SS instructions.
BC BCT BXH BXLE	Conditional Branch instructions branch or not depending upon the value in the Condition Code. They are very often after a Compare instruction. For example: BH LABEL Branch to LABEL if a previous operation set the Condition Code to a value consistent with a comparison where the first operand was greater than the second. Note: BH (Branch High) is a form to the BC instruction. Also, there are looping branch instructions that are used to implement iterative code (BCT, BXH, BXLE).

Table 10 Basic Instructions

5.6 Simple Integer Arithmetic Program

```
1                PRINT          NOGEN

2                EQUREGS

3   ADD          SUBENTRY

4                L              R2,ONE

5                A              R2,TWO

6                XPRNT          MSG,L'MSG

7                XDECO          R2,OUT

8                XPRNT          OUT,L'OUT

9                SUBEXIT

10  MSG          DC             C'Adding Numbers'

11  ONE          DC             F'1'

12  TWO          DC             F'2'

13  OUT          DS             CL12

14               END
```

Figure 4 Example Program

The *Hello World* program isn't very interesting. It doesn't actually do any calculations and mainly relies on system macros and pseudo instructions instead of real machine instructions. In Figure 4, however, we see a more advanced program. It has all the basic components of the *Hello World* program above but, rather than merely printing a message, it adds two binary numbers, converts the result to decimal and prints the answer.

The differences between this program and the *Hello World* program are:

1. On line 4, we load the 4 byte (32 bit) signed binary value located in memory at label ONE into register 2. Note: although registers are actually 64 bits wide, this form of the Load instruction only loads into the low order 32 bits of the register. The high order 32 bits are unchanged.

2. On line 5, we add the 4 byte signed binary value from memory at label TWO to the low order contents of register 2. The high order 32 bits are unchanged.

3. One line 6, we write a title. We give the XPRNT pseudo-instruction the address of the beginning of MSG and its length.

4. On line 7, we convert the binary value in R2 to printable decimal characters and stores them, right justified padded to the left with blanks, in the 12 byte character string in memory at label OUT. The contents of R2 are in signed binary and cannot be printed directly. XDECO is an Assist package pseudo-instruction that converts binary into printable decimal characters.

5. On line 8, we print the contents of OUT.

6. On line 9 we exit the program.

7. Lines 11 and 12 reserve storage for two full word (4 byte, 32 bit) binary values and initializes them to the binary equivalent of 1_{10} and 2_{10}, respectively. DC statements reserve storage *and* initialize it. The code *F* tells the assembler to initialize a full word (4 bytes, 32 bits) with the binary equivalent of the decimal number contained within the quotes. Note that the assembler uses single-quote marks rather than double quotes.

8. Line 13 reserves, but does not initialize, a character string of length 12. A DS differs from a DC in that a DS merely reserves memory, it does not initialize it. The contents of these 12 bytes are random until a program stores something in them.

9. The END statement is an assembler directive that indicates the end of the input program. It does not generate exit code. That is done by the SUBEXIT macro.

6. Instruction Formats

An instruction format refers to the layout of an instruction and its operands. Each computer architecture has its own set of instruction formats. Some are very simple, such as those used in RISC (Reduced Instruction Set Computer) machines such as the in SPARC (Scalable Processor Architecture), while some are very complex, such as those used in CISC (Complex Instruction Set Computer) machines such as the Intel Pentium and the now deceased Digital VAX architecture.

Instruction formats can be viewed at two levels. At the assembly language level they are the syntax that maps where the different operands are placed in the source code form of an instruction. They tell us, for each instruction, the operands to be used and how to write them in a fully explicit notation.

On the second level, instruction formats are layouts for the actual executable binary format for the instructions generated when the assembler translates source code into binary.

Each instruction belongs to an instruction format family. The executable binary code for all instructions in a family of instructions follows the same pattern or layout. Components of the source code format for an instruction map to a specific bits in the binary machine code format.

First, we will discuss instruction formats from the assembly language perspective and then from the machine language perspective. For example, a generic RX format instruction has the fully explicit *assembly language format* of:

```
OpCode R1,D2(X2,B2)
```

This is the syntax of how you would write a fully explicit RX instruction. It begins with an OpCode, a short sequence of characters that indicate the instruction to be executed. For example, A for Add, S for subtract, L for load, and ST for store.

Next is the layout for the operands. All RX instructions have two operands. The first is in a register and the second is in memory. In the format above, the first operand is designated as R1. In the syntax, this means that the first operand is a register. The letter *R* means register and the number indicates if it is the first, second, etc. operand. Note: this notation is tells us the format to of how to write an RX instruction. The designation *R1* does not mean you must use the actual machine register 1. It merely means that the first operand is a register.

Next, following the comma, you see the layout for the second operand as indicated by the number 2 on each token. The second operand for an RX instruction is in memory whose address is calculated from a base (B) register, displacement (D) and, optionally, and index register (X). Very often the index register is specified a R0 which, in an addressing context means no register.

So, if you wanted to write an Add instruction that added the contents of the 4 bytes of memory located 400 bytes from the address in your base register (say, R13) to the contents of register 5 you would write:

    A R5,400(R0,R13)

Note that the index register was designated as R0 which means there will be no contribution from the index position. Assembly language formats such as shown above are known as *fully explicit* notation. That is, the format where the programmer fills in *all* the details. In practice, however, the programmer usually uses symbolic labels and other aids which the assembler converts into the details of base register, index, register, displacement, length and so forth.

For each instruction format, there is a similar generic syntax showing how to write an instruction of that format.

When the assembler reads an instruction such as the above, it must translate it into binary. Now we must look at the machine language format for the instruction. The machine language format for all instructions is:

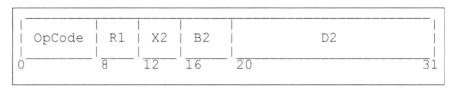

The numbers across the bottom indicate the starting bit positions in this 32 bit machine language instruction format. Instructions are typically either 16, 32 and 48 bits long. For each instruction format, there will be a layout that is similar to the above.

In the RX layout you can see that the first 8 bits are reserved for the opcode, bits 8 through 11 are where the number of the register that is the first operand is placed (four bit can represent values from zero to fifteen – the complete set of general purpose registers). The next two four bit fields are for the index and base registers, respectively and the final twelve bits are for the displacement.

In the original 360 architecture, there were five basic instruction formats known as RR (register-register), RX (register-index), RS (register-storage), SI (storage-immediate) and SS (storage-storage). In IBM parlance, *storage* means memory. In the more recent versions of the architecture, additional formats have been added but they are philosophically rooted in the original five. At present, there are 21 instruction formats.

6.1 Registers

In the original IBM 360 architecture there were sixteen 32 bit general purpose registers (GPR) and four 64 bit floating point registers. In the current architecture there are sixteen 64 bit general purpose registers and sixteen 64 bit floating point registers.

Those instructions from the original architecture which operated on 32 bit general purpose registers now use the low order 32 bits of the 64 bit registers. The high order 32 bits are normally not affected. Only newer instructions use the full 64 bit GPRs.

Additionally, the current architecture includes a number of control and memory access registers which are not covered in this text as they are mainly operating system oriented.

6.2 Operands and Data Addressing

Instructions consist of an opcode and one or more operands. Opcodes in the original architecture were all one byte numbers indicating which instruction to execute. In the newer architectures, opcodes can be longer than one byte. Most instructions have operands which determine the data upon which the instruction operates. Operands can be in registers or in memory or part of the instruction itself. When an operand is in a register, the operand is specified simply by giving the register number (0 through 15). This requires only 4 bits.

However, in the original architecture, when an operand is in memory, the memory address is specified as a combination of a base register, an unsigned displacement and, in some instructions, an optional index register. The address is calculated by adding the contents of the base register, the value of the displacement and, if present, the contents of the index register. The resulting number is the address of the operand in memory.

Displacements in the original architecture are all 12 bits unsigned numbers ranging in value from 0 to 4095. In some newer instructions, the displacements may be 20 bit signed numbers.

Registers are always specified with 4 bits (a range of 0 to 15). So, to specify an operand that is a memory, an instruction format needs, at a minimum, between 16 and 20 bits (a 12 bit displacement and one or two register specifications at 4 bits each).

Some instructions have both operands in registers while others have operands in memory and registers. If an instruction has both operands in registers, only 8 bits are required to specify both operands. Instructions that have one or more operands in memory are, therefore, longer than instructions where both operands are in registers.

In some cases, an operand may be a constant that is part of the instruction. In the original architecture these were always one byte in length. In newer versions, in some instructions, more than one byte is used.

The terms *base register* and *index register* do not refer to another class of registers. They selected from any of the 16 general purpose registers. In practice, however, there are limitations on which registers you may select.

First, registers R1 and R2 are altered by some instructions and thus not suitable as base register candidates. Similarly, some registers have, by convention, program linkage assignments which limit their usage. Generally speaking, base registers are chosen from the range R3 through R13 and R15. For most of this text, we assume that the SUBENTRY macro has been used which always selects R13 as the base register.

One important note concerning registers is that if you specify R0 as either a base or an index register, it means *no* register. That is, the contents of R0 will not be used in any address calculations. Further, if you place R0 in a position where a branch address is required, it means *no* branch (see BCR, BCTR, BALR, BASR). R0 may, however, be used for other purposes such as arithmetic.

In most cases, the displacement and base register will be automatically filled in by the assembler when we specify an operand as a label as we saw in Figure 4.

For the most part, in instructions where it is available, the index register is rarely used. When it is used, it is for array-like operations where the base and displacement point to the start of an array and the index register gives an offset into it. Unless you tell the assembler to the contrary, the assembler will, by default, set the index register to R0 meaning no register. This was the case in Figure 4 for the Load (L) and Add (A) instructions, both of which have an index register in their format. In both cases in the examples, the assembler placed R0 into the index positions.

In later versions of the architecture, the basic addressing modes were extended to include 20 bit signed displacements (12 bit displacements are always unsigned, positive values) and relative addressing.

In relative addressing, the address of the operand is calculated relative to the address of the current instruction. Relative addressing is used mainly in branch instructions and in the Load Address Relative Long (LARL) instruction. The relative address value is specified in halfword units. Most relative address values are located in immediate operands.

6.3 Operand Notations

For each instruction there is a standard shorthand notation used by the documentation to describe the instruction. This format tells you the mnemonic opcode and the number and nature of the operands.

In this shorthand, you will see code letters that indicate what kind of operands the instruction uses. Instructions may have from one to three operands but most have two. Operands can be in registers, immediate data (part of the instruction itself) or in memory.

In the standard shorthand notation, operands are specified with the letters R, I, B, X, M, L and D. For example, the assembly language fully explicit format for the 32 bit signed binary Add instruction is given as:

```
A R1,D2(X2,B2)
```

The first letter (A) is the instruction mnemonic (Add). The codes that follow tell us what each operand or operand component is and the numbers tell us which operand we are looking at (first, second, third).

Notation	Meaning
R	general purpose register
I	immediate byte operand
B	base register
D	displacement
X	index register
M	mask
L	length
DH	high 8 bits of an extended displacement
DL	low 12 bits of an extended displacement

Table 11 Operand Notations

In the Add instruction above, the code R1 means that the first operand is a register while the second operand is composed of a displacement (D2), an index register (X2), and a base register (B2). In the case of the Add instruction, the 32 bits from memory are added to the low order 32 bits of the register specified as the first operand. The designation R1 (or R2 or R3 in other instructions) means the first (or second or third, respectively) operand is a register. It does not necessarily mean that the first operand is the actual machine register 1 - but it could be. The basic codes are given in Table 11.

For the most part, anytime you see D, B, and, possibly, X in an operand designation, it is part of a memory address (shift instructions are a special case where this does not apply). The code I means that the instruction contains an embedded byte or bytes of data that are the operand itself (referred to as *immediate* operands). The code L means that the instruction contains a value which indicates the length of an operand. The code M means that the operand is a four bit field called a *mask* that is used to indicate under which conditions a branch should take place. The codes DH and DL are used for newer, longer, signed forms of the D (displacement) component of an address (DL is the low order portion of the displacement and DH is the high order portion).

6.4 Basic Assembly Language Operand Formats

In the base architecture, instructions are either two, four or six bytes in length. The basic instruction format families and the instruction lengths are:

```
RR (register-register - 2 bytes)
RX (register-index    - 4 bytes)
RS (register-storage  - 4 bytes)
SI (storage-immediate - 4 bytes)
SS (storage-storage   - 6 bytes)
```

Again, IBM uses the term storage to mean memory.

As we have shown, at the most basic level, the operands of an instruction may be fully specified by the programmer with registers, displacements, masks and lengths. At this level, the programmer fills in all the operand fields. The assembler uses this data to construct the binary machine language instruction (usually shown in hexadecimal). When the programmer fills in all the fields in this manner, it is called *fully explicit* notation.

In practice, when writing assembler language source code we use a combination of fully explicit and symbolic operand notations. This enables the programmer to specify operands:

symbolically so that the assembler calculates the base, displacement, index, mask and lengths for you,

explicitly where the programmer specifies the base, displacement, index, mask and lengths or,

a mixture of symbolic and explicit notation.

6.5 Basic Explicit Operands

The simplest form of addressing is register addressing. In an instruction, if an operand is in a register, you simply specify the register number. If the operand is in memory, you specify the base and displacement or, in the case of RX instructions, the base, displacement and index.

Both operands are registers in RR format instructions (the BCR instruction in an exception). In RX instructions the first operand is normally register and the second is in memory (the BC instruction is an exception). RS instructions the first and third operands are registers and the second is in memory. In SS instructions, both operands are in memory. In SI instructions, one operand is in memory and one is a constant that is part of the instruction itself (the immediate operand).

For RR examples, see Figure 5. Note that the mnemonics for RR instruction opcodes always end in the letter R. A mnemonic is a short sequence of letters to make information easier to remember.

The first example involves the *Add Register* instruction, AR, as shown in see Figure 5. The instruction adds the contents of the register specified as the second operand to the contents of the register specified as the first operand and leaves the result in the first operand.

```
AR R2,R3 *Contents of R3 added to R2, result in R2
SR R3,R4 *Contents of R4 subtracted from R3, result in R3
LR R4,R5 *Contents of R5 copied to R4
```

                    Figure 5 RR Examples

In the example, you can see that register 2 is the first operand and register 3 is the second operand so the value (contents) in register 3 will be added to the value (contents) in register 2 and the answer (result) will be left in register 2.

Note: technically, the assembler requires you to use only numbers to specify registers so the example should not use the letter *R* in the register designations. However, in most cases, we will assume that the macro EQUREGS has been invoked at the beginning of each program. This macro tells the assembler that R0 means 0, R1 means 1, and so forth.

In the second example we see the *Subtract Register* (SR) instruction. Similar to the AR instruction, the SR instruction subtracts the contents of register 4 from the contents of register 3 and the result is placed in register 3.

In the final example we see the LR or *Load Register* instruction. This instruction copies the contents of the second operand to the first.

On the other hand, if an operand is in memory, you must specify it's location usually by means of a base, displacement and, possibly (in RX instructions), an index register.

```
D2(B2)          base and displacement
D2(X2,B2)       base, index and displacement
```
Figure 6 Memory Operands

In the most fully explicit expression of a memory operand, you fill-in both the base register and displacement yourself (and, possibly, the index). The syntax for a base/displacement memory operand looks like the examples in Figure 6.

In Figure 6, D2 is the displacement, B2 is the base register and X2 is the index register. The number 2 following each indicates if this is part of the second operand. In the example, 2 is shown as the operand number since many memory operands are second operands. In the original instruction set, third operands are never of the base displacement variety however they may be first operands.

In the original architecture, index registers were only available in RX instructions. In later versions, the closely related RXE, RXF and RXY formats were added. These also use index registers. Often index registers are specified as R0. If R0 is used in an addressing context, it means no register. Note, however, that register R0 can be used for arithmetic and other things but it has a special meaning when used for addressing.

Since the index register is seldom used, R0 is often seen in this position and the operand address, in effect, is calculated from the base register and displacement only.

Note: in an operand where no index register is used, you could, technically, place the base register number in the index position and a zero in the base register position with no effect on the address calculated. However, in many machines this would result in a tiny performance reduction.

Figure 7 gives a few examples of base/displacement addressing with and without index registers. In each, the value of the displacement is 1234_{10}, the base is R5 and the index is either R6 or R0. Programmer written displacements are normally specified in decimal.

If R5 has 1000_{10} in it and R6 has 100_{10} in it, the effective addresses (the result of the address arithmetic calculations) are 2234_{10}, 2334_{10} and 2234_{10}, respectively.

```
1234(R5)      base and displacement
1234(R6,R5)   base, index and displacement
1234(R0,R5)   base, no index, displacement
```

Figure 7 Example Memory Addressing

Another way to specify an operand is called *immediate addressing*. In this case, the operand is actually part of the instruction itself and not in a register or memory.

In the basic instruction set, immediate operands are always one byte in length. In the original architecture, in all but one case, immediate operands are the second operands.

In some instructions such as the shift instructions, the second operand is shown as a base/displacement but it is actually used to calculate the number of bits by which to shift. In these instructions, the displacement is added to contents of the register specified as the base register and the result is the amount of the shift. The result is not used to access memory. Since in practice, most programs shift by a constant amount it is common to see code such as

```
SRA R5,10
```

which means, *shift the bits in register 5 right by 10 bits*. When you specify a number alone in a base/displacement/index format operand, it is as though you specified 10(R0) or 10(R0,R0) which is to say, displacement 10, no base register, and no index register.

On the original architecture, the SVC (Supervisor Call) instruction, was designated as an RR instruction but the 8 bits normally containing the register specifications are instead treated as a one byte constant. The SVC is also the only RR instruction whose mnemonic does not end in R.

In newer versions, there is one variation of the SS format with an immediate operand designated as the third operand. All other instructions using an immediate operand are SI instructions.

There are several ways to code an immediate operand but it is usually specified either as a character constant such as C'A' (The letter A) or as a hexadecimal constant such as X'FF' (a byte all of whose bits are ones).

In some newer instruction formats, an immediate operand can be 16 or 32 bits in length.

6.6 Symbolic Addressing

In reality, assembly language programmers usually avoid the use of explicit base and displacement format when writing programs. Instead, they use labels which refer to program addresses symbolically and have the assembler calculate the displacement and select the base register (there can be more than one active available base register – the one which would generate the smallest displacement is normally selected).

Labels can be assigned to either instructions or data. The assembler initially scans your program and builds an internal table of the size, location, data type and contents of everything you write. For each label it sees, it records how many bytes it is from the start of your program. When you use a label in an instruction, it is the job of the assembler to use this information to select the optimal base register from those it has been told are available and then to calculate the displacement from the base register selected to the address associated with the label.

For example, if R13 is a base register and is pointing (has as its contents) the address of the first byte of your program, displacements to labels will be calculated as distances from the start of your program. Thus, a label which is attached to byte 100 relative to the start of your program will have a displacement of 100 from R13 in a base/displacement reference in your program to that label. However, if R13 is pointing at byte 8 in your program, the same label will have a displacement of 92 from R13. It is common for base registers not to point to the start of a program.

When you write a program you need to tell the assembler not only which register or registers it can use as base registers but also where they are pointing. In practice, this is not difficult in small programs. You use an assembler directive called USING to notify the assembler which register(s) can be used as base registers and where they point relative to the start of your program.

When we say a register *points* a place in a program, we mean that the register contains the address of that place. For the examples in this book, the base register will be R13 because it is, by default, established and initialized by the SUBENTRY macro.

What this all means is that instead of you calculating a lot of base and displacement values, the assembler will do it for you. For example, suppose you have a program in which you want to:

1. load a value from memory at label I into register 7

2. add to register 7 the value from memory at label J

3. store the result to memory at label K

Assume all values are 32 bit (4 byte) signed, fixed point binary values. Assume that your program is using R13 as its base register. Assume that label I is 400_{10} bytes from the start of the program, label J is 404_{10} bytes from the start, and label K is 408_{10} bytes from the beginning. Figure 8 gives a code fragment for this (other parts of the program have been omitted).

```
1       L          R7,I
2       A          R7,J
3       ST         R7,K
...  ...
4  I    DC         F'10'
5  J    DC         F'20'
6  K    DS
```

Figure 8 Symbolic Addressing

The first instruction is the RX form of the Load instruction. It loads the 32 bit value from the address specified by the second operand label (I) into the register specified as the first operand. Thus, the four byte value from memory at I is loaded into register 7.

When the assembler encounters the Load instruction, it scans and parses its operands. The first operand, R7, is simple. However, the second operand, I, is more complex.

The assembler finds label I in the program. Then it calculates how many bytes from the beginning of the program the label is located at. For this example, let us say that I is at offset 400_{10} from the beginning of the program. Next the assembler calculates the relative offset of label I from the base register (SUBENTRY only establishes one base register: R13).

The macro SUBENTRY establishes R13 as your base register and initializes it to point to byte 8 of your program. Note: R13 does not point at the beginning of your program but 8 bytes into it!

So, given R13 that the base register is pointing at byte 8 and that the label I **is** located at location 400_{10} from the actual start of your program, the assembler will generate the explicit code:

```
L    R7,392(R0,R13)
```

The displacement is calculated relative to the base register, not the start of the program. While your label is 400_{10} bytes from the start of the program, it is only 392_{10} bytes from the value in the base register. Hence, the displacement is 392_{10}.

Since the *load* instruction is an RX instruction, it has an index register position but, as is typical, we are not using it so R0 is placed there.

```
1     L     R7,392(R0,R13)
2     A     R7,396(R0,R13)
3     ST    R7,400(R0,R13)
      ...
4  I  DC    F'10'
5  J  DC    F'20'
6  K  DS    F
```

Figure 9 Explicit Addressing

Similarly, the other instructions from Figure 9 will be translated to machine language as if they had been written as shown in Figure 8. Obviously, it is easier to have the assembler calculate the displacements than to do the calculations yourself.

The end result of submitting your program to the assembler is a translation of your program into binary machine language. In the earliest days of computing, programmers actually wrote in binary. Happily, those days are long gone. Instead, the assembler translates your symbolic code to executable binary code.

6.7 Basic Instruction Formats

We now explore the actual instruction format beginning with the original instruction formats: RR, RX, SI, SS, and RS. The formats in the original instruction set have the following similarities regardless of the instruction type:

1. Each instruction begins with an 8 bit opcode that identifies the instruction to be executed. Newer instructions, however, often have longer extended opcodes.

2. Registers, both base and index, are always represented as four bit fields (that's because there are sixteen registers numbered 0 through F and you only need four bits to represent any one of these).

3. Displacements are twelve bit unsigned integers. Some of the newer instruction types, however, may have larger, signed displacements.

4. Length specifications are stored in one byte. The entire 8 bits may be the length or the byte may be subdivided into two four bit length fields, depending on the instruction.

5. All immediate operands are one byte. In some recently added instruction types, this is not true.

6. Instructions are either two, four or six bytes long. This is true for all basic instruction types.

In the following sections we will examine each instruction format binary layout.

6.7.1 RR Format

All but one (SPM – Set Program Mask) of the RR format instructions have two operands, both of which are either general purpose registers (GPR) or, in the case of branch instructions, a mask and a general purpose register. All RR instructions are 16 bits in length and consist of an 8 bit op-code and two four bit fields used to designate the operands. RR format instructions are referred to as *register to register* instructions. RR instructions are shown in assembly language format as:

```
OpCode R1,R2
OpCode M1,R2
```

Where *opcode* is the operation code mnemonic. The R1 field indicates that the first operand is a register and R2 tells us that the second operand is also a register. M1 tells us that the first operand is a 4 bit mask. A mask is a 4 bit pattern that tells a conditional branch instruction the conditions under which it should branch. A typical RR instruction is:

AR R5,R6

AR is a signed binary add instruction where the low order 32 bits from the second register (R6) are added to low order 32 bits of R5 with the results remaining in R5. RR instruction mnemonics normally end in the letter R *(e.g.* AR, SR, LR, DR, and so forth).

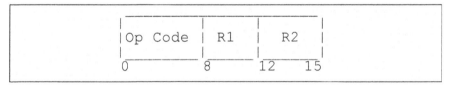

Figure 10 RR Format

RR machine language format, as shown in Figure 10 is the simplest. It consists of an opcode in the first eight bits (bits zero through seven) and, in most cases, two register specifications in bits 8 through 11 and bits 12 through 15, respectively. Since each of the register fields is four bits, it can have a value from 0000_2 to 1111_2 (R0 to R15). For example, consider the instruction:

```
AR R5,R6
```

The opcode for the AR instruction, in hexadecimal, is 1A so the machine language translation of the above is the two bytes:

    1A56

This is the translation of the symbolic format code to actual executable code. When you run the assembler, you will see this translation on the left hand side of the assembler output file (the *.PRN* file in the z390 emulator).

In the Branch Conditional Register (BCR) instruction, the 4 bits of the first operand are not a register but, rather, a 4 bit mask which is used to determine under what conditions the instruction will branch. The branch address is contained in the register specified as the second operand.

6.7.2 RX Format

RX format instructions have two operands. The opcode is always the first byte. The first operand is a register (shown as R1) or a mask (shown as M1). The second operand, shown as D2(X2,B2), is used to calculate the address of the operand in memory. The R1/M1 operand is specified in a 4 bit field. The address of the second operand is calculated from the base register, displacement and index register. The displacement is a 12 bit field containing an unsigned constant between 0 and 4095. If the index register is specified as register zero (often the case), it means there is no index register. RX instructions are always four bytes long.

RX instructions are specified in assembly language as:

    OpCode R1,D2(X2,B2)
    OpCode M1,D2(X2,B2)

A typical RX instruction would be:

    A R5,100(R0,R13)

Which means to add the 32 bits from memory at the address calculated from the second operand to the 32 bits in R5 leaving the answer in R5. The RX machine language format is shown Figure 11.

Address calculation in the original architecture always results in a positive, unsigned number.

The RX instruction:

    A R5,240(R0,R13)

is translated to:

The 8 bit op code (5A) is followed by the four bits specifying the first operand (R5), followed by the four bits of the index register (R0), followed by the base register (R13 - 13_{10} is D_{16}) followed by the twelve bit displacement 240_{10} which is $0F0_{16}$.

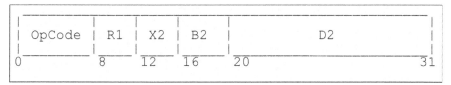

Figure 11 RX Format

6.7.3 RS Format

In RS format instructions there are normally three operands, two are registers and one is a base/displacement pair. There is no index register. The first and third operands are registers and the second operand is a base/displacement memory address calculation. RS instructions are four bytes long and called *register-storage* instructions.

RS instructions are specified in assembly language format as:

```
OpCode R1,R3,D2(B2)
```

A typical example of an RS instruction would be the Load Multiple (LM) instruction which loads multiple 32 bit registers from consecutive words in memory. In this case, the R1 operand indicates which register is the first to load and the R3 operand indicates the last. The address of the first 32 bit word to be loaded is calculated from the base and displacement.

So, to load R3, R4, R5 and R6 from 4 consecutive words in memory, you would write something like:

```
LM R3,R6,1000(R13)
```

The machine language format of an RS instruction is shown in Figure 12.

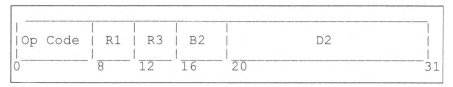

Figure 12 RS Format

The machine language format consists of an 8 bit opcode, followed by 4 bits to designate the register used as the first operand, followed by 4 bits to designate the register being used as the *third* operand, followed by 4 bits to designate the base register and then 12 bits for the displacement. The base and displacement constitute what is called the second operand even though it appears third in the actual machine language format.

The instruction:

```
LM R1,R5,200(R13)
```

where the opcode for LM is 98_{16} in machine language looks like:

```
9815D0C8
```

By now you should be able to identify the opcode (98_{16}), the first operand is R1, the third operand is R5, the base register is D_{16} (R13) and the displacement is $0C8_{16}$.

The bit shift instructions (SLA, SRA, SRDA, SLDA, SLL, SRL, SLDL and SRDL) are all RS instructions but the calculation resulting from second operand base/displacement pair is not used to address memory. Instead, it is the number of positions to shift the bits in the target register. Further, in these instructions, the third operand is not used and always appears as zero in the machine language format.

6.7.4 SI Format

In SI format instructions the first operand is the address of a single byte in memory which is calculated from a base/displacement pair. The second operand, if present, is a one byte constant that is part of the instruction itself and called the *immediate* operand. SI instructions are 4 bytes long.

SI instructions are specified as:

```
OpCode D1(B1),I2
OpCode D1(B1)
```

A typical assembly language format example might be:

```
CLI 100(R13),C'A'
```

which compares the byte at the memory address calculated by the displacement and base register with the character value A.

The machine language format of an SI instruction is shown in Figure 13. Both the value addressed by the memory operand and the immediate operand are one byte in length.

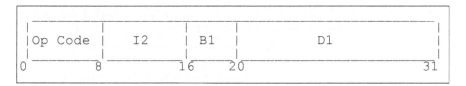

Op Code	I2	B1	D1
0	8	16 20	31

Figure 13 SI Format

For example, there is an instruction known as CLI - Compare Logical Immediate. It compares a byte in memory with the immediate byte and sets 2 bits called the *Condition Code* to indicate if the byte in memory is equal, less than or greater than the immediate operand.

So, if you want to test if a byte in memory has the value character A, the symbolic instruction might be:

```
CLI MEMB,C'A'
```

This instruction compares the byte in memory at the label MEMB with the immediate byte whose value is the letter A. After MEMB is translated to an appropriate base and displacement pair, the instruction might look something like:

```
CLI 64(R13),C'A'
```

The opcode for CLI is 95_{16} so the machine language instruction for the above would look like:

```
95C1D040
```

where $C1_{16}$ is the letter A in hex, D_{16} is the base register and 040_{16} is the displacement. Note that in the instruction, the I2 operand actually appears first and the first operand D1(B1) appears second.

Some SI instructions such as Halt IO (HIO), Set System Mask (SSM), Start IO (SIO), Test and Set (TS), Test Channel (TCH) and Test IO (TIO) do not use the immediate operand. The Diagnose instruction (no mnemonic) is an SI instruction with no operands.

6.7.5 SS Format

SS instructions come in two flavors: those with one 8 bit length field and those with two 4 bit length fields.

6.7.5.1 Single 8 Bit Length Field

In SS instructions, both operands are in memory and specified with base/displacement calculated addresses. In addition, there is a one byte field that gives the length of the target operand.

The length byte is a positive integer in the range 1 to 256 in the assembly language format (what the programmer writes). But in the machine language format, the value for the length byte is as one less than the assembly code value (0 to 255). During execution, a 0 length is interpreted as a 1, a 1 as 2, and so forth. This permits lengths ranging from 1 to 256 rather than 0 to 255. It was assumed by the system designers that there would be little need to move zero bytes.

SS instructions are six bytes in length and called *storage-storage* instructions. SS-8 instructions are specified in assembly language format as:

```
OpCode D1(L,B1),D2(B2)
```

where L is an 8 bit length code. An example would be the Move Character (MVC) instruction which copies one or more bytes beginning at the address specified by the second operand to the bytes beginning at the address specified by the first operand. The length field (shown as 20 in this example) contains the number of bytes to be copied:

```
MVC 1000(20,R13),2000(R13)
```

6.7.5.2 Two 4 Bit Length Fields

This is really the same format as above except the 8 bit length byte is viewed as two four bit fields. Thus, the instruction has two lengths. As before, the length values stored in the machine language instruction are interpreted as one greater than what is actually present so a 0 means 1 and 1 means 2 and so forth. The maximum length of each operand is 16. The first length field applies to the first operand and the second to the second.

SS-4 instructions are specified as:

```
OpCode D1(L1,B1),D2(L2,B2)
```

where L1 and L2 are the 4 bit length codes associated with operand 1 and operand 2, respectively.

A typical example would be an Add Packed instruction (AP) which performs a BCD or decimal addition between two memory resident operands. The operands can be of different lengths but the first operand, where the result is stored, must be large enough to hold the answer. In the following example, the first operand is 5 bytes and the second is 3:

```
AP 1000(5,R13),2000(3,R13)
```

All SS instructions are 6 bytes in length. The original SS machine language formats are shown in Figure 14.

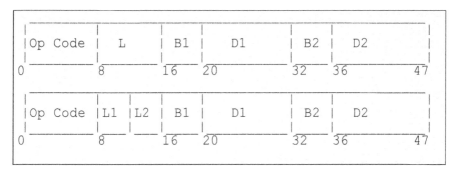

Figure 14 SS Formats

As can be seen, in one format, the length byte is taken as an unsigned 8 bit number. In the other variation, the length byte is interpreted as two unsigned 4 bit numbers.

The instruction::

```
MVC  100(8,R13),200(R13)
```

Where the opcode of an MVC is $D2_{16}$ would, in machine language, look like:

```
D207D064D0C8
```

You can see the opcode is D2, the length is 07, the first base is D_{16}, the first displacement is 064_{16}, the second base is D_{16} and the second displacement is $0C8_{16}$.

Notice that the length is not 8. When represented in machine language, the length is always one less. Thus 0 means 1, 1 means 2 and so forth.

As noted, some SS instructions divide the length byte into two 4 bit fields in order to get 2 lengths. This is mainly used with the class of arithmetic instructions known as decimal or packed. For example, the SS instruction Add Decimal (or Add Packed) with the mnemonic AP has two lengths. The length subfields give the length of the first and second operands, respectively. So, a typical AP instruction might look like:

```
AP  VAL1(5),VAL2(3)
```

This means to add the three byte field from the second operand (VAL2) to the contents of the 5 byte field specified as the first operand (VAL1) and leave the result in the first operand. Translated to explicit format the above might look like:

```
AP  32(5,R13),64(3,R13)
```

which would, given the opcode of FA_{16} yield the machine instruction:

where FA_{16} is the opcode, 4 is the first 4 bit length code (one less than 5, as before), 2 is the second length, D is the first base, 020_{16} is the first displacement, D is the second base and 040_{16} is the second displacement.

6.7.5.3 Added SS Formats

In later versions of the architecture additional SS formats were added as shown in Figure 15. These tend to be uncommon instructions such as Load Multiple Disjoint (LMD), Shift and Round Decimal (SRP), Move to Primary (MVCP), Move to Secondary (MVCS) and Move With Key (MVCK).

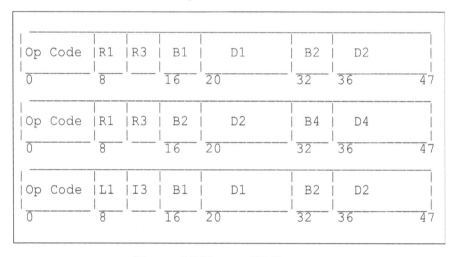

Figure 15 Newer SS Formats

6.8 Newer Instruction Formats

As time passed, the architecture evolved. The original 24 bit (16 megabyte) address space grew to 31 bits (2 gigabytes) and then to 64 bits (16 exabytes); the original 32 bit general purpose registers became 64 bits and so on. To take advantage of these changes, instructions were added along with new instruction formats. A good example of what happened can be seen in the evolution of the signed, fixed point binary Add instruction.

In the original architecture there were three instructions you could use to add signed binary integers as shown in Table 12. The first two of these, AR and A, add two 32 bit signed fixed point binary values yielding a 32 bit signed fixed point binary result. The AH instruction adds a 16 bit signed fixed point binary value to a 32 bit register value and yields a signed 32 bit binary result.

Mnemonic	Format	1st	2nd	2nd Operand	Result	Op

		Operand	Operand	Displacement		Code
AR	RR	32 bit GPR	32 bit GPR	N/A	32 bit GPR	1A
A	RX	32 bit GPR	32 bit memory	unsigned 12 bit	32 bit GPR	5A
AH	RX	32 bit GPR	16 bit memory	unsigned 12 bit	32 bit GPR	4A

Table 12 Original Signed Add Instructions

In the current architecture, however, there are several additional variations of this operation as shown in Table 13.

Mnemonic	Format	1st Operand	2nd Operand	2nd Operand Displacement	Result	Op Code
AR	RR	32 bit GPR	32 bit GPR	N/A	32 bit GPR	1A
AGR	RRE	64 bit GPR	64 bit GPR	N/A	64 bit GPR	B908
AGFR	RRE	64 bit GPR	32 bit GPR	N/A	64 bit GPR	B918
A	RX	32 bit GPR	32 bit Memory	unsigned 12 bit	32 bit GPR	5A
AY	RXY	32 bit GPR	32 bit memory	signed 20 bit	32 bit GPR	E3/5A
AG	RXY	64 bit GPR	64 bit GPR	signed 20 bit	64 bit GPR	E3/08
AGF	RXY	64 bit GPR	32 bit memory	signed 20 bit	64 bit GPR	E3/18
AH	RX	32 bit GPR	16 bit memory	unsigned 12 bit	32 bit GPR	4A
AHY	RXY	32 bit GPR	16 bit memory	signed 20 bit	32 bit GPR	E3/7A
AHI	RI	32 bit GPR	16 bit immediate	N/A	32 bit GPR	E3/7A

Table 13 Signed Binary Add Instructions

As can be seen in Table 13, the original three binary add instructions have now grown to ten but not much has really changed. They merely take into account the possibility of several combinations of 32 and 64 bit operands and results along with the newer signed 20 bit displacement. An Add instruction with an immediate operand was also added. Note that the original instructions all had eight bit opcodes while the newer instructions use either 16 bit opcodes found in the first 16 bits of the instruction (such as AGR) or an 8 bit opcode in the first 8 bits of the instruction and an additional 8 bits located in the last byte of the instruction.

Just as with the Add instruction, other instructions in the original architecture have been augmented. The basic concept of the instruction, in most cases, is essentially unchanged. In this book, we will mainly use examples from the original architecture for the sake of simplicity.

The following sections give an overview of the newer machine language formats.

6.8.1 RI Format

RI (register and immediate) and RIL (register and immediate long) formats were not part of the original set of formats. Both have extended opcodes in addition to the eight bit opcode contained in the first byte of the instruction. The extended portion of the opcode is located in bits 12 through 15 of the instruction. RI instructions have a 16 bit immediate operand while RIL instructions have 32 bit immediate operands.

RI instructions mainly use the 16 bit immediate operand as a constant in operations such as Add Halfword Immediate (AHI) while RIL format instructions use the longer 32 bit immediate operand as a signed relative address such as in the Branch Relative and Save (BRAS/BRASL) linkage instructions shown in section 8.3.3.

The Branch Relative on Condition (BRC) and Branch Relative on Condition Long (BRCL) are examples that use a Condition Code mask M1 rather than a register as the first operand.

In the RI format is shown in Figure 16.

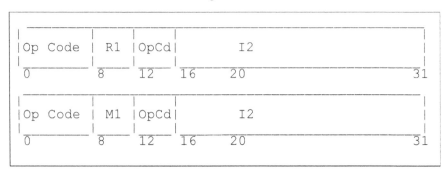

Figure 16 RI Format

6.8.1.1 RIL Format

The RIL format is 6 bytes long as shown in Figure 17. The immediate operand is 32 bits in length and used mainly for

---

66

signed, relative addressing. When used for relative addressing, the value of the immediate operand is in halfwords.

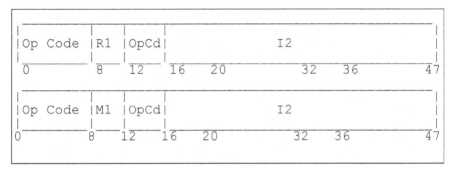

Figure 17 RIL Formats

6.8.2 RIE Format

The RIE format, shown in Figure 18 is used in only two instructions: the Branch Relative on Index High and the Branch Relative on Index Low or Equal (BRXHG/BRXLG) where the immediate operand is used as a signed relative branch address in multiples of halfwords.

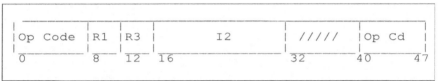

Figure 18 RIE Format

6.8.3 RRE Format

RRE (register register extended), shown in Figure 19, is similar to RR instructions but the opcode is 16 bits long. Bits 16 through 23 of these instructions are not used. This format is used in many instructions that extend the original RR format instruction set to accommodate two 64 bit register operands or one 64 and one 32 bit register operands. Examples include Add (AGR and AGFR).

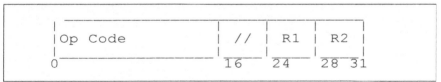

Figure 19 RRE Format

6.8.4 RSL Format

The RSL format, shown in Figure 20, is used only with the Test Decimal (TP) instruction.

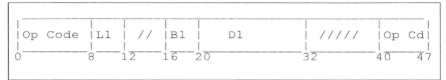

Figure 20 RSL Format

6.8.5 RRF Format

The RRF format, shown in Figure 21, is used mainly with floating point instructions.

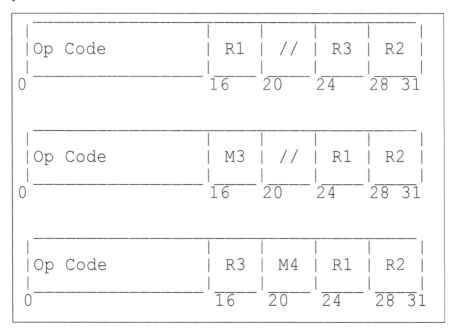

Figure 21 RRF Format

6.8.6 RSI Format

The RSI format, shown in Figure 22, is used with only two instructions: Branch Relative on Index High and Branch Relative on Index Low or Equal (BRXH/BRXLE). These instructions use 32 bit arithmetic. The relative address in the immediate operand is in halfword units.

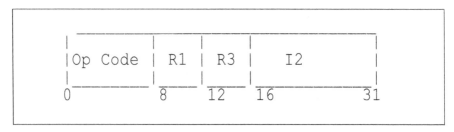

Figure 22 RSI Format

6.8.7 RSY Format

The RSY format, shown in Figure 23, is similar to the RS format but has additional opcode information and an extended 20 bit displacement. While 12 bit displacements are treated as unsigned, positive numbers, 20 bit displacements are treated as 20 bit signed numbers. A 12 bit displacement can range in value from 0 to 4095 while a 20 bit displacement can range from -524,288 to +524,287.

6.8.8 RXE Format

The RXE format, shown in Figure 24, is used mainly with floating point operations.

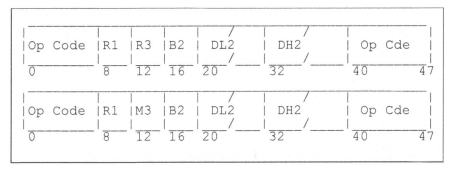

Figure 23 RSY Format

6.8.9 RXF Format

The RXF format, shown in Figure 25, is used mainly with floating point operations.

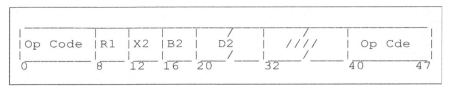

Figure 24 RXE Format

6.8.10 RXY Format

RXY instructions, shown in Figure 26, are similar to RX instructions except they have a 20 bit signed displacements and a 16 bit opcode. One or both of the operands are 64 bit values.

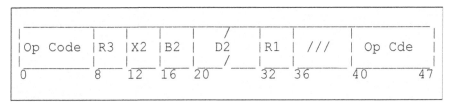

Figure 25 RXF Format

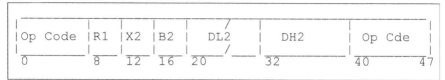

Figure 26 RXY Format

6.8.11 S Format

The S format, shown in Figure 27, has one memory resident operand. The Test and Set (TS) is the most commonly used of this format. Originally, TS was labeled as an SI instruction but the I operand was never used.

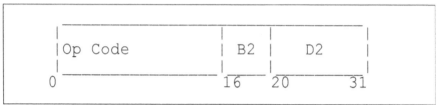

Figure 27 S Format

6.8.12 SIY Format

SIY instructions, shown in Figure 28, are similar to SI instructions but use a signed 20 bit displacement. Many original SI instructions have SIY counterparts such as Compare Logical (CL/CLY).

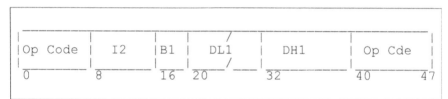

Figure 28 SIY Format

6.8.13 SSE Format

SSE instructions, shown in Figure 29, are mainly used for machine control, not general programming.

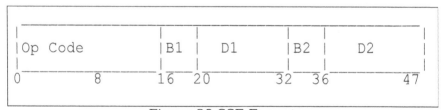

Figure 29 SSE Format

7. Status Word (PSW)

7.1 Purpose

The PSW (Program Status Word) has been part of the IBM mainframe architecture since the beginning. Originally, it was a 64 bit (8 byte) special purpose CPU register. Currently, in the latest Z models, it is a 128 bit (16 byte) CPU register. The longer format is mainly due to the extension of addressing from 24 to 64 bits over the years. In the Z390 emulator, the PSW is 64 bits in length and the address portion is 31 bits in length. The PSW contains several important values and flags describing the state of the system at any given instant. Some of the important fields in the PSW in the ESA/390 level architecture are outlined in the following sections.

7.2 Addressing modes

In the current architectural levels, bits 31 and 32 determine the addressing mode. If both are zero, addressing is in 24 bit mode. If 31 is zero and 32 one, 31 bit addressing is in effect. When both are one, 64 bit mode is in effect.

The address of the next instruction to be fetched for execution is contained in the PSW. In 24 bit addressing compatibility mode, this address is found in bits 40 through 63. In 31 bit addressing mode, the address is in bits 33 through 63 of the PSW. In 64 bit addressing mode the address is in bits 65 through 127.

7.3 Condition Code

The Condition Code is located at bits 18 and 19 of the PSW. The Condition Code reflects the result of a prior operation. It can have a value of 0, 1, 2 and 3 at any given point in time. Many (but not all) instructions set the Condition Code.

For example, after a fixed point binary Add instruction, the Condition Code is 0 if the result is zero, 1 if the result is less than zero, 2 if the result is greater than zero and 3 if the operation generates an overflow. After a Compare instruction, the Condition Code will be 0, 1 or 2 if the first operand is equal to, greater than, or less than the second. A value of 3 after a Compare is not possible.

7.4 Program Mask

The Program Mask is located in bits 20 through 23. The Program Mask determines which program exceptions (errors) will be recognized or ignored. They are shown in Table 14.

```
Bit 20 Enable fixed point overflow exception
Bit 21 Enable decimal overflow exception
```

When the bit is 1, the exception is enabled. When 0, the exception is ignored. If enabled, the exception will interrupt your program.

7.5 Problem / Supervisor State Bit

The Problem State bit is located at bit 15. When 1, the machine is operating in unprivileged problem state. In problem state, not all instructions may be executed. When 0, the machine is in supervisor state and all instructions may be executed. The operating system routines often run in supervisor state and has access to all instructions.

7.6 Instruction Addressing

The PSW always contains the address of the next instruction to be executed. This is often referred to as the *updated address portion of the PSW*. When an instruction is fetched, before it is executed, the address portion of the PSW is updated (incremented) to point to the address of the byte immediately following the instruction just fetched and yet to be executed. Thus, the PSW points to where the next instruction should be located. The address portion of the PSW always points to the *next* instruction, not the current instruction. In case of an error and a system dump, the PSW address will likely be pointing at the instruction following the one causing the error.

Any of the branch instructions can alter the address portion of the PSW. In effect, a branch means loading a new value into the address portion of the PSW. When you alter this value, the next instruction to be executed will be fetched from this location.

8. Flow of Control & Branch Instructions

8.1 Flow of Control

Every program needs a way to control the order in which instructions are executed. Normally, computers fetch and execute instructions consecutively from ascending memory locations.

This, however, this is not always desirable. Sometimes you need to skip blocks of code based on whether a condition is true or false, or to loop back through a block of code a number of times, or branch to a subroutine and return when the subroutine has finished.

In the original architecture there were several branch instructions to handle these situations. They include instructions that branch if a condition is true, instructions that iterate and instructions that are used to call subroutines.

We begin with the most common form of branch of instruction, the conditional branch which branches, or not, depending on the value of the Condition Code.

8.2 Conditional Branch Instructions

The conditional branch instructions branch, or transfer control, based upon the value of the Condition Code. For example, if you want to skip around a section of code if the result of the previous arithmetic operation is negative, the instruction to accomplish this is the Branch Conditional.

In the original architecture there were two Branch Conditional instructions, the BC and the BCR. In later generations additional instructions were added which build on the originals.

8.2.1 Branch Conditional (BC/BCR)

The two basic Branch Conditional instructions are the BC (an RX instruction) and BCR (the RR version of the BC). In both instructions the destination (where to branch to) is specified by the second operand. The explicit formats are:

```
BC   M1,D2(X2,B2)
BCR  M1,R2
```

In the BC instruction, the destination address is calculated from the base, index and displacement in the usual manner. In the BCR, the destination address is contained in the register specified as the second operand.

In both instructions, the first operand is called a *mask*. It resides in the 4 bits where there would normally be a register specification in both the RX and RR formats.

The mask tells the computer which value or values of the Condition Code should cause the instruction to branch. Note: the Condition Code has only one value at a time but you may want to branch if its value is one of a set of values. If the Condition Code has one of these values, the branch takes place. If the Condition Code does not have one of these values, execution resumes with the instruction immediately following the branch instruction.

The mask is 4 bits long and each bit corresponds to one of the 4 possible settings for the Condition Code. If a mask bit is 1, this means the branch will take place if the Condition Code has the corresponding value. If the mask has no 1s in any position corresponding to the current value of the Condition Code, no branch takes place. If all mask bits are 1, the branch always takes place (unconditional branch).

For example, after a signed Add instruction, the Condition Code will have one of the values shown in Table 15.

```
0   Answer was zero
1   Answer was less than zero
2   Answer was greater than zero
3   Answer caused an overflow

          Table 15 CC after signed Add
```

Let us say you want your program to branch to some label if the result of the Add was zero. To do this you need mask of 1000_2 as shown in Figure 30. The first operand, B'1000', specifies a 4 bit constant. The first position in the mask corresponds to a Condition Code value of 0, the second to 1, the third to 2 and the fourth to 3. In this case, the branch to label LAB1 will occur if the Condition Code is 0. Otherwise, execution will continue at the instruction following the BC.

```
AR R3,R4
BC B'1000',LAB1
```
Figure 30 BC Example

Alternatively, what if you want to branch if the result in R3 is zero or less than zero? In this case, you could place a second BC instruction after the first such as:

```
BC B'1000',LAB1
BC B'0100',LAB1
```

which will work since the BC instruction itself does not alter the Condition Code. The first instruction will branch if the Add resulted in zero and the second will branch if the Add resulted in a negative value. However, this is wasteful. Instead, you combine all the conditions for which you want to branch into one mask on one BC instruction. Thus, the BC to branch if the result is zero or negative becomes the single instruction:

```
BC B'1100',LAB1
```

All of the possible combinations of mask settings following an arithmetic instruction are shown in Table 16.

```
B'0000' Never branch
B'0001' Branch if overflow
B'0010' Branch if > zero
B'0011' Branch if > zero or overflow
B'0100' Branch if < zero
B'0101' Branch if < zero or overflow
B'0110' Branch if not zero or overflow
B'0111' Branch if not zero
B'1000' Branch if zero
B'1001' Branch if zero or overflow
B'1010' Branch if zero or > zero
B'1011' Branch if not < zero
B'1100' Branch if zero or < zero
B'1101' Branch if not > zero
B'1110' Branch if not overflow
B'1111' Branch always
```

Table 16 Mask settings after a signed add

However, if the instruction preceding the BC were a Compare, the meaning of the mask would be described differently. For example, mask B'1000' would mean branch if *result is zero* after an Add but it means *branch if equal* after a Compare. Likewise, mask B'0010' means branch *greater than zero* after an Add but branch *if first operand is greater than second* after a Compare.

```
BC B'0001',LAB   or   BC 1,LAB
BC B'0010',LAB   or   BC 2,LAB
BC B'0011',LAB   or   BC 3,LAB
BC B'0100',LAB   or   BC 4,LAB
BC B'0101',LAB   or   BC 5,LAB
BC B'0110',LAB   or   BC 6,LAB
BC B'0111',LAB   or   BC 7,LAB
BC B'1000',LAB   or   BC 8,LAB
BC B'1001',LAB   or   BC 9,LAB
BC B'1010',LAB   or   BC 10,LAB
BC B'1011',LAB   or   BC 11,LAB
BC B'1100',LAB   or   BC 12,LAB
BC B'1101',LAB   or   BC 13,LAB
BC B'1110',LAB   or   BC 14,LAB
BC B'1111',LAB   or   BC 15,LAB
```

Table 17 Decimal mask settings

Generally speaking, the Condition Code is 0, 1, 2 or 3 after arithmetic instructions is the result was zero, less than zero, greater than zero or overflow. After Compare instructions it is 0,

1, or 2 is the first operand is equal to the second, less than or greater than the second, respectively. After logical operations the Condition Code will be 0 if the result was zero and 1 if not. A number of other instructions set it in ways that are specific to the individual instructions.

Condition Code	Decimal Mask Value
0	8
1	4
2	2
3	1

Table 18 Decimal mask equivalents

The mask can be specified in any manner that results in a value between zero and fifteen. The most popular methods are either as a decimal number or as a bit string. When a decimal number is given, its corresponding binary pattern determines the branch conditions as seen in Table 17.

Extended	Basic	Meaning
B D2(X2,B2)	BC 15,D2(X2,B2)	Branch always
BR R2	BCR 15,R2	Branch always
NOP D2(X2,B2)	BC 0,D2,(X2,B2)	No operation
NOPR R2	BCR 0,R2	No operation
After Compare Instructions (A:B)		
BH D2,(X2,B2)	BC 2,D2(X2,B2)	Branch A high
BL D2(X2,B2)	BC 4,D2(X2,B2)	Branch A low
BE D2(X2,B2)	BC 8,D2(X2,B2)	Branch A equals B
BNH D2(X2,B2)	BC 13,D2(X2,B2)	Branch A not high
BNL D2(X2,B2)	BC 11,D2(X2,B2)	Branch A not low
BNE D2(X2,B2)	BC 7,D2(X2,B2)	Branch not equal
After Arithmetic Instructions		
BO D2(X2,B2)	BC 1,D2(X2,B2)	Branch on overflow
BP D2(X2,B2)	BC 2,D2(X2,B2)	Branch plus
BM D2(X2,B2)	BC 4,D2(X2,B2)	Branch minus
BZ D2(X2,B2)	BC 8,D2(X2,B2)	Branch zero
BNP D2(X2,B2)	BC 13,D2(X2,B2)	Branch not plus
BNE D2(X2,B2)	BC 7,D2(X2,B2)	Branch not zero
After Test Under Mask		
BO D2(X2,B2)	BC 1,D2(X2,B2)	Branch if ones
BM D2(X2,B2)	BC 4,D2(X2,B2)	Branch if mixed
BZ D2(X2,B2)	BC 8,D2(X2,B2)	Branch if zeros
BNO D2(X2,B2)	BC 14,D2(X2,B2)	Branch if not ones

Table 19 Extended mnemonics

A simple way to construct a decimal mask is to remember that the bit positions in the mask each have a decimal equivalent. By adding the decimal equivalents of the bit positions, a final decimal mask can be created. The equivalents are shown in Table 18. So, if you want to branch if the Condition Code is either 0 or 3, the decimal mask would be 9 (8+1).

The BCR instruction is similar to the BC. The first operand is the four bit mask with the same meanings as in the BC instruction. The second operand is a register which contains the branch address. However, should the second operand be specified as R0, no branch will ever take place since R0 means no register when used in an addressing context.

Additionally, there are builtin extended mnemonic branch instructions. These are no additional instructions but variations of the basic Branch Conditional instruction where the assembler will fill in the mask for you. These are shown in Table 19. The purpose of these is to make your program more readable. Instead of using the mask codes, you use a mnemonic which is indicative of the purpose. The assembler interprets these as either a BC or BCR with a predetermined mask. Some mask settings (such as 8) have more than one extended representation: BE after a Compare instruction (Branch Equal) and BZ after an arithmetic instruction (Branch Zero). Because the mask is the same, they are interchangeable.

8.2.2 Branch Relative on Condition (BRC)

```
BRC M1,I2
```

The Branch Relative on Condition instruction is a newer RI format (see section 6.8.1) instruction which is similar to the BC instruction. However, the branch address is calculated by adding twice the value of the signed 16 bit immediate operand to the current instruction address. Hence the term *Relative* in its name. Since all instructions must begin on an even memory address, an odd relative offset would make no sense. Doubling the relative offset also increases the range of the offset. The value in the relative operand is specified in halfwords.

8.2.3 Branch Relative on Condition Long (BRCL)

```
BRCL M1,I2
```

The Branch Relative on Condition Long is an RIL format (see section 6.8.1.1 instruction similar to the BRC instruction except that the immediate operand is 32 bits in length. The value in the relative operand is specified in halfwords.

8.2.4 Conditional Branch Program Example

In Figure 31, R1 is loaded with binary equivalent of 10_{10} on line 4. On line 5, the text *LOOP EXAMPLE* is printed. On line 6, one is subtracted from R1 and the result, on the next line, is compared with zero. The Compare instruction sets the condition code to indicate if the first operand is equal to, less than or greater than the second operand. The Branch Conditional on line 8 branches to LOOP if the Condition Code indicates that the contents of R1 are greater than zero, otherwise execution continues at line 9. The net effect is that the phrase LOOP EXAMPLE is printed 10 times. Note: the Compare is actually unnecessary as the Subtract sets the condition code to indicate the result.

```
1                        PRINT           NOGEN
2      EXMPL             SUBENTRY
3                        EQUREGS
4                        L               R1,TEN
5      LOOP              XPRNT           MSG,L'MSG
6                        S               R1,ONE
7                        C               R1,ZERO
8                        BC              B'0010',LOOP
9                        SUBEXIT
10     MSG               DC              C'LOOP EXAMPLE'
11     ZERO              DC              F'0'
12     ONE               DC              F'1'
13     TEN               DC              F'10'
14                       END
```

Figure 31 Conditional Branch Example

8.3 Branch and Link Instructions

The Branch and Link family of instructions were designed for legacy subroutine linkage conventions. The original instructions used were BAL/BALR. To these have been added new instructions (BAS/BASR and BRAS/BRASL) that accommodate newer, extended addressing modes.

Additionally, there are new linkage instructions which use the system stack which was not part of the original architecture. These include the Branch and Stack (BAKR), Program Call (PC) and Program Return (PR) instructions.

8.3.1 Branch and Link (BAL/BALR)

The BAL and BALR instructions branch unconditionally. They do not depend on the condition code. A branch is made to the address specified by the second operand which, in the case of a BAL, is a base, index and displacement address and, in the case of a BALR, to the address contained in the register designated as the second operand. With the BALR, however, if the second operand is specified as R0, no branch takes place.

In both versions of the instruction, the memory address of the byte immediately following the BAL or BALR is placed into the register specified as the first operand. This is the linking operation: it stores the address where return should be made.

These instructions were on the earliest models of the 360 architecture where addresses were always 24 bits. In current machines, where the registers are 64 bits in length, when a program is operating in 24 bit addressing mode, the 24 bit updated PSW instruction address is placed in the rightmost 24 bits of the first operand register (bits 40 through 63 of the 64 bit register), while the following fields from the PSW are stored in bits 32 through 39 of the register:

1. The Instruction Length Code (bits 32 and 33)

2. The Condition Code (bits 34 and 35)

3. The Program Mask (Bits 36 through 39)

This effectively mimics the operation of the early 24 bit address machines. The low order 32 bits of the 64 bit first operand register mimic a 32 bit register from the early architecture. In these are stored eight bits of status information from the PSW followed by 24 bits of address. Since early machines only used 24 bit for addressing, the high order 8 bits were available for other uses. In this case, they stores information about the status of the program as the subroutine call was being made. This information could be used to restore the status upon return.

However, in 31 bit addressing mode, bit 32 of the 64 bit first operand becomes one and the remaining low order 31 bits (bits 33 through 63) are loaded with the updated instruction address from the PSW.

In both 24 and 31 bit addressing modes, bits 0 through 31 (the high order bits) of the 64 bit register specified as the first operand are unchanged.

In 64 bit addressing mode, the full 64 bit updated address portion of the PSW is placed in the 64 bit register specified as the first operand.

The main use for these instructions is to branch to a subroutine and, in the same operation, load a register with the address of the return point as shown in this example:

```
L    R15,=V(SUB1)  * load address of subroutine
BALR R14,R15       * branch to subroutine
```

This example is typical of a legacy assembly language subroutine call. The figure =V(SUB1) is a literal which will cause the assembler to allocate 4 bytes of memory that will be set by the system loader, as the program containing this instruction is loaded into memory, with the address of the subroutine whose name is SUB1. Thus, R15 will contain the address of the first byte of the subroutine SUB1. On execution, the BALR will branch to the address in R15 and, at the same time, load into R14 the address of the byte immediately following the BALR. The subroutine, when finished, branches back to this address. The BAL operates similarly except the second operand address is calculated from a base, index, and displacement.

A second non-branching use for the BALR is to load the address of the byte immediately following the BALR into a register such as:

```
BALR R13,R0    * Load updated PSW addr into R13
```

In this case, no branch takes place because register R0 is designated as the destination address. There is no equivalent BAL usage. This form is often used to load base registers such as:

```
BALR R12,R0
USING *,R12
```

The BALR loads R12 and the USING tells the assembler that R12 points 'here' where 'here' is the byte immediately following the BALR.

As noted, the BAL/BALR in 24 bit addressing mode place additional information in the high order 8 bits of the first operand. Many legacy programs depended on this information. In 31 and 64 bit addressing modes, this information is lost. Thus, the similar BAS and BASR instructions were added and are now preferred when not using 24 bit addressing mode.

8.3.2 Branch and Save (BAS/BASR)

```
BAS  R1,D2(X2,B2)
BASR R1,R2
```

These are similar to the BAL and BALR instructions and are intended to replace them. They both load the updated address portion of the PSW into the first operand and branch to the address specified by the second operand. As with the BALR, if the second operand of the BASR is specified as R0, no branch takes place.

In both instructions, the updated address portion of the PSW is loaded into the register specified as the first operand depending upon the addressing mode. In 24 bit addressing mode, bits 32 through 39 of the 64 bit register are set to zero. In 31 bit addressing mode, bit 32 is set to one. In 24 and 31 bit addressing mode, bits 0 through 31 of the first operand remain unchanged. In 64 bit mode, the entire register specified as the first operand receives the address.

8.3.3 Branch Relative and Save (BRAS/BRASL)

```
BRAS   R1,I2
BRASL  R1,I2
```

These instructions are comparable to the BAS/BASR instructions. The register specified as the first operand is loaded with the updated address portion of the PSW in the same manner as the BAS/BASR.

In the BRAS instruction there is a 16 bit immediate field which is treated as a signed binary number. In the BRASL, there is a 32 bit immediate field which is likewise treated as a signed number. BRAS is an RI format instruction while BRASL is an RIL format instruction (see section 6.8.1).

In both instructions, the branch address is computed by adding the twice the value of the immediate field to the current instruction address. That is, the immediate field is treated as the number of half words to jump relative to the current instruction address. All instructions must begin on half-word boundaries.

8.4 Looping Branch Instructions

Looping normally involves three separate actions: an arithmetic calculation, a comparison and a conditional branch. For example, to loop through a section of code ten times you need a counter (usually a register) initialized to zero, an add instruction to increment the counter, a compare instruction to see if the counter has reached nine followed by a conditional branch instruction to iterate if it hadn't.

Since this is such a common sequence of events, the architecture provides several instructions that perform all three operations in one instruction.

There are three looping instructions families with several variations in how the branch address is calculated and the number of bits in the operands. These are:

1. Branch Index Low or Equal: the loop continues so long as an index is less than or equal to a limit;

2. Branch Index High: the loop continues so long as the index is greater than a limit; and

3. Branch on Count: loop until a counter reaches zero.

The operands in these instructions (the count, index and limit values) can be either 32 or 64 bits, depending on the instruction. The branch address is specified either as a register, a base/displacement, or a relative address (on offset from the current instruction's address).

8.4.1 Branch Index Low or Equal (BXLE)

The first of these is the BXLE instruction, Branch on Index Low or Equal. The instruction is an RS instruction which has the explicit format:

```
BXLE R1,R3,D2(B2)
```

The instruction operates as follows: first, an increment is added to the contents of the register specified as the first operand. The value in the first operand is then compared with a limit value and a branch takes place to the address specified by the second operand, the result of the D2(B2) calculation, if the result of the comparison indicates that the contents of the first operand are less than or equal to the limit value.

The third operand, the R3 in the above, is used to determine both the increment and the limit values. If the register designated as R3 is even, it is the even register of an even odd pair of registers. In this case, the even register of the pair contains the increment and the odd register contains the limit value. If the register designated as R3 is odd, its contents are used as both the limit and the increment.

1		PRINT	NOGEN
2		EQUREGS	
3	SUM100	SUBENTRY	
4			
5		SR	R2,R2
6		L	R3,ONE
7		L	R4,ONE
8		L	R5,HUNDRED
9	LOOP	AR	R2,R3
10		BXLE	R3,R4,LOOP
11		XDECO	R2,OUT
12		XPRNT	OUT,L'OUT
13		SUBRETURN	
14		LTORG	
15	ONE	DC	F'1'
16	HUNDRED	DC	F'100'
17	OUT	DS	CL12

Figure 32 BXLE Loop Example

There are several instructions that use even/odd register pairs. The valid pairs are:

```
R0/R1
R2/R3
R4/R5
R6/R7
R8/R9
R10/R11
R12/R13
R14/R15
```

The program in Figure 32 gives an example of a BXLE. This program adds the first 100 numbers into R2 and then prints the result. Lines 5 through 8 we initialize the registers. On line 5, R2 is set to zero by subtracting it from itself. R3 will be the BXLE's counting register which is set to 1. R4 will be the increment register, also set to 1 and R5 is the limit register, set to 100.

The contents of R3 are added to the contents of R2 in line 9. The BXLE (line 10) then increments R3 by 1 (from contents of R4) and compares the result with 100 (contents of R5). The BXLE branches to LOOP so long as the value in R3 is less than or equal to 100. When R3 becomes 100, execution continues with the XDECO which converts the fixed point binary value in R2 to printable digits in the 12 byte string OUT. The XPRNT prints the result to the screen. The second operand of the XPRNT is the length of the string OUT.

The data declarations on line 15 and 16 create two full word fixed point binary values in memory initialized with the values 1 and 100, respectively. The declaration on line 17 reserves storage for a character string of length 12 but does not initialize it (DC statements initialize, DS statements only reserve memory).

The advantage of the BXLE instruction is that it combines the increment, comparison and conditional branch into one instruction and thus, in a loop iterated many times, results in considerably faster execution. The disadvantage is that it ties up several registers in the process. But, in many circumstances, it is justified.

In the BXLE, the addition and comparison operations treat the operands as 32 bit signed integers but any overflow that may be caused by the addition is ignored.

8.4.1.1 Branch Index Low or Equal 64 bit (BXLEG)

```
BXLEG R1,R3,D2(B2)
```

In addition to the BXLE, there is the newer BXLEG instruction. This is of machine format RSY (see section 6.8.7). In this instruction, for purposes of addition and comparison, the operands are treated as 64 bit signed integers. Overflow is likewise ignored. Otherwise, the instruction behaves similarly to the BXLE. Note that RSY instructions use longer, signed displacements.

8.4.1.2 Branch Relative on Index Low or Equal (BRXLE)

```
BRXLE R1,R3,I2
```

The Branch Relative on Index Low or Equal is an RSI format (see section 6.8.6) instruction similar to the BXLE. In the case of the BRXLE instruction, the branch address is calculated by adding the twice the value of the 16 bit signed immediate operand to the current instruction address. Thus, the instruction, if it branches, branches relative to the current address. The immediate operand specifies the number of half-words to branch. The index, increment and limit are treated as signed 32 bit quantities.

8.4.1.3 Branch Relative on Index Low or Equal (BRXLG)

```
BRXLG R1,R3,I2
```

This instruction is of format RIE and is the same as BRXLE except the index, increment and limit are treated as signed 64 bit quantities.

8.4.2 Branch Index High (BXH)

```
BXH R1,R3,D2(B2)
```

Closely related to the BXLE is the Branch Index High - BXH. The BXH operands are the same in scope and function as the BXLE except that the branch takes place when the contents of the register specified as the first operand are *greater* than the limit value. If not, the branch does not take place.

8.4.2.1 Branch Index High 64 bit (BXHG)

```
BXHG R1,R3,I2
```

Corresponding to the BXH is the newer RSY format BXHG instruction in which the increment, limit and index registers are treated as signed 64 bit quantities.

8.4.2.2 Branch Relative on Index High (BRXH/BRXHG)

```
BRXH R1,R3,I2
BRXHG R1,R3,I2
```

The BRXH is similar to the BXH (32 bit operands) and the BRXHG is similar to the BXHG (64 bit operands) however both instructions calculate the branch address by adding twice the value of the 16 bit signed immediate operand to the current instruction address.

8.4.3 Branch on Count (BCT/BCTR)

```
BCT  R1,D2(X2,B2)
BCTR R1,R2
```

A similar set of looping instructions are the BCT and BCTR or Branch on Count instructions. In both of these, one is subtracted from the contents of the register specified as the first operand. If the result is not zero, a branch is made to the address specified by the second operand. When the result is zero, execution advances to the next instruction following the BCT or BCTR. The first operand is treated as a 32 bit signed quantity.

In the case of the BCTR, the second operand is a register whose contents are the branch address except when the second operand is specified as register zero. In this case no branch takes place (R0 being used in an addressing context). In the case of the second operand being R0, the BCTR becomes, in effect, a decrement instruction on the register specified as the first operand.

Using a BCT instruction, the program from Figure 32 becomes the program in Figure 33. As before, we zero the contents of R2 (line 5) and load 100 into R5, the count register. On line 7 we add the counting register into the total (R2). The BCT instruction decrements R5 and branches to LOOP if R5 is not zero.

```
1                       PRINT        NOGEN
2                       EQUREGS
3       SUM100          SUBENTRY
4
5                       SR           R2,R2
6                       L            R5,HUNDRED
7       LOOP            AR           R2,R5
8                       BCT          R5,LOOP
9                       XDECO        R2,DBL
10                      XPRNT        DBL,L'DBL

11                      SUBRETURN
12                      LTORG
13      HUNDRED         DC           F'100'
14      DBL             DS           CL12
15                      END
```

Figure 33 BCT Loop Example

8.4.3.1 Branch on Count (BCTG/BCTGR)

```
BCTG   R1,D2(X2,B2)
BCTGR  R1,R2
```

These instructions are essentially the same as the BCT/BCTR but treat the first operand as a 64 bit signed quantity. The BCTG uses a 20 bit signed displacement rather than an unsigned 12 bit displacement as is the case with the BCT.

8.4.3.2 Branch Relative on Count (BRCT/BRCTG)

```
BRCT   R1,I2
BRCTG  R1,I2
```

The BRCT is the same as the BCT (32 bit operand), and the BRCTG is the same as the BCTG (64 bit operand), except that, in both cases, the branch address is calculated by adding twice the value of the signed 16 bit displacement to the current instruction address.

9. Data Definitions & Aggregates

9.1 Define Constant and Define Storage (DC and DS)

In an assembly language program, you allocate memory either statically by means of data declaration instructions that tell the assembler how many bytes to allocate and the attributes of the data, or dynamically by using system services. In this section, we deal with static data allocation generated by DC and DS instructions.

In many cases, you will associate a label with each item of data. For each data definition, the assembler keeps track of the address of the first byte of the data along with several attributes stated or implied by the data definition statement (such as length, data type, alignment, repetition factor, initialization, and so forth).

In IBM assembly language, there are two ways to allocate and label memory. The first is with a *DC* instruction and the second is with a *DS* instruction. A DC (define constant) instruction allocates and initializes memory in your program whereas a DS (define storage) instruction allocates memory without initialization. Actually, the term *define constant* is misleading. A DC instruction allocates and initializes an area of memory but the programmer is free to alter it during execution.

DS and DC instructions are actually assembler directives and not executable instructions as an Add or Subtract would be. They instruct the assembler to reserve bytes in the memory image of your program where data will be stored.

In both forms you often (but not always) place a unique label complying with assembler naming rules (see section 4.4) on the instruction. Labels begin in column 1. Following the label, you include one or more spaces followed by either DC or DS, followed by one or more spaces followed by a series of codes that indicate the data type, initial value (if any), duplication factor (similar to dimensionality in a high level language), and, if not otherwise implied, the length of the item being allocated. Based on these codes, the assembler will allocate memory at the current location in your program and will remember the attributes with which you defined the item for future use.

When reserving memory, codes used in the DS/DC instructions tell the assembler the type of data being allocated. The most common codes are given in Table 20. Each code indicates a data type, and implied length and alignment of the data item being defined.

Several of the codes may have an additional type extension code that further defines the data being allocated. For our purposes, only the type extension D will be considered. It may be added to the fixed point binary F code and address data codes A and V. The D extension makes the underlying data type a doubleword (8 bytes) rather than the default 4 bytes. Thus, the data type FD is fixed point binary doubleword. AD and VD are double word address values.

In Table 20, several data specification types show an implied length of 1 byte. In other data specifications, however, there is a larger implied length. For example, a fixed point binary integer, type F, is normally 32 bits or 4 bytes and thus has an implied length of 4.

Type	Implied Length (bytes)	Alignment	Format
C	1	byte	characters
X	1	byte	hexadecimal digits
B	1	byte	binary digits
F	4	word	fixed point binary
H	2	halfword	fixed point binary
D	8	doubleword	long floating point
P	1	byte	packed decimal
Z	1	byte	zoned decimal
A	4	word	address value
V	4	word	external address value

Table 20 Basic DS/DC Data Types

Alignment refers to the addresses at which allocated memory may be placed. Some data types require that the address of their first byte be evenly divisible by 4 (word alignment), 8 (doubleword alignment) or 2 (half word alignment). This is for performance reasons as some memory operations execute quicker if the data is aligned to boundaries. Byte alignment means the item can begin on any address.

When allocating a unit of memory using a code with a required alignment, if the next available byte is not of the required alignment for the data type being allocated, the assembler will automatically skip one or more bytes in order that the item be correctly aligned.

For example, if the next address available is divisible by 2 but not 4 and you are allocating a full word fixed point value (type F), the assembler will skip two bytes before allocating your data. Normally you won't notice this but if you look carefully in the .*PRN* file for the program, you will see the extra location counter increment necessary to achieve alignment.

In some cases, especially where you need to know the exact number of bytes being used in an otherwise contiguous memory area, these extra padding bytes are important. Simply adding the sizes of the items allocated may not be accurate due to embedded padding bytes.

If you use the DS instruction, you do not provide initialization (if you do, it will be ignored). If you use DC, you give the initial value that will be loaded into the memory location when the program begins. Initialization is normally a single-quoted string beginning immediately after the data type. The value in the string must be appropriate for the data type.

Figure 34 gives some examples of DS and DC instructions. The first three DS instructions reserve 4, 2 and 8 bytes respectively. None of the data items at these labels is initialized and, consequently, the contents of each are undefined until the program stores a value in them.

DAT4 is a double word (8 bytes). It uses the D extension to indicate that it is a 64 bit fixed point binary.

Both DAT5A and DAT5B are 10 bytes but they have different attributes. DAT5A is one instance of a character string of length 10 while DAT5B is 10 contiguous instances of a character string of length 1.

DAT6 is 120 bytes: 10 instances (duplication factor) of a character string of length 20. The number preceding the data type is the duplication factor.

```
DAT1    DS    F                       * fullword uninitialized
DAT2    DS    H                       * halfword uninitialized
DAT3    DS    D                       * doubleword uninitialized
DAT4    DS    FD                      * doubleword uninitialized
DAT5A   DS    CL10                    * 10 bytes
DAT5B   DS    10CL1                   * 10 bytes
DAT6    DS    10CL20                  * 120 bytes
LAB1    DC    F'123'                  * binary full word
LAB2    DC    C'HELLO WORLD'          * character string
LAB3    DC    B'1011101010001001'     * bit string
LAB4    DC    X'2F3C'                 * hexadecimal string
LAB5    DC    P'1234'                 * packed decimal string
LAB6    DC    F'789'                  * full word fixed
*                                     * point binary
LAB7    DC    FD'1234'                * doubleword fixed
```

```
*                                   * point binary
LAB8    DC       CL20'HELLO'         * 20 bytes
```
Figure 34 Example DS/DC Statements

The memory amounts reserved at labels LAB1 through LAB8 are 4, 11, 2, 2, 3, 4, 8 and 20 bytes respectively.

The data at LAB5 is 3 bytes long because there are 4 digits and a sign (C) in the internal representation. Since each digit and the sign require a half byte and all allocations must be in units of full bytes, three bytes are required with a leading zero. (01 23 4C).

In addition to the label and the data type, you may also specify a duplication factor. This is the number of items of the type you want to allocate. So, if you say *18F* you are asking for 18 fullwords. Your label (lets say LOC) will be the address of the first fullword and the remaining 17 will be at successive 4 byte offsets from this location (LOC+4, LOC+8, LOC+12, and so forth).

9.2 Literals

Often for the sake of clarity or convenience, constants are not separately declared in DC instructions but contextually defined with what are called *literals*. This is a shorthand notation which causes the assembler to make the data declaration for you.

You use literal notation in an instruction in place of a label. A literal looks like a DC instruction operand but is always preceded by an equals sign. Note: there is another form of notation for *immediate* operands which looks similar. However, immediate operands are *not* preceded by the equals signs. The two should not be confused.

The assembler keeps track of all the literals your program has used. The assembler will declare these constants, by default, at the end of your program or at a point immediately after a LTORG directive. This is referred to as the literal pool. If you use the same literal more than once, it will only be declared once.

```
L      R1,=F'123'                   * loads R1 with 123
MVC    MESSAGE,=C'Hello World'      * moves string to MESSAGE
MVC    RESULT,=X'40202120'          * moves edit pattern to RESULT
CLI    LAB,C'X'                     * immediate - no = sign
```
Figure 35 Literals

Figure 35 gives several examples of literals. In the first example, literal is the second operand of the load (L) instruction. The effect of this instruction is to load register one with the full word fixed point binary equivalent of the decimal number 123. The remaining examples show character string constants, hexadecimal constants and a single character constant.

Normally, all literals will be defined at the physical end of your program. However this is not always desirable and hence the LTORG directive. The LTORG directive has to do with base register addressing.

Sometimes a program may need to use a very large data area, one that will extend beyond the range of any base and displacement combination. However, as long as the first byte of the data area is within range of a base and displacement, it can be used without problem (you load the address of the area into a register and then address it directly with this register).

If, however, you allowed the literals to be placed at the end of such a program, they would be after the large data area and thus out of range of any base and displacement. So we use the LTORG directive to control placement of the literal pool and place the pool prior to the start of the large data area.

```
NAME                    DS                      0CL75
FIRST                   DS                      CL25
MIDDLE                  DS                      CL25
LAST                    DS                      CL25
```
Figure 36 Name Record

9.3 Records

It is often desirable to organize data into records whose components can be addressed individually or collectively. This can be done by means of DSECTs (dummy sections) or data definitions. DSECTS are discussed in section 18.6.

For example, if you want to create a record named NAME with components FIRST, MIDDLE and LAST, each 25 bytes in length, you could do so as shown in Figure 36. In this example the label NAME has a length attribute of 75 but a repetition attribute of zero so, consequently, it allocates no space in the object module and the location counter is unchanged.

The labels FIRST, MIDDLE and LAST each allocate 25 bytes of data in the object module (for a total of 75).

However, a reference to NAME, since it has a length attribute of 75, refers the 75 bytes beginning at NAME so NAME actually incorporates FIRST, MIDDLE and LAST. This is important for data movement. In the following line of code, all 75 bytes from NAME (including FIRST, MIDDLE and LAST) are copied to OUT:

```
MVC OUT,NAME
```

The assembler when it sees NAME codes the address as the first byte of FIRST (NAME takes no space and thus shares the same memory address as FIRST) but it takes the length from the length attribute of NAME which is 75.

Another related usage would be mapping individual constituent bytes of a larger data item with smaller labeled items.

For example, the four bytes of a fixed point binary field in memory could be individually addressed by name. In Figure 37, the label VAR, once again, takes no storage for itself however the four individual character data items following it do allocate the required 4 bytes. Thus, a Load or Store instruction on VAR would load or store 4 bytes however each individual byte could be manipulated by name with the labels V1, V2, V3 or V3 (for example, in calculating a hash function).

VAR	DS	0F
V1	DS	C
V2	DS	C
V3	DS	C
V4	DS	C

Figure 37 Data Mapping

Note that the declaration of VAR in Figure 37 may result in a change in the location counter in order to achieve alignment. This will happen if the next byte in the program is not on the correct memory boundary. In this case, he memory address must be evenly divisible by four. The assembler will skip up to three bytes in order that the label VAR is on a full word boundary. In fact, it is not uncommon in code to see DS statements, possibly unlabeled, with zero repetitions of aligned data types such a H, F and D in order to achieve boundary alignment alone. See Table 20 Basic DS/DC Data Types.

In another example, you might have two data sets (files) on disk. One of these is an index file and contains fixed length records each of which consists of two pointers and a name record. The other is a data file containing information on the person named.

Each record contains a person's name (first, middle and last) and a pointer to their data record in the other file. It also contains a pointer to the next index record in the index file. The index file is maintained on disk as a list structure so as to make it easy to keep it alphabetized when new names are added. The disk pointers are 32 bit unsigned numbers which give the relative record number of the record to which they are point.

The data declarations are shown in Figure 38. The name of the entire index file entry is INDEX. Its components include two pointers, one to the next file index record (IPTR) and the associated personal data file record (DPTR). Each record also contains a name record consisting of FIRST, MIDDLE and LAST. The total length is 83 bytes.

Note the initial DS 0F which aligns what follows to begin to a full word boundary. If the DS 0F had not been present, it is possible that INDEX may have been assigned to a non-fullword boundary because it is a character string and requires no alignment. However, IPTR does require a full word and would have resulted in padding bytes to be inserted until a fullword boundary was achieved. As a consequence, INDEX and IPTR would not share the same address.

Also Note also that the fullword binary numerics are declared first. Had they been declared after the 75 bytes of NAME, the assembler would have inserted a padding byte so that they would begin on a full word boundary and, consequently, the overall record would be 84 bytes. Since we probably don't want padding bytes in our disk records, it is important to watch for alignment issues in data definitions.

	DS	0F
INDEX	DS	0CL83
IPTR	DS	F
DPTR	DS	F
NAME	DS	0CL75
FIRST	DS	CL25
MIDDLE	DS	CL25
LAST	DS	CL25

Figure 38 Aligned Record

10. Assist Macro Input/Output

Normally, input/output on the IBM mainframe architecture involves mastering a set of somewhat complex underlying operating system macros some of which are covered in Chapter 21. However, for purposes of this text, the simplified Assist pseudo instructions XREAD, XPRNT, XDECO, XDECI, XDUMP, XHEXO, and XHEXI are used.

In some systems the Assist package is implemented as macros, in others, such as the z390 package, they are pseudo-instructions. That is, they appear in code as though they were actual instructions.

These macros or pseudo-instructions handle reading, printing, conversion from fixed point binary to printable decimal and the reverse, memory dumps, conversion from fixed point binary to printable hexadecimal, and printable hexadecimal to fixed point binary. These are considerably simpler to use than the underlying system macros.

10.1 Input / Output using XREAD and XPRNT

In the z390 emulator, by default, the XREAD pseudo-instruction reads from a file with the same name as the file containing the assembly language source program but with the .XRD extension. The output file from the XPRNT pseudo-instruction has the same name as your assembly language source program file but with the .XPR extension. XPRNT output will also appear in the console window. Note the spelling of XPRNT.

The general format of the XREAD is:

```
[LABEL] XREAD INFIELD,LENGTH
```

The LABEL is optional. INFIELD is the address of the area of memory into which data will be read. This address may be specified in the same manner as a second operand in an RX instruction but is usually just a label. The length is specified as either a constant or as a register enclosed in parentheses. If specified as a register, the value in the register at runtime is the length used.

On a PC, the z390 emulator converts ASCII input lines to EBCDIC with carriage-returns and line-feeds removed. Short records are padded to the right with blanks (40_{16} in EBCDIC) to fill the input area to the length specified. Long input records (that is, those that exceed the length stated in the XREAD) are truncated. In the event of an error, the program aborts with an abend (abnormal end) code of S013. If you attempt to read beyond end-of-file, the Condition Code is set to 1, 0 otherwise.

Figure 39 gives an example of a program that reads and prints lines until there is no more input. The BC on line 4 branches to DONE when the Condition Code becomes 1 indicating end of file. Otherwise, the program prints and loops (line 6).

10.2 XDUMP

The XDUMP pseudo instruction dumps the contents of the general purpose registers, the floating point registers and all or part of the program memory segment to the output window. This is an aid for debugging and discussed in greater detail in Chapter 20. Output from an XDUMP will also appear in a file with the .LOG extension in the z390 emulator.

```
                [LABEL] XDUMP [D1(X1,B1),[LENGTH]]

1                        PRINT           NOGEN

2       README          SUBENTRY

3       LOOP            XREAD           IN,20

4                       BC              B'0100',DONE

5                       XPRNT           IN,20

6                       BC              B'1111',LOOP

7       DONE            SUBEXIT

8       IN              DS              CL20

9                       END
README.XRD

Arms, and the man I sing, who, forc'd by fate,
And haughty Juno's unrelenting hate,
Expell'd and exil'd, left the Trojan shore.
Long labors, both by sea and land, he bore,
And in the doubtful war, before he won
The Latian realm, and built the destin'd town;
His banish'd gods restor'd to rites divine,
And settled sure succession in his line,
From whence the race of Alban fathers come,
And the long glories of majestic Rome.

README.XPR

Arms, and the man I
And haughty Juno's u
Expell'd and exil'd,
Long labors, both by
And in the doubtful
The Latian realm, an
His banish'd gods re
And settled sure suc
From whence the race
And the long glories
```

Figure 39 XREAD/XPRNT Example

The operands are a memory location in base, index, displacement format and a length as a constant (not in a register). If the length is omitted, a default value of 4 will be used. This describes the extent of the memory area to be dumped. If no operands are given, the entire memory area associated with the program is dumped.

10.3 XDECO/XDECI

These pseudo instructions are used to convert from binary to printable zoned decimal and the reverse.

XDECO converts from fixed point binary to printable zoned decimal and has the format:

```
[LABEL]     XDECO R1,D2(X2,B2)
```

The first operand designates the register containing the signed 32 bit fixed point binary number to be converted to printable decimal. The second operand gives the address of a 12 byte character field that will receive the converted number. The number will be right justified with a leading minus sign if negative and padded to the left with blanks. The label is optional.

The XDECI converts from zoned decimal to fixed point binary and has the format:

```
[LABEL]     XDECI R1,D2(X2,B2)
```

The first operand designates the register to receive the number converted to signed fixed point binary and the second operand designates the address of a field in memory containing the zoned decimal number. The first operand is normally not machine general purpose register R1 as R1 is altered by the instruction (see below).

XDECI scans the input string. If the first character is neither a numeric nor a plus nor a minus sign, the instruction halts and machine register R1 is set to the address of the first character and the Condition Code is set to 3. Note: R1 in this case means the actual register R1, not the first operand.

Otherwise, the instruction scans the input character string until a non-decimal character is encountered (for example, a blank). It converts the zoned decimal number prior to the non-decimal character to signed fixed point binary number which it places in the first operand. The Condition Code is set to 0 if the converted number is zero, 1 if the number is less than zero and 2 if the number is greater than zero. If there are more than 9 digits in the zoned decimal number, the Condition Code is set to 3 and the first operand is unchanged. In all cases, machine register R1 is set to the address of the first character which is not a digit.

10.4 XHEXO/XHEXI

These operations are similar to XDECO/XDECI except hexadecimal numbers are converted and plus or minus signs are not allowed.

11. Binary Arithmetic

11.1 A Program to Add Numbers

Next we modify, in stages, the *Hello World!* program from Chapter 5. Our new program will be called ADD.MLC whose purpose it will be to add a set of numbers.

First make a copy of *hello.MLC* and name it *add.MLC*. This is file we will modify by first adding a table of numbers initialized with values between 1 and 5. Figure 40 shows the first modification with the added table of initialized numbers. We have also modified the message from *Hello World!* to *Adding Numbers*. Note that Figure 40 shows line numbers on the right but these are for reference and are not part of the actual source code.

```
1                   PRINT           NOGEN
2       ADD         SUBENTRY
3                   EQUREGS
4                   XPRNT           MSG,L'MSG
5                   SUBEXIT
6       MSG         DC              C'Adding Numbers'
7       ONE         DC              F'1'
8       TWO         DC              F'2'
9       THREE       DC              F'3'
10      FOUR        DC              F'4'
11      FIVE        DC              F'5'
12                  END
```

Figure 40 ADD.MLC Step 1

Each of the storage definitions on lines 7 through 11 allocates a full word (4 bytes) whose contents are initialized to the signed fixed point binary equivalent of the decimal numbers in the quoted fields. Note that the fields use single quotes, not double quotes. The total storage allocated is 20 bytes. At this point the program does nothing but print MSG.

Next we need to calculate the total of the four numbered we added. Since we are working with 32 bit signed fixed point binary integers, we will need a register in which to do the calculations. A register is required because the 32 bit binary arithmetic instructions are all of the RR or RX variety and, consequently, one or both of the operands must be a register.

Although any register is legal, we normally select a register in the range R2 through R12. This is because registers R0, R1 and R13, R14 and R15 have significance with regard to program linkage. R2 is a good choice but be careful, it can sometimes be altered by some system calls and instructions (for example, the

TRT instruction) but this will not be the case here so we will select R2.

R2 is our *accumulator*. That is, we will add each of the values into it until it has the final total and then we will print the total. Obviously we first need to put zero into the register. This can be done in either of two ways. One way is to load a full word constant zero into the register. This would use a 4 byte Load instruction and require a corresponding 4 byte constant in memory. This is shown in Figure 41.

The Load instruction (line 4) loads the full word from the memory address specified by the second operand into the register specified as the first operand. It is an RX instruction and the assembler calculates the memory address by a base and displacement. The index register will be zero. The SUBENTRY macro has already established R13 as the base register.

Alternatively, we could use a literal as shown in Figure 42 but this is really the same thing as the assembler makes an equivalent storage declaration for us.

```
1                     PRINT           NOGEN
2        ADD          SUBENTRY
3                     EQUREGS
4                     L               R2,ZERO   *Zero R2
5                     XPRNT           MSG,L'MSG
6                     SUBEXIT
7        MSG          DC              C'Adding Numbers'
8        ZERO         DC              F'0'
9        ONE          DC              F'1'
10       TWO          DC              F'2'
11       THREE        DC              F'3'
12       FOUR         DC              F'4'
13       FIVE         DC              F'5'
14                    END
```

Figure 41 ADD.MLC Step 2

The preferred alternative is to simply subtract the register from itself as shown in Figure 43. This is the quickest and uses the least memory (two bytes: RR instructions are all two bytes in length). The SR instruction subtracts the contents of the register specified as the second operand from the contents of the register specified as the first operand and leaves the result in the first operand. In this case, the result is zero. As we have not used R2 in our program, it would normally contain a random value from the last program that used it. But in the z390 emulator all register bytes are initialized to $F4_{16}$. Regardless of its prior value, subtraction from itself yields zero.

Next we need to add each of the values into R2. To do this, we could use five Add (A) instructions as shown in Figure 44. The Add instruction is an RX instruction that adds a full word aligned signed binary value from memory at the address specified as the second operand to the value in the register specified as the first operand and leaves the result in the first operand. The easiest way to specify a memory operand is with a label so that the assembler calculates the base/displacement. Thus, we use five Add instructions, each referencing a separate label.

1		PRINT	NOGEN
2	ADD	SUBENTRY	
3		EQUREGS	
4		L	R2,=F'0' *Zero R2
5		XPRNT	MSG,L'MSG
6		SUBEXIT	
7	MSG	DC	C'Adding Numbers'
8	ONE	DC	F'1'
9	TWO	DC	F'2'
10	THREE	DC	F'3'
11	FOUR	DC	F'4'
12	FIVE	DC	F'5'
13		END	

Figure 42 Add.MLC Step 3

1		PRINT	NOGEN
2	ADD	ENTRY	
3		EQUREGS	
4		SR	R2,R2 *Zero R2
5		XPRNT	MSG,L'MSG
6		SUBEXIT	
7	MSG	DC	C'Adding Numbers'
8	ONE	DC	F'1'
9	TWO	DC	F'2'
10	THREE	DC	F'3'
11	FOUR	DC	F'4'
12	FIVE	DC	F'5'
13		END	

Figure 43 ADD.MLC Step 4

After the Add instructions, the final total is in R2 as a signed fixed point binary number. We need to print it but binary is not printable. To print it we need to convert it from binary to zoned decimal. The Assist package has a convenient instruction that does this for us named XDECO used as shown in Figure 45. XDECO takes the place of several actual instructions which are

discussed below in Section 23.7. XDECO is a pseudo RX
instruction in the Assist package that converts the signed fixed
point binary integer in the register specified as the first operand
to a 12 byte signed, right justified, decimal character string
(zoned decimal) padded to the left with blanks. It places the
result in memory beginning at the address specified as the
second operand.

```
1                       PRINT           NOGEN
2       ADD             SUBENTRY
3                       EQUREGS
4                       SR              R2,R2    *Zero R2
5                       A               R2,ONE
6                       A               R2,TWO
7                       A               R2,THREE
8                       A               R2,FOUR
9                       A               R2,FIVE
10                      XPRNT           MSG,L'MSG
11                      SUBEXIT
12      MSG             DC              C'Adding Numbers'
13      ONE             DC              F'1'
14      TWO             DC              F'2'
15      THREE           DC              F'3'
16      FOUR            DC              F'4'
17      FIVE            DC              F'5'
18                      END
```

Figure 44 ADD.MLC Step 5

Note that the operand on the DS instruction labeled OUT is
CL12. This format means *character length 12* or, one character
string with a length attribute of 12. Another way of allocating it
would be an operand of 12C which means 12 character strings of
length one (one is the implied, default length of a character).
However, this later notation would not work with the L'OUT
figure in the XPRNT which evaluates to the length attribute of
OUT. The value of L'OUT would be 1, not 12. Used in this manner
12 is a duplication count, not a length.

We assemble, link and execute the code from Figure 45 with the
command:

        assist add

Note that you do *not* include the .MLC ending. The command
assembles the program and, if there are no errors, runs it. The
assist command tells the assembler to use the Assist package of
pseudo-instructions. The results are shown in Figure 46 (long
lines truncated). Prior to the lines printed by the ADD program,
you see the separate steps the process entails: assembly

(MZ390), linking LZ390 and execution by the emulator EZ390. Note that the answer, 15, is twelve characters long with 10 leading blanks (your reader may not accurately render this due to proportional fonts).

```
1                       PRINT           NOGEN

2         ADD           SUBENTRY

3                       EQUREGS

4                       SR              R2,R2   *Zero R2

5                       A               R2,ONE

6                       A               R2,TWO

7                       A               R2,THREE

8                       A               R2,FOUR

9                       A               R2,FIVE

10                      XPRNT           MSG,L'MSG

11                      XDECO           R2,OUT

12                      XPRNT           OUT,L'OUT

13                      SUBEXIT

14        MSG           DC              C'Adding Numbers'

15        ONE           DC              F'1'

16        TWO           DC              F'2'

17        THREE         DC              F'3'

18        FOUR          DC              F'4'

19        FIVE          DC              F'5'

20        OUT           DS              CL12

21                      END
```

Figure 45 ADD.MLC Step 6

```
C:\Documents and Settings\user>echo off
13:13:21 add   MZ390 START USING z390 V1.5.01b ON J2SE 1.6.0_18
13:13:21 add   MZ390 ENDED   RC= 0 SEC= 0 MEM(MB)= 43 IO=733
13:13:22 add   LZ390 START USING z390 V1.5.01b ON J2SE 1.6.0_18
13:13:22 add   LZ390 ENDED   RC= 0 SEC= 0 MEM(MB)= 15 IO=35
13:13:22 add   EZ390 START USING z390 V1.5.01b ON J2SE 1.6.0_18
Adding Numbers
          15
13:13:22 add   EZ390 ENDED   RC= 0 SEC= 0 MEM(MB)= 19 IO=22
```

Figure 46 Assemble & Execute ADD.MLC

11.2 Analyzing the PRN File

When you assembled the program, a file named *add.PRN* was created. It contains important information about your program. It shows your source program and its translation to machine language. A part of the *.PRN* file from Figure 46 is shown in Figure 47. Column headings have been added at the top (these do not appear in the actual *.PRN* file - they are for illustration). The columns from the *.PRN* file are:

1. Column 1 is what is known as the location counter. It is in hexadecimal and gives, relative to location zero, the starting byte address of each line of code in the machine language image being created by the assembler. Each time a machine language instruction is generated or an area of memory is allocated, the location counter will increment by an amount equal to the effective size of the instruction or data area. To achieve memory address alignment, bytes are occasionally skipped so the location counter increment can sometimes be larger than the size of the instruction or data area (all instructions must begin on halfword boundaries, F type data definitions on fullword boundaries and so forth).

2. Column 2 is also in hexadecimal and is the translation of the assembly language statement (up to the first 8 bytes) of the source code shown column 6. Not all assembly language source statements generate machine language so this column may be blank.

3. Column 3 is the effective address, relative to zero, of the first operand of the machine language instruction if the first operand is a memory address. If the first operand is not a memory address (for example, a register) this column is blank. The *effective address* is the location counter address.

4. Column 4 is the effective address, relative to zero, of the second operand if the second operand is a memory address. It is blank otherwise.

5. Column 5 indicates the macro level (first number in the parentheses), the original source code statement line number (second number in the parentheses), and, finally, the actual line number taking into account statements inserted by macro expansions.

6. Column 6 contains your original source code statements.

The reason why we need to know how to read the .PRN file is because it is used in debugging. Very often when we have an error, we need to examine the contents of a memory dump (see Chapter 20 and the .PRN file is our road map to the dump.

For example, look at the line with the location counter value of 72_{16} (leading zeros omitted). But there are two lines with location counter value of 72_{16} ! The first of these, corresponding to original source code line 3 (column 5), is the value of the location counter at the point when the assembler reads the EQUREGS statement.

EQUREGS is the name of a macro. The assembler goes to the macro library and inserts the 16 lines of macro code at this point.

Note that source code line number after the EQUREGS has line jumps from 15 to 33. This increase indicates that lines not shown were inserted.

Col 1	Col 2	C3 Col 4	Col 5	Col 6	
000000			(1/1)1	PRINT	NOGEN
000000			(1/2)2 ADD	SUBENTRY	
000072			(1/3)15	EQUREGS	
000072	1B22		(1/4)33	SR	R2,R2 *Zero
000074	5A20D0B0	0000B8	(1/5)34	A	R2,ONE
000078	5A20D0B4	0000BC	(1/6)35	A	R2,TWO
00007C	5A20D0B8	0000C0	(1/7)36	A	R2,THREE
000080	5A20D0BC	0000C4	(1/8)37	A	R2,FOUR
000084	5A20D0C0	0000C8	(1/9)38	A	R2,FIVE
000088	E020D0A2000E	0000AA	(1/10)39	XPRNT	MSG,L'MSG
00008E	5220D0C4	0000CC	(1/11)40	XDECO	R2,DBL
000092	E020D0C4000C	0000CC	(1/12)41	XPRNT	DBL,L'DBL
000098			(1/13)42	SUBEXIT	
0000AA	C1848489958740D5		(1/14)49 MSG	DC	C'Adding Numbers'
0000B8	00000001		(1/15)50 ONE	DC	F'1'
0000BC	00000002		(1/16)51 TWO	DC	F'2'
0000C0	00000003		(1/17)52 THREE	DC	F'3'
0000C4	00000004		(1/18)53 FOUR	DC	F'4'
0000C8	00000005		(1/19)54 FIVE	DC	F'5'
0000CC			(1/20)55 DBL	DS	CL12
0000D8			(1/21)56	END	

Figure 47 ADD.PRN

Macro expansions (that is, the lines inserted) are not being shown because of the PRINT NOGEN directive.

In this case, the code inserted by the EQUREGS does not generate machine language code – the statements consist entirely of assembler directives. Hence, the location counter is unchanged on the line after the EQUREGS.

Most macros, however, do generate executable assembly language code. Note that the location counter jumps from zero at the beginning of the program to 72_{16} following the SUBENTRY. This is because the SUBENTRY macro generated 72_{16} bytes of machine language.

The next line (line 33) has the machine language code $1B22_{16}$ which represents the SR instruction. As an RR instruction, the format consists of one byte (2 hex digits) containing the opcode and one byte containing the operands. The opcode is 1B as determined from the listing of instructions in Table 40.

With regard to the second byte of the instruction (22_{16}), the first operand is designated by the first four bits and the second operand by the second four bits. Since a hex digit corresponds to four bits, the first hex digit (2) is the first operand and the second hex digit (2) is the second operand. Hence, the code $1B22_{16}$ is the machine language result for *SR R2,R2*.

Since all RR instructions are two bytes in length, the location counter advances by 2 from 72_{16} to 74_{16}.

The next instruction is *A R2,ONE* which says to fetch the 4 bytes beginning at the label ONE and add them to the 4 bytes in register R2, leaving the result in R2. The Add instruction is an RX instruction and, as is the case with nearly all RX instructions (except the BC), has the format shown in section 6.7.2 above (the BC has a mask where R1 normally appears)

From the Add instruction we get the hexadecimal machine language code of $5A20D0B0_{16}$. The first byte (5A) is the opcode. The next byte contains the first operand (R2) and the index register (R0). The third byte contains the base register (D_{16} or R13) and the first 4 bits of the displacement (0). The full displacement is $0B0_{16}$ or 176_{10}.

The fully explicit notation for the Add would correspond to:

        A R2,176(R0,R13)

Because we specified the second operand with the label ONE, the assembler has calculated that the address of ONE is at a displacement of $B0_{16}$ (leading zero omitted) relative to the contents of register 13. This means that, when the program runs, the address of ONE will be the sum contents of R13 plus $B0_{16}$ (176_{10}).

So the question becomes, what's in R13? If you look at the location counter you will see that ONE is at location $B8_{16}$ from the *start* of the program but the displacement of ONE, relative to the contents of R13, is $B0_{16}$. Thus, R13 must have 8 in it!.

When we assemble our programs we do not know where in memory they will be placed. So, instead, the assembler tabulates addresses as though programs were all loaded at location zero. When the program runs, the first byte of our program will be located at an actual run time address which will not be zero. (In fact, the emulator makes it appear that our programs are always loaded at runtime at address location 8000_{16}.)

During the first few instructions of our program when our program actually runs, the SUBENTRY macro determines where in memory our program actually is located and sets the base register (R13) accordingly. This can be seen in Figure 3. It shows the expansion of the SUBENTRY macro.

Several things happen in Figure 3. First, the BAL on line 4, loads R15 with the updated address portion of the PSW. This is the actual *run time* address of the eighth byte of the program. On line 11, the LR instruction copies this value from R15 to R13. Note: system macros use ordinary numbers for the registers, not numbers preceded by the letter R. The USING tells the assembler that R13 is our base register.

Thus, when the program runs, R13 has the actual, real-live address of the eighth byte of our program. Because R13 is designated as the base register (line 12 in Figure 3), the assembler calculates all displacements relative to byte 8 which at run time is 8008_{16} (in the emulator). Thus, if a label is 100 bytes from byte 8 in the assembler location counter listing, it will be 100 bytes from 8008_{16} at run time.

As noted, the assembler uses R13 as the base register due to the USING on line 12 in Figure 3. *USING* is an assembler directive that does not generate code but tells the assembler which register to use as a base register and where the base register is pointing. In this case, it tells the assembler that R13 is pointing at HELLO+8, the eighth byte of the program. Since the SUBENTRY macro will always expands the same way in each program (except for the program name and date time stamp), if we use SUBENTRY, R13 will always be our base register, it will always point to the eighth byte of the program, and all displacements relative to the base register will be eight less than the location counter value for the label. SUBENTRY is not the only entry macro. Others may be used which could establish a different base register.

Thus, the assembler, knowing that R13 can be used as a base register and that it is pointing 8 bytes into the program, seeing the label ONE in the Add instruction, calculates, correctly, that the label is at $B0_{16}$ or 176_{10} bytes from the 8th byte of the program. Thus we see a displacement of $0B0_{16}$ and a base register of R13 in the machine code.

The index register in the Add instructions in Figure 47 are all specified as R0. When R0 is used in an addressing context, it means no register. There is an R0 and you can use it for arithmetic but if you use it in an address, it means no value is contributed regardless of the actual value in R0. Normally, the index register in an address will be R0 unless you explicitly tell the assembler to use it.

11.3 Data Addressing Alternatives

The program in Figure 45 used several labels to address the data. An alternative program, which generates identical machine language code, can be seen in Figure 48. Here only one label (ONE) is used for each of the second operands in the Add instructions but with an increment that takes into account the number of bytes from the label ONE to the desired operand.

Since F type data each take four bytes of memory, the data for F'2' begins at ONE+4, the next, F'3', is at ONE+8 and so on. Since each DC inmstruction generates exactly four bytes of data, these are arranged at consecutive memory locations.

Note that in some circumstances, padding bytes may be placed between data items. This occurs when the next data item requires an address alignment which the next byte lacks. In these cases, enough bytes are skipped after the last byte of the previous item to attain the required alignment. In the case of the example here, since F type data is aligned to addresses evenly divisible by 4 (word alignment) and the length of each is 4, each item is on consecutive word aligned boundaries. No padding bytes will occur.

```
1                PRINT       NOGEN
2      ADD       SUBENTRY
3                EQUREGS
4                SR          R2,R2   *Zero R2
5                A           R2,ONE
6                A           R2,ONE+4
7                A           R2,ONE+8
8                A           R2,ONE+12
9                A           R2,ONE+16
10               XPRNT       MSG,L'MSG
11               XDECO       R2,DBL
12               XPRNT       DBL,L'DBL
13               SUBEXIT
14     MSG       DC          C'Adding Numbers'
15     ONE       DC          F'1'
16               DC          F'2'
17               DC          F'3'
18               DC          F'4'
19               DC          F'5'
20     DBL       DS          CL12
21               END
```

Figure 48 ADD1.mlc

108

In Figure 48, the assembler adds the offsets (4, 8, 12, and 16) to the displacement associated with label ONE in order to address the words 4, 8, 12 and 16 bytes from ONE. Thus, the actual machine code generated is identical to that in Figure 45.

11.4 Even More Addressing Alternatives

In reality, few programmers would code as shown in either Figure 45 or Figure 48, at least not if any significant number items need to be summed. Instead, a loop would be used. The usual way to implement a loop to add full word fixed point binary values is with a register that is incremented by 4 for each iteration and whose value is added to the base address of the table of values to be summed.

To do this, first, we need an additional register, we need to initialize it, to increment it, and to control the number of iterations. For a register we can select any register not otherwise in use except R0 since we will use the register chosen as an index register and R0 means no register in that position.

For the loop mechanism, we also need a way to test whether we are done and iterate if we are not. To test the contents of our index register, we will use the Compare instruction. To cause the program to loop, we will use a Branch on Conditional (BC) instruction.

Figure 49 shows the revised program. We've selected R3 as our loop index register which we initially set to zero (line 5). We've also added a new label: LOOP which is where we branch to until we've added all the numbers.

On line 6, we have a modified form of the Add instruction. The first operand is the same as before but in the second operand we specify an index register as indicated by the (R3) following the label ONE. What this means is that the base and displacement will point to label ONE and the contents of R3 will be added to this result. R3 becomes our index register. It acts very much like an index variable in an array reference.

Initially, R3 contains zero so the effective address is ONE. After the first iteration, however, R3 will contain 4 and the effective address will be ONE+4 and so on.

The Add instruction on line 7 increments the index register R3 by 4 (using literal notation). Next, on line 8, we compare the contents of R3 with the value 16 using the RX Compare instruction. The Compare instruction sets the Condition Code to indicate the result of the comparison.

In the BC instruction (line 9) we set the mask (see section 8.2) so that the BC instruction will branch to label LOOP if the Condition

Code indicates that the Compare instruction found that the value in R3 was *less than or equal* to 16.

```
1                    PRINT        NOGEN
2       ADD          SUBENTRY
3                    EQUREGS
4                    SR           R2,R2   *Zero R2
5                    SR           R3,R3   *Zero R3
6       LOOP         A            R2,ONE(R3)
7                    A            R3,=F'4'
8                    C            R3,=F'16'
9                    BC           B'1100',LOOP
10                   XPRNT        MSG,L'MSG
11                   XDECO        R2,DBL
12                   XPRNT        DBL,L'DBL
13                   SUBEXIT
14      MSG          DC           C'Adding Numbers'
15      ONE          DC           F'1'
16                   DC           F'2'
17                   DC           F'3'
18                   DC           F'4'
19                   DC           F'5'
20      DBL          DS           CL12
21                   LTORG
22                   END
```

Figure 49 ADD2.MLC

If the contents of R3 are equal to 16, the Condition Code is set to 0, if contents of R3 are less than 16, the Condition Code is set to 1, otherwise, the Condition Code is set to 2. The BC instruction mask causes a branch if the Condition Code is either 0 or 1. When the contents of R3 exceed 16, the branch will not take place and the instruction following the BC instruction, the XPRNT (line 10), will execute.

Looping code similar to this is very common in programming. In fact, so common that several instructions were added to the architecture to combine the increment/compare/branch operations as was discussed in section 8.4.

The LTORG directive at the end tells the assembler to place any undeclared literals at this place in your program. These include the =F'4' and =F'16'. Note: if you do not include a LTORG, the assembler will place any literals it has accumulated at the end of your program anyway.

11.5 Using Extended Mnemonics

Figure 50 is a similar example. It is a program to sum the integers from 1 to 100. It initializes R2 to 0 and R3 to 1 (lines 4 & 5). It adds R3 to R2 then increments R3 (lines 6 & 7). Then it tests R3 against the value 100 (line 8) and branches (line 9) back to LOOP if the contents of R2 are less than 101 or falls through to the next instruction (XDECO) when the contents of R3 become equal to 101.

```
1                   PRINT       NOGEN
2       SUM100      SUBENTRY
3                   REGS
4                   SR          R2,R2    * zero R2
5                   L           R3,=F'1' * init R3
6       LOOP        AR          R2,R3
7                   A           R3,=F'1' * incr R3
8                   C           R3,=F'101'
9                   BL          LOOP
10                  XDECO       R2,DBL
11                  XPRNT       DBL,L'DBL
12                  SUBRETURN
13                  LTORG
14      DBL         DS          CL12
15                  END
                Figure 50 Loop Example
```

In Figure 50 we see another form of the BC instruction being used: the extended mnemonic form. The BL (Branch Low) on line 9 is really a BC with a mask of B'0100'. There are several of these forms accepted by the assembler as shown in Table 18. They help make your program more readable but are, in reality, an ordinary BC instruction with the appropriate mask filled in by the assembler.

111

12. More Binary Arithmetic

12.1 64 Bit versus 32 Bit Instructions

The original architecture supported 16 and 32 bit binary integers by means of 32 bit general purpose registers. Newer versions of the machine, however, now have 64 bit general purpose registers so the newer architectures now support for 64 bit arithmetic operations. As a result, in addition to the original instructions that operated on 32 bits, there are now several new instructions to handle several possible combinations of operand lengths. Generally speaking, when a 32 bit instruction operates on a 64 bit GPR, it only operates on the lower 32 bits. The upper 32 bits are usually unchanged.

OpCode	Type	1st Operand	2nd Operand
A	RX	32 bit register	32 bit memory
AR	RR	32 bit register	32 bit register
AH	RX	32 bit register	16 bit memory

Table 21 Basic Signed Binary Add

In the original architecture there were just three fixed point Add instructions instructions as shown in Table 21. Currently, however, there are 11 as shown in Table 22 (new instructions shaded).

OpCode	Type	1st Operand	2nd Operand	Result
A	RX	32 bit register	32 bit memory	32 bit register
AR	RR	32 bit register	32 bit register	32 bit register
AH	RX	32 bit register	16 bit memory	32 bit register
AGR	RRE	64 bit register	64 bit register	64 bit register
AGFR	RRE	64 bit register	32 bit register	64 bit register
AY	RXY	32 bit register	32 bit memory	32 bit register
AG	RXY	64 bit register	64 bit memory	64 bit register
AGF	RXY	64 bit register	32 bit memory	64 bit register
AHY	RXY	32 bit register	16 bit memory	32 bit register
AHI	RI	32 bit register	16 bit immediate	32 bit register
AGHI	RI	64 bit register	16 bit immediate	64 bit register

Table 22 All Signed Binary Add Instructions

Newer instructions also have additional addressing modes that allow for immediate operands as well as extended (20 bit) signed displacements. For the most part, however, they are merely extensions of the original design.

12.2 Condition Code After Binary Operations

All signed arithmetic Add and Subtract instructions set the Condition Code to indicate the result of the operation as shown in Table 23. Multiply and divide instructions do not set the condition code, it remains unchanged.

12.3 Overflows

The signed binary add and subtract instructions can encounter situations where the result of the operation would overflow the register. This happens in 32-bit addition when the result exceeds the maximum or minimum allowed for a signed positive 32 bit number, +2,147,483,647 and -2,147,483,648, respectively. In the case of 64 bit numbers, these values are +18,446,744,073,709,551,615 and -18,446,744,073,709,551,616.

Result	Condition Code
zero	0
< zero	1
> zero	2
overflow	3

Table 23 Condition Codes

Overflows can also occur with the Shift Left Arithmetic (SLA, SLAG) and Shift Left Double Arithmetic (SLDA) instructions (when a bit unlike the sign bit is shifted into the sign bit position (the high order bit). As this would result in a sign change, it is considered to be an overflow.

When an overflow, the Condition Code is set to 3 and a fixed-point-overflow exception interrupt is raised. This normally results in program termination unless bit 20 (in the Program Mask) of the PSW is 1 in which case the interrupt is disallowed.

OpCode	Type	1st Operand	2nd Operand	Result
S	RX	32 bit register	32 bit memory	32 bit register
SR	RR	32 bit register	32 bit register	32 bit register
SH	RX	32 bit register	16 bit memory	32 bit register
SGR	RRE	64 bit register	64 bit register	64 bit register
SGFR	RRE	64 bit register	32 bit register	64 bit register
SY	RXY	32 bit register	32 bit memory	32 bit register
SG	RXY	64 bit register	64 bit memory	64 bit register
SGF	RXY	64 bit register	32 bit memory	64 bit register
SHY	RXY	32 bit register	16 bit memory	32 bit register

Table 24 Signed Subtract Instructions

12.4 Subtraction

Similar to the Add instructions A and AR, are the original Subtract instructions S and SR. The S instruction is of type RX and the SR is of type RR. Both subtract the contents of the second operand from the register specified as the first operand leaving the result in the first operand. Both operate on 32 bit signed (2s complement) binary integers. The full set of Subtract instructions is given in Table 24.

12.5 Unsigned Binary Arithmetic

The architecture provides for unsigned arithmetic known as logical instructions as shown in Table 26 and Table 27. All logical instructions treat both operands as unsigned binary integers. An overflow cannot occur. Instead, the Condition Code indicates if a carry took place as shown in Table 25. The similar table for Subtract Logical indicates a borrow. This information can be used to construct extended precision binary integer arithmetic for which the Add Logical with Carry (ALCR, ALC, ALCGR, and ALCG) instructions were specifically added.

Result	Condition Code
zero, no carry	0
not zero, no carry	1
zero, carry	2
not zero, carry	3

Table 25 CC after logical add

OpCode	Type	1st Operand	2nd Operand	Result
AL	RX	32 bit register	32 bit memory	32 bit register
ALR	RR	32 bit register	32 bit register	32 bit register
ALGR	RRE	64 bit register	64 bit register	64 bit register
ALGFR	RRE	64 bit register	32 bit register	64 bit register
ALY	RXY	32 bit register	32 bit memory	32 bit register
ALG	RXY	64 bit register	64 bit memory	64 bit register
ALGF	RXY	64 bit register	32 bit memory	64 bit register
ALCR	RRE	32 bit register	32 bit register	32 bit register
ALC	RXY	32 bit register	32 bit memory	32 bit register
ALCGR	RRE	64 bit register	64 bit register	64 bit register
ALCG	RXY	64 bit register	64 bit memory	64 bit register

Table 26 Logical Add Instructions

12.6 Multiply

The original 32 bit binary integer multiply instructions are the M and MR. In both, the first operand specifies the even register of an even/odd pair of registers. In the original architecture these were 32 bit registers but in the current implementation only the low order 32 bits of the 64 bit general purpose registers participate. The high order bits are unchanged. The multiplicand is a 32 bit signed integer which resides in the odd register of the pair. The multiplier is a 32 bit signed integer which resides either in the register designated as the second operand (MR) or at the memory address specified (M). The contents of the even register are ignored.

OpCode	Type	1st Operand	2nd Operand	Result
SL	RX	32 bit register	32 bit memory	32 bit register
SLR	RR	32 bit register	32 bit register	32 bit register
SLGR	RRE	64 bit register	64 bit register	64 bit register
SLGFR	RRE	64 bit register	32 bit register	64 bit register
SLY	RXY	32 bit register	32 bit memory	32 bit register
SLG	RXY	64 bit register	64 bit memory	64 bit register
SLGF	RXY	64 bit register	32 bit memory	64 bit register
SLBR	RRE	32 bit register	32 bit register	32 bit register
SLB	RXY	32 bit register	32 bit memory	32 bit register
SLBGR	RRE	64 bit register	64 bit register	64 bit register
SLBG	RXY	64 bit register	64 bit memory	64 bit register

Table 27 Logical Subtract Instructions

The result is a 64 bit signed binary number which is placed in the low order 32 bits of the even/odd register pair with the high order 32 bits of the result in the low order 32 bits of the even register and the low order 32 bits of the result placed in the low order 32 bits of the odd register. No overflow can take place and the Condition Code remains unchanged.

For example, If R5 contains 20_{10} and R6 contains 3_{10}, we can multiply them with the instruction:

    MR R4,R6

The result will be in R4 and R5. As the answer is 60_{10}, the result is effectively in R5. R6 will contain results only in the case when answers exceed 32 bits.

There is also an MH instruction where a 16 bit signed number from memory is multiplied by the 32 bit signed contents of the register specified as the first operand. The low order 32 bits of the result replace the contents of the first operand. No overflow can occur and the Condition Code remains unchanged. The rules of algebra determine the sign of the result (except in overflows) but zero is always positive. There is no negative zero in 2s complement notation.

OpCode	Type	1st Operand	2nd Operand	Result
M	RX	32 bit register	32 bit memory	32 bit register
MR	RR	32 bit register	32 bit register	32 bit register
MH	RI	32 bit register	16 bit memory	64 bit register
MHI	RRE	32 bit register	16 bit immediate	32 bit register
MGHI	RI	64 bit register	16 bit immediate	64 bit register
MSR	RRE	32 bit register	32 bit memory	32 bit register
MSGR	RRE	64 bit register	64 bit register	64 bit register
MSGFR	RRE	64 bit register	32 bit memory	64 bit register
MS	RX	32 bit register	32 bit memory	32 bit register
MSY	RXY	32 bit register	32 bit memory	32 bit register
MSG	RXY	64 bit register	32 bit memory	64 bit register
MSGF	RXY	64 bit register	64 bit memory	64 bit register

Table 28 Signed Multiply Instructions

In more recent systems, several additional Multiply instructions have been added that permit various combinations of operand lengths as well as newer addressing modes. The complete set of signed multiply Instructions is given in Table 28.

Also, in newer systems a set of Multiply Logical instructions have been added that treat both operands and the result as unsigned numbers. The complete list is shown in Table 29.

OpCode	Type	1st Operand	2nd Operand	Result
ML	RXY	32 bit register	32 bit memory	64 bit register
MLR	RXE	32 bit register	32 bit register	64 bit register
MLGR	RXE	64 bit register	64 bit register	128 bit register
MLG	RXY	64 bit register	64 bit memory	128 bit register

Table 29 Logical Multiply Instructions

12.7 Divide

The original binary integer divide instructions are D and DR. These are shown in Table 30 along with the newer versions of the instruction. Table 31 gives the logical or unsigned versions. In both, the register specified as the first operand, the dividend, is the even register of an even odd pair. Because in the original architecture these were 32 bit registers, in the current implementation only the low order 32 bits of the general purpose registers participate. The high order bits are unchanged. The low order portions of both registers are treated as one 64 bit signed binary integer with the high order part of the number in the even register. There is no halfword divide instruction.

OpCode	Type	1st Operand	2nd Operand	Result
D	RX	32 bit register	32 bit memory	32 bit register
DR	RR	32 bit register	32 bit register	32 bit register
DSGR	RRE	64 bit register	64 bit register	64 bit register
DSGFR	RRE	64 bit register	32 bit memory	64 bit register
DSG	RXY	64 bit register	32 bit memory	64 bit register
DSGF	RXY	64 bit register	64 bit memory	64 bit register

Table 30 Signed Divide Instructions

The divisor is a 32 bit signed number located in the register specified as the second operand (DR) or at the memory location specified by the second operand address.

OpCode	Type	1st Operand	2nd Operand	Result
DL	RXY	32 bit register	32 bit memory	64 bit register
DLR	RXE	32 bit register	32 bit register	64 bit register
DLGR	RXE	64 bit register	64 bit register	128 bit register
DLG	RXY	64 bit register	64 bit memory	128 bit register

Table 31 Unsigned Divide Instructions

The result consists of a remainder located in the even register of the first operand and the quotient located in the odd register. The sign of the quotient is determined by the rules of algebra and the remainder has the same sign as the dividend except that zero is always positive. A divide by zero will raise a fixed-point divide exception if enabled . The condition code is unchanged.

For example, if location VAR1 contains the 32 bit number 10, and location VAR2 contains the 32 bit number 3, you can divide the value at VAR1 by the value at VAR2 with the following:

```
L     R2,VAR1
SRDA  R2,32
D     R2,VAR2
```

The results will be 1 in R2 (the remainder) and 3 in R3 (the quotient).

Only the low order 32 bits of the even/odd registers participate in the D and DR instructions and they are treated as a single 64 bit number.

We load the dividend into the even register and then do a shift double arithmetic to the right by 32. This has the effect of shifting the dividend from the even register to the odd register but propagating across the even register the sign bit.

The SRDA instruction shifts the low order 32 bits of each register as though they were one 64 bit register.

13. Character Instructions

13.1 Basic Character Instructions

The original architecture had instructions to manipulate strings of character data up to 256 bytes in length. In later versions of the architecture, these were extended to handle larger strings but we begin with the most basic.

13.1.1 Moving Characters (MVC)

```
MVC  D1(L,B1),D2(B2)
```

The basic character move instruction is the MVC instruction. It is an SS instruction and copies up to 256 bytes beginning at the address given as the second operand to the address given as the first operand. The addresses may overlap.

In the machine language coding of an MVC (as is also the case with other SS character instructions), the length is expressed as an 8 bit field whose coded value is one less than the actual length to be moved. Thus, in the machine language format, a length value of 0 means move 1 byte and a length value of 255 means move 256 bytes, and so on. In the assembly language source code, however, the actual length is coded (one will be subtracted from this value by the assembler in constructing the machine language translation).

```
1         MVC  L1,L2            * 20 bytes from L2 copied to L1
2         MVC  L1(10),L2        * 10 bytes from L2 copied to L1
3
4         LA   R2,L1
5         LA   R3,L2
6
7         MVC  0(20,R2),0(R3)   * 20 bytes from L2 copied to L1
8         MVC  10(10,R2),0(R3)  * 10 bytes from L2 copied to L1
9  *                            * beginning at position 10
10
11        MVC  L1(1),=C' '      * blank copied to 1st byte.
12        MVC  L1+1(19),L1      * overlapped move: L1 is made
13 *                            * all blanks
14
15 L1     DS   CL20
16 L2     DC   C'ABCDEFGHIJKLMNOPQRST'
```
Figure 51 MVC Examples

In the case where no length is supplied, the implied length attribute of the first operand is used. The operands are specified in base/displacement format. There is no index register. Several examples are given in Figure 51.

13.1.2 Move Immediate (MVI)

```
MVI D1(B1)I2
```

The MVI (Move Immediate) instruction copies the immediate byte from the instruction to a byte in memory. In SI (storage immediate) instructions, the second operand is always a single byte which is itself part of the instruction.

Because of the EX instruction (see section 16.5, the second operand actually appears in the machine format before the first operand as shown in Figure 13. However, when writing in assembly language source code, the second operand appears second. Figure 52 has some examples.

```
MVI       L1,C'A'            * sets byte at L1 to letter A
MVI       L1,X'C1'           * sets byte at L1 to A
                             * (C1 is hex for A)
MVI       L1,B'11000001'     * sets byte at L1 to A
                             * (binary code for A)
MVI       L1,193             * sets byte at L1 to A
                             * (decimal equivalent)
                 Figure 52 MVI Examples
```

Note that the second operand of an SI instruction is always a constant. It is never a literal (for example, C'A' and never =C'A').

An extended version of this instruction, MVIY, was added in later generations of the architecture. It is a type SIY instruction and has a 20 bit signed displacement.

13.1.3 Move Character Long (MVCL)

```
MVCL R1,R2
```

The MVCL instruction is an RR instruction that was added to the original architecture to support extended length character move operations. Both operands must designate the even register of an even-odd pair.

The instruction copies the bytes beginning at the address specified by the even register of the second operand (R2) to the bytes beginning at the address specified by the even register of the first operand (R1).

The odd register of the first operand contains the first operand's length expressed in the low order 24 bits of the odd register. The odd register of the second operand contains an 8 bit padding byte followed by a 24 bit length. Up to 16M bytes can be copied.

If the first operand is longer than the second, the first is padded to the right by the padding byte. The instruction is interruptible. The instruction checks for destructive overlap. That is, are bytes from the first operand used as source bytes after bytes have been moved into same.

If there was no destructive overlap the Condition Code is 0 if both lengths are equal, 1 if the first operand is shorter than the second, and 2 if the first operand is longer than the second. The Condition Code is 3 and no copying is performed if a destructive overlap is detected.

13.1.4 Move Inverse (MVCIN)

```
MVCIN D1(L,B1),D2(B2)
```

The MVCIN instruction is an SS instruction with a format the same as the MVC except that the first operand addresses the leftmost byte of the target while the second operand addresses the rightmost byte of the source. The source is copied to the target with the order of bytes inverted. Both operands have the same length.

13.1.5 Other Move Instructions

Later models introduced the Move Long Extended (MVCLE) instruction of type RS which uses longer length fields. There is also a similar Move Long Unicode (MVCLU). The instruction Move String (MVST) of type RRE moves characters until a pre-determined byte is detected.

Additionally, there are the Move Numerics (MVN), Move Zones (MVZ), and Move With Offset (MVO) instructions, all of type SS, generally associated with manipulating packed decimal data.

13.1.6 Compare Logical Character (CLC)

```
CLC D1(L,D1),D2(B2)
```

The original instruction for comparing strings of bytes is the CLC (compare logical character) instruction. It is an SS format instruction using a single 8 bit length field as shown in the format in Figure 14.

The instruction successively compares each byte from each operand (first with first, second with second, and so forth). The instruction continues so long as the bytes compared are equal. If all bytes are found to be equal, the condition code is set to 0 and the instruction halts.

When bytes are compared, they are treated as unsigned 8 bit values. The byte with the larger absolute value is considered the greater of the two. The condition code is set to indicate the result:

```
CC=0 All bytes in both operands are equal;
CC=1 First operand less than the second;
CC=2 First operand greater than the second;
CC=3 Not possible.
```

If the instruction encounters a pair of unequal, the instruction halts and the condition code is set to reflect the inequality. If the byte from the first operand is less than the byte from the second operand, the condition code is set to 1, otherwise, 2. Figure 53 gives examples.

```
       CLC   L1,L2               * CC will be 1
       CLC   L1,L3               * CC will be 2
       CLC   L1(3),L2       * CC will be 0 - 3 bytes compared

L1     DC    C'ABCDEF'
L2     DC    C'ABCDEX'
L3     DC    C'ABCDEA
```

Figure 53 CLC Examples

As with the MVC, the length encoded in the machine language format is one less than the actual length. If the length is not specified, the assembler will use the length attribute of the first operand.

13.1.6.1 Compare Logical Immediate (CLI)

The CLI, compares one byte in memory with the instruction's immediate byte and sets the condition code accordingly. For example:

```
    CLI LAB,C'A'
```

In this case, the byte in memory at label LAB is compared with the immediate byte containing the EBCDIC code for the letter A. The condition code is set to reflect the result in the same manner as for the CLC above.

Alternatively, the following has the same effect:

```
    CLI LAB,X'C1'
    CLI LAB,B'11000001'
```

where the hexadecimal code $C1_{16}$ and the bit string 11000001_2 are the hexadecimal and bit string equivalents of the letter A. Any notation that results in the same bit pattern in the immediate byte is acceptable but not all are easily readable.

13.1.7 Compare Logical Character Long (CLCL)

```
CLCL R1,R2
```

Two instructions were added to the architecture when the IBM 360 evolved into the IBM 370. These are the CLCL (Compare Logical Character Long) and MVCL (Move Character Long). In the original architecture, the CLC and MVC instructions were limited to character strings no longer than 256 bytes. The CLCL and MVCL instructions have a string length limit of 16 MB.

The maximum string length on the early machines was said to be based on the maximum amount of time an instruction could execute on a low end version of the IBM 360 without the possibility of missing an interrupt. Both the MVC and CLC are uninteruptable and, should more than one interrupt take place while they were executing, the first interrupt might be overwritten by the second.

The CLCL instruction is an RR instruction. Both operands must designate the even register of an even-odd pair. The instruction compares the bytes beginning at the address specified by the even register of the first operand (R1) with the bytes at the address specified by the even register of the second operand (R2). The odd register of the first operand contains the first operand's length expressed in the low order 24 bits of the odd register. The odd register of the second operand contains an 8 bit padding byte followed by a 24 bit length. Up to 16M bytes can be compared.

Comparison is byte by byte. The shorter operand is considered to be extended to the right by the padding byte, if needed.

The comparison terminates when an inequality is found or at the end of the longer operand. If the operation ends with an inequality, the even registers of both operands contain the addresses of the unequal bytes. The length fields in the odd registers of both operands give the number of bytes remaining to be compared when the operation ended. The instruction is interruptible.

The Condition Code will be set to 0 if both operands are equal, 1 if the first operand is less than the second, and 2 if the first operand is greater than the second.

13.1.8 Additional Character Compare instructions

Several additional character compare instructions have been added to the architecture over the years. They are: Compare Logical Characters Under Mask (CLM, CLMY, CLMH). Characters to be compared are determined by a mask. Compare Logical Long Extended (CLCLE). An extended long character string comparison similar to CLCL. Compare Logical Long Unicode (CLCLU). Compares long Unicode character strings. Compare Logical String (CLST). Compares long strings delimited by a predetermined byte. Compare Until Substring Equal (CUSE). Search for equal substrings.

13.2 Translate (TR) and Translate and Test (TRT)
13.2.1 Translate and Test

Scanning is a frequent program need so the 360 architecture provided a single instruction to do this known as the TRT (Translate and Test) instruction.

The TRT uses a table (given as the second operand) and a string (the first operand). The table is nominally 256 bytes long.

Source bytes from the string are successively (left to right) used to index into the table. That is, the unsigned numeric value of a source string byte is added to the base address of the table and this is the address of the table byte. The byte found in the table at this offset decides what should happen:

1. If the byte in the table is zero, the operation continues;

2. If the byte in the table is non-zero, the operation terminates and the byte from the table is placed in the low order byte of register R2 and the address of the byte from the source string causing the halt is placed in register R1;

3. If all tested bytes are zero, the condition code becomes zero and the instruction terminates.

4. If a tested byte is non-zero, the Condition Code becomes 1 if the byte from the source string was not the final byte of the source string. The Condition Code is set to 2 if the source string byte was the final byte of the source string. The source string is not altered.

While this may sound complicated it isn't. Take, for example, the case where you want to scan a source string for the first non-blank character, a not uncommon thing to do. To use a TRT, you need a table that will cause the TRT to continue scanning if blanks are encountered and to halt if a non-blank character is found. Putting it simply, you need a table where all the values are non-zero except the value corresponding to the offset of a blank character (40_{16} or 64_{10}).

While the concept of the table is simple, it is also clear that typing 256 DC statements is not pleasant. However, the assembly language provides short cuts:

1. Build a table all of whose bytes are non-zero (X'01', for example);

2. Go back into the table at offset 64_{10} and change the value to X'00'.

This is shown in Figure 54 where first you build a table of 256 bytes all initialized to X'01'. Then, you go back into the table and replace the byte corresponding to the offset of blank (40_{16}, 64_{10}) with X'00'.

```
TAB         DC          256X'01'
            ORG         TAB+C' '
            DC          X'00'
            ORG
```

Figure 54 TRT Table with ORG

The ORG directive resets the assembler's location counter to the value we specify. In this case, we reset the location counter to the start of TAB plus C' ' which is the equivalent of saying 40_{16} or 64_{10} but C' ' is easier to understand. Now the location counter is back in the table at the offset corresponding to a blank. Here you place the X'00' which replaces the X'01' that was there.

Next, you need to cause the location counter to spring back to where it was after you initially built the table or subsequent code will overwrite the remainder of the table. An ORG with no argument resets the location counter to the highest value it has ever held. Hence the naked ORG (the no argument form).

The effect of all this is to create a table of X'01' codes except at the offset position for blank.

The example in Figure 55 reads and scans input records for the first word delimited by blanks, and prints the word.

```
            PRINT
1           NOGEN
2           START   0

3    REGS
4    *
5    * PROGRAM TO SCAN AN INPUT IMAGE FOR FIRST
6    * WORD DELIMITED BY A BLANK
7
            SUBENTR
8    SCAN   Y
9
10   LOOP   XREAD   REC,L'REC              * read a record
11          BC      B'0100',ATEND          * EOF?
12          XPRNT   REC,L'REC              * write the record
13
14          LA      R3,REC
15
16          TRT     0(L'REC,R3),TAB
17          BE      EXIT                   * only blanks found
18
19          LA      R4,REC+32              * end addr
20          LR      R3,R1                  * addr of non-blank
21          LA      R5,WORD                * target
22
23   L1     MVC     0(1,R5),0(R3)          * copy a byte
24
25          LA      R3,1(R0,R3)            * increment source addr
26          LA      R5,1(R0,R5)            * increment target addr
27
28          CR      R3,R4                  * at end?
29          BNL     PRNT                   * yes
30          CLI     0(R3),C' '             * blank?
31          BE      PRNT                   * yes - end of word
32          B       L1                     * loop
33
34   PRNT   XPRNT   WORD,L'WORD            * print word
35          MVI     WORD,C' '              * blank to 1st position
36          MVC     WORD+1(L'WORD-1),WORD  * ripple move
37          B       LOOP                   * again
38
39   *
40   * EOJ processing
41   *
42   ATEND  XPRNT   MSG,L'MSG
```

```
43
44  EXIT    SUBEXIT
45  *
            Literal
46  *       s
47  *
48          LTORG
49
50  REC     DS      CL30                        * actual input record
51  WORD    DC      CL30' '
52  MSG     DC      C'***** DONE *****'
53  TAB     DC      256X'01'
54          ORG     TAB+C' '
55          DC      X'00'
56          ORG
57  END     BEGIN
```

Figure 55 TRT Example

Notes on Figure 55:

1. Lines 10 and 11 read input. The program is written so as to
   return to line 10 (label LOOP) to read until there is no more
   input. When the XREAD runs out of input, the Condition Code
   is set to 1 and the program branches to ATEND.

2. The TRT on line 16 scans the string whose address is in was
   loaded into R3 (line 14) and whose length is L'REC - the
   length of the data at label REC. The TRT table is at label TAB.

3. TAB. If all characters in REC are blank (Condition Code 0), the
   program branches to EXIT.

4. The address of the byte after REC is loaded into R4 - this will
   be a limit.

5. The address of the non-blank character in REC that caused the
   halt is copied from R1 to R3. The address of a target field to
   receive the first non-blank word is loaded into R5.

6. The MVC on line 23 copies one byte from the location pointed
   to be R3 to the target pointed to by R5.

7. R3 and R5 are incremented by one in lines 25 and 26. Using
   an LA instruction to increment the contents of a register by a
   small amount is not uncommon. The LA does not access
   memory: it merely calculates an address. Thus, in the case of
   line 25, the 'address' calculated is the contents of R3 plus one
   (R0 does not contribute). The result is stored in R3. The same
   is done for R5. These lines advance the addresses in R3 and
   R5.

---

8. Lines 23 through 32 loop through the non-blank characters moving each non-blank character to the output field WORD until the end of REC is encountered or a blank is found.

9. Line 28 compares the address in R3 with the limit address R4 and branches to PRNT if it is greater than or equal (Branch Not Low) the value in the limit register R4.

10. Line 30 compares the byte pointed to by R3 with a blank (end of word?) and branches to PRNT if so. Otherwise (line 32), it branches to L1 to move the next character.

11. Line 34 prints the word extracted from the input image.

12. The MVI on line 35 places a blank in the first byte of WORD and then the MVC on line 36 propagates it across the field (this is called a ripple move) thus blanking out WORD. It does this by moving byte 1 to byte 2, then byte 2 to byte 3, and so forth, thus propagating the first byte, the blank.

13. The program branches to LOOP to read a new line.

14. Sample input lines are shown in Figure 56. These are placed in a file with the same file name as the program but with the .XRD file extension. Output (not shown) consists of the words TEST1, TEST2 and TEST3 on separate lines, left justified.

A related instruction, Translate and Test Reverse (TRTR) was added in later models. It performs the operation of the TRT but in the reverse direction.

```
        TEST1                      *
                    TEST2          *
    TEST3                          *
```

Figure 56 Input Lines

13.2.2 Translate

The translate instruction (TR) has characteristics that are similar to the TRT. It has a source string, the first operand, and it has a 256 byte table addressed as the second operand. Like the TRT, each byte, successively, from the source string is used to address a byte in the table at an offset equal to the numeric value of the source string byte.

However, in the translate instruction, the byte from the table replaces the byte in the source string. Also, the translate processes the entire source string and does not halt until all bytes have been processed. It does not set the condition code or alter any registers.

An example use for the TR instruction would be to convert from lower to upper case or to replace some punctuation characters with blanks.

In newer architectures, several variations were added: Translate Extended (TRE) which halts upon encountering a programmer specified test byte. Translate One To One (TROO), Translate One To Two (TROT), Translate Two to One (TRTO), and Translate Two To Two (TRTT) are variations that operate on multiple bytes and longer string lengths.

13.3 Insert Character (IC/ICY)

The Insert Character instructions IC (format RX) and ICY (format RXY) load the byte addressed by the second operand into the low order 8 bits of the register specified as the first operand. Other bits of the first operand register are unchanged. The IC instruction uses an unsigned 12 bit displacement while the ICY uses a 20 bit signed displacement. Neither alters the condition code. Additionally, there is the Insert Characters Under Mask instruction (ICM) which selectively loads up to 4 characters from memory into a register.

13.4 Store Character (STC/STCY)
The STC instruction stores the low order byte from the register designated as the first operand at the address specified by the second operand. It is of RX format. The similar STCY instruction is of format RXY and uses a 20 bit signed displacement. A related instruction, Store Characters Under Mask (STCM) stores a variable numbers of bytes.

```
STC R1,D2,(X2,B2)
```

14. Load Instructions

The architecture provides a number of instructions to load the contents of registers and these are detailed next. For purposes of programming examples, only the basic load instructions will be used but a complete list is given in Table 32.

14.1 Load (L)

The basic load instruction loads a 32 bit word from memory into a general purpose register. The word in memory should be on a word boundary (a memory address evenly divisible by 4). The Condition Code is unchanged. Load is of format RX.

```
L  R5,L1
```

Additional variations on the Load instruction are shown in Table 32. These vary on the size of the data loaded and the memory addressing method. Instructions not offered on the original architecture are shown shaded.

14.2 Load (LR)

The contents of the register specified as the second operand are copied to the register specified as the first operand. The Condition Code is unchanged. LR is of format RR.

```
LR  R5,R6
```

14.3 Load Multiple (LM)

One or more general purpose registers are loaded from consecutive words beginning at the memory address specified as the second operand. The Condition Code is unchanged. The LM is of type RS. The registers to be loaded begin with the register specified as the first operand through and including the register specified as the third operand. If the register specified as the first operand is greater than the register specified as the third operand, wrap around occurs. If the first and third operands both specify the same register, only 4 bytes are loaded.

```
LM  R1,R5,L1   * R1,R2,R3,R4 and R5 are loaded
LM  R6,R4,L2   * R6,R7, … R0,R1, … R4 are loaded.
```

14.4 Load and Test (LTR)

The contents of the register specified as the second operand are loaded into the register specified as the first operand and the Condition Code is set to reflect the value of the fixed point binary integer word copied. Often both operands are specified as the same register in which case the only effect is to set the Condition Code. The LTR is format RR. The Condition Code is set as follows:

```
CC=0 Zero;
CC=1 Negative;
CC=2 Positive.
```

14.5 Load Positive (LPR)

The absolute value of the signed binary value in the register specified as the second operand is loaded into the register specified as the first operand. Both operands may be the same register. The Condition Code is set. The LPR is format RR. The largest negative number has no positive equivalent and this case can generate an overflow. The Condition Code is set as follows:

```
CC=0 Zero, no overflow
CC=1 Not possible
CC=2 Greater than zero, no overflow
CC=3 Overflow
```

14.6 Load Negative (LNR)

The 2s complement of the absolute value of the signed fixed point binary integer contained in the register specified as the second operand is loaded into the register specified as the first operand. The Condition Code is set. LNR is of format RR. The Condition Code is set as follows:

```
CC=0 Zero
CC=1 Negative
CC=2 Not possible
CC=3 Not possible
```

14.7 Load Complement (LCR)

The LCR loads into the register designated as the first operand the 2s complement of the contents of the register designated as the second operand. Both register designations may be the same in which case the contents of the designated register are complemented. A value of zero in is unchanged (the 2s complement of 0 is 0). The Condition Code is set as follows:

```
CC=0 Result 0
CC=1 Result negative
CC=2 Result positive
CC=3 Overflow
```

14.8 Load Address (LA)

The load address instruction is an RX instruction which calculates the address specified by the second operand and places the result into the register specified as the first operand. No memory access is made. The instruction only performs the address arithmetic. In 24 bit addressing mode the result is 24 bits while in 31 bit addressing mode the result is 31 bits. All address arithmetic is done with positive numbers only.

The LA is also used as a fast way to load small constants into registers and to do limited positive binary arithmetic. It can also be used to add the positive contents of two registers in one operation. Examples:

1. Load the constant 22 into R5: **LA R5,22(R0,R0)** Since R0 does not participate in address arithmetic, the effective result of the address calculation is 22 which is loaded into R5. This is considerably faster than a load instruction with a 4 byte memory operand.
2. Increment the contents of R5 by 10 (contents of R5 must be positive and no more than 24 or 31 bits in length, depending upon the current addressing mode). **LA R5,10(R0,R5)**
The value in R5 and 10 are added and the result replaces the contents of R5. Again, R0 does not participate. This is considerably faster than an Add instruction with a four byte memory operand.
3. Add the contents of R2 and R3 and place the result in R5. Assumes that R2 and R3 have positive values not greater than 24 or 31 bits (depending on addressing mode) and the result will be less than 31 or 24 bits in length (depending on addressing mode) LA R5,0(R2,R3) For small positive values, this instruction replaces as SR and two AR instructions and is very fast (address arithmetic is the fastest form of arithmetic).

OpCode	Type	1st Operand	2nd Operand	Result	Operation
			Load		
L	RX	32 bit register	32 bit memory	32 bit register	
LR	RR	32 bit register	32 bit register	32 bit register	
LGR	RRE	64 bit register	64 bit register	64 bit register	2nd operand is loaded unchanged into the first operand except for the LGFR and LGF where the result is sign extended.
LGFR	RRE	64 bit register	32 bit memory	64 bit register	
LY	RXY	32 bit register	16 bit immediate	32 bit register	
LG	RXY	64 bit register	64 bit register	64 bit register	
LGF	RXY	64 bit register	32 bit memory	64 bit register	
LPQ	RXY	2 64 bit registers	128 bit memory	2 64 bit registers	
			Load Address		
LA	RX	64 bit register	21/31/64 bits	64 bit register	Address computed by 2nd operand loaded into 1st operand.
LAY	RXY	64 bit register	21/31/64 bits	64 bit register	
			Load and Test		
LTR	RR	32 bit register	32 bit register	32 bit register	2nd operand loaded into 1st operand to set Condition Code
LTGR	RRE	64 bit register	64 bit register	64 bit register	
LTGFR	RRE	64 bit register	32 bit register	64 bit register	
			Load Complement		
LCR	RR	32 bit register	32 bit register	32 bit register	2s complement of 2nd operand loaded into 1st operand.
LCGR	RRE	64 bit register	64 bit register	64 bit register	
LCGFR	RRE	64 bit register	64 bit register	64 bit register	
			Load Multiple		
LM	RS	32 bit register(s)	32 bit memory word(s)	32 bit register(s)	One or more registers are loaded from locations in memory. For LM and LMY, the high
LMY	RSY	32 bit register(s)	32 bit memory word(s)	32 bit register(s)	
LMG	RSY	64 bit register(s)	64 bit memory word(s)	64 bit register(s)	

OpCode	Type	1st Operand	2nd Operand	Result	Operation
LMD	SS	64 bit register(s)	32 bit memory word(s)	64 bit register(s)	
LMH	RSY	64 bit register(s)	32 bit memory word(s)	64 bit register(s)	order 32 bits of the registers are

Load Positive

OpCode	Type	1st Operand	2nd Operand	Result	Operation
LPR	RR	32 bit register	32 bit register	32 bit register	Absolute value of 2nd operand loaded into 1st operand.
LPGR	RRE	64 bit register	64 bit register	64 bit register	
LPGFR	RRE	64 bit register	32 bit register	64 bit register	

Load Byte

OpCode	Type	1st Operand	2nd Operand	Result	Operation
LB	RXY	32 bit register	memory byte	32 bit register	
LGB	RXY	64 bit register	memory byte	64 bit register	

Load Reversed

OpCode	Type	1st Operand	2nd Operand	Result	Operation
LRVR	RRE	32 bit register	32 bit memory	32 bit register	The 2nd operand is loaded into the first with the bytes reversed.
LRVGR	RRE	64 bit register	64 bit memory	64 bit register	
LRVH	RXY	16 bit register	16 bit memory	16 bit register	
LRV	RXY	32 bit register	32 bit memory	32 bit register	
LRVG	RXY	64 bit register	64 bit memory	64 bit register	

Load Negative

OpCode	Type	1st Operand	2nd Operand	Result	Operation
LNR	RR	32 bit register	32 bit register	32 bit register	The 2s compliment negative of the 2nd operand is loaded into the 1st operand.
LNGR	RRE	64 bit register	64 bit register	64 bit register	
LNGFR	RRE	64 bit register	32 bit register	64 bit register	

Load Logical Thirty One Bits

OpCode	Type	1st Operand	2nd Operand	Result	Operation
LLGTR	RRE	64 bit register	32 bit register	64 bit register	The low order 31 bits of the 2nd operand are loaded into the 1st.
LLGT	RXY	64 bit register	32 bit memory	64 bit register	

Load Halfword

OpCode	Type	1st Operand	2nd Operand	Result	Operation
LH	RX	32 bit register	16 bit memory	32 bit register	The halfword addressed by

OpCode	Type	1st Operand	2nd Operand	Result	Operation
LHY	RXY	32 bit register	16 bit memory	32 bit register	
LHG	RXY	64 bit register	16 bit memory	64 bit register	the 2nd operand is loaded into the 1st operand.
LHI	LHI	32 bit register	16 bit immediate	32 bit register	
LGHI	LGHI	64 bit register	16 bit memory	64 bit register	

Load Logical

OpCode	Type	1st Operand	2nd Operand	Result	Operation
LLGFR	RRE	64 bit register	32 bit register	64 bit register	
LLGF	RXY	64 bit register	32 bit memory	64 bit register	
LLGC	RXY	64 bit register	8 bit memory	64 bit register	Bits from the 2nd operand are loaded into the 1st operand without regard to sign.
LLGH	RXY	64 bit register	16 bit memory	64 bit register	
LLIHH	RI	64 bit register	16 bit immediate	64 bit register	
LLIHL	RI	64 bit register	16 bit immediate	64 bit register	
LLILH	RI	64 bit register	16 bit immediate	64 bit register	
LLILL	RI	64 bit register	16 bit immediate	64 bit register	

Table 32 Load Instructions

15. Store Instructions

In this section we discuss the basic store instructions. The complete list of Store instructions is given in Table 33.

15.1 Store (ST)

The store instruction stores the 32 bit contents of a register to a word in memory. It is an RX instruction. The memory address should be a word boundary. The Condition Code is unchanged. ST is of format RX.

```
ST R1,D2(X2,B2)
```

15.2 Store Multiple (STM)

One or more general purpose registers are stored to consecutive words beginning at the memory address specified as the second operand. The Condition Code is unchanged. The STM is of format RS. The registers to be stored begin with the register specified as the first operand through and including the register specified as the third operand. If the register specified as the first operand is greater than the register specified as the third operand, wrap around occurs. If the first and third operands both specify the same register, only 4 bytes are stored. Examples:

```
STM R1,R5,L1  * R1,R2,R3,R4 and R5 are stored
STM R6,R4,L2  * R6,R7, … R15, R0,R1, … R4 stored
```

OpCode	Type	1st Operand	2nd Operand	Result	Operation
			Store		
ST	RX	32 bit register	32 bit memory	32 bit memory	1st operand is stored to memory addressed by 2nd operand.
STY	RXY	32 bit register	32 bit memory	32 bit memory	
STG	RXY	64 bit register	64 bit memory	64 bit memory	
			Store Character		
STC	RX	8 bit register	memory byte	memory byte	1 or more bytes from the 1st operand stored to memory
STCY	RXY	8 bit register	memory byte	memory byte	
STCM	RS	32 bit register	1 to 4 memory bytes	1 to 4 memory bytes	
STCMY	RSY	32 bit register	1 to 4 memory bytes	1 to 4 memory bytes	
STCMH	RSY	32 bit register	1 to 4 memory bytes	1 to 4 memory bytes	
			Store Halfword		
STH	RX	16 bit register	2 bytes memory	2 bytes memory	16 bits of 1st operand stored to memory
STHY	RXY	16 bit register	2 bytes memory	2 bytes memory	
			Store Multiple		
STM	RS	1 to 16 32 bit registers	1 to 16 memory words	1 to 16 memory words	
STMY	RSY	1 to 16 32 bit registers	1 to 16 memory words	1 to 16 memory words	
STMG	RSY	1 to 16 64 bit registers	1 to 16 memory double words	1 to 16 memory double words	Multiple registers stored to memory.
STMH	RSY	1 to 16 32 bit registers	1 to 16 memory words	1 to 16 memory words	
STPQ	RXY	2 64 bit registers	2 double words	2 double words	
			Store Reversed		
STRVH	RXY	16 bit register	2 bytes memory	2 bytes memory	Bytes from the 1st operand are stored in reverse order
STRV	RXY	32 bit register	4 memory bytes	4 memory bytes	
STRVG	RXY	32 bit register	8 memory bytes	8 memory bytes	

OpCode	Type	1st Operand	2nd Operand	Result	Operation

Table 33 Store Instructions

16. Bit Operations

Bit operations involve modification or manipulation of individual bits in an operand. The basic Boolean operations of AND, OR, and EXCLUSIVE OR were originally implemented as RR, RX, SI or SS instructions. The COMPLEMENT and SHIFT instructions work only on operands in registers. Newer architectures have added additional versions of these instructions.

16.1 Boolean Instructions

In the Boolean instructions (AND, OR, and EXCLUSIVE OR), the designated operation takes place between the corresponding bits of each operand and the result replaces the first operand. If the corresponding bits in both operands are one, the result is one, zero otherwise.

16.1.1 AND (N, NR, NI, NC)

In the bitwise AND instructions, corresponding bits from each operand are and'ed together. If both bits are 1, the resulting bit is 1. If either or both bits are 0, the resulting bit is 0.

The bitwise AND instructions are:

1. NR - RR format - the 32 bits of the operand in the register designated as the second operand are and'ed with the bits of the register designated as the first operand and the result is placed in the first operand.

2. N - RX format - the 32 bits from the word in memory addressed by the second operand are and'ed with the bits in the register designated as the first operand and the result is placed in the first operand.

3. NI - SI format - the 8 bits in the immediate operand are and'ed with the bits of the byte in memory designated as the first operand and the resulting byte replaces the byte in memory.

4. NC - SS format - from 1 to 256 bytes beginning at the address specified by the second operand are and'ed with the corresponding bytes beginning at the address specified by the first operand with the resulting bytes replacing the bytes from the first operand.

Table 34 shows all AND operations. Versions added in later models are shaded.

OpCode	Type	1st Operand	2nd Operand	Result	Operation
NR	RR	32 bit register	32 bit register	32 bit register	
N	RX	32 bit register	32 bit memory	32 bit register	
NI	SI	8 bit memory	8 bit immediate	8 bit memory	
NC	SS	Memory String	Memory String	Memory String	2nd operand bitwise ANDed with 1st operand and result remains in 1st operand. In NIHH, NIHL, NILH, NILH, and NILL, only 16 bits of the 1st operand altered.
NGR	RRE	64 bit register	64 bit memory	64 bit register	
NY	RXY	32 bit register	32 bit memory	32 bit register	
NG	RXY	64 bit register	64 bit memory	64 bit register	
NIY	SIY	8 bit memory	8 bit immediate	8 bit memory	
NIHH	RI	16 bit register	16 bit immediate	16 bit register	
NIHL	RI	16 bit register	16 bit immediate	16 bit register	
NILH	RI	16 bit register	16 bit immediate	16 bit register	
NILL	RI	16 bit register	16 bit immediate	16 bit register	

Table 34 Additional AND Instructions

16.1.2 OR (O, OR, OI, OC)

In the bitwise OR instructions, the corresponding bits from both operands are or'ed. If either or both corresponding bits are one, the resulting bit is one. If both bits are zero, the resulting bit is zero.

The bitwise OR instructions are:

1. OR - RR format - the 32 bits of the operand in the register designated as the second operand are or'ed with the bits in the register designated as the first operand and the result is placed in the first operand.

2. O - RX format - the 32 bits from the word in memory addressed by the second operand are or'ed with the bits in the register designated as the first operand and the result is placed in the first operand.

3. OI - SI format - the 8 bits in the immediate operand are or'ed with the bits of the byte in memory addressed by the first operand and the resulting byte replaces the byte in memory.

4. OC - SS format - from 1 to 256 bytes beginning at the address specified by the second operand are or'ed with the corresponding bytes beginning at the address specified by the first operand with the resulting bytes replacing the bytes from the first operand.

Table 35 shows all OR instructions. The versions added in later models are shaded.

OpCode	Type	1st Operand	2nd Operand	Result	Operation
OR	RR	32 bit register	32 bit register	32 bit register	
O	RX	32 bit register	32 bit memory	32 bit register	
OI	SI	8 bit memory	8 bit immediate	8 bit memory	
OC	SS	Memory String	Memory String	Memory String	2nd operand bitwise ORed
OGR	RRE	64 bit register	64 bit memory	64 bit register	with 1st operand and result
OY	RXY	32 bit register	32 bit memory	32 bit register	remains in 1st operand.
OG	RXY	64 bit register	64 bit memory	64 bit register	In NIHH, NIHL, NILH,
OIY	SIY	8 bit memory	8 bit immediate	8 bit memory	NILL, and NILL, only 16 bits of
OIHH	RI	16 bit register	16 bit immediate	16 bit register	the 1st operand
OIHL	RI	16 bit register	16 bit immediate	16 bit register	altered.
OILH	RI	16 bit register	16 bit immediate	16 bit register	
OILL	RI	16 bit register	16 bit immediate	16 bit register	

Table 35 OR Instructions

16.1.3 Exclusive OR (X, XR, XI, XC)

In the bitwise Exclusive OR instructions, corresponding bits from both operands are exclusive or'ed with one another. If both bits are zero or if both bits are one, the resulting bit is zero. If one bit is zero and the other is one, the resulting bit is one.

The basic bitwise EXCLUSIVE OR instructions are:

1. XR - RR format - the 32 bits in the register designated as the second operand are exclusive or'ed with the bits of the register designated as the first operand and the result is placed in the first operand.

2. X - RX format - the 32 bits from the word in memory addressed by the second operand are exclusive or'ed with the bits in the register designated as the first operand and the result is placed in the first operand.

3. XI - SI format - the 8 bits in the immediate operand are exclusive or'ed with the bits of the byte in memory designated as the first operand and the resulting byte replaces the byte in memory.

4. XC - SS format - from 1 to 256 bytes beginning at the address specified by the second operand are exclusive or'ed with the corresponding bytes beginning at the address specified by the first operand with the resulting bytes replacing the bytes from the first operand.

Table 36 shows all versions of the Exclusive Or. Versions added in later models are shaded.

OpCode	Type	1st Operand	2nd Operand	Result	Operation
XR	RR	32 bit register	32 bit register	32 bit register	
X	RX	32 bit register	32 bit memory	32 bit register	
XI	SI	8 bit memory	8 bit immediate	8 bit memory	
XC	SS	Memory String	Memory String	Memory String	2nd operand is bitwise XORed with 1st operand and result remains in 1st operand. In NIHH, NIHL, NILH, and NILL, only 16 bits of the 1st operand altered.
XGR	RRE	64 bit register	64 bit memory	64 bit register	
XY	RXY	32 bit register	32 bit memory	32 bit register	
XG	RXY	64 bit register	64 bit memory	64 bit register	
XIY	SIY	8 bit memory	8 bit immediate	8 bit memory	
XIHH	RI	16 bit register	16 bit immediate	16 bit register	
XIHL	RI	16 bit register	16 bit immediate	16 bit register	
XILH	RI	16 bit register	16 bit immediate	16 bit register	
XILL	RI	16 bit register	16 bit immediate	16 bit register	

Table 36 XOR Instructions

16.2 Shift

The shift operators move bits either left or right in one or more registers. They are classed as either logical or arithmetic.

Logical shifts treat all bits the same. There is no special treatment of the sign bit position. No overflow can occur. On both left and right shifts, zero bits replace the bits shifted from both low and high order positions.

Arithmetic shifts take into account the sign bit. When shifting to the left, if a bit unlike the sign bit is shifted into the sign bit position, an overflow occurs. On a right shift, bits like the sign bit replace the shifted bits.

In the original architecture, shifts were performed on a single 32 bit register or on an even/odd pair of 32 bit registers. For most of the shift instructions, this is still true. Of the twelve shift instructions, only four operate on a single 64 bit register.

For all the shift instructions the first operand designates the register to be shifted and the second operand indicates the number of bit positions to be shifted.

The number of bit positions to shift is calculated from the base register and displacement of the second operand. If the base register is specified as zero, the amount of the shift is the displacement. If the base is specified as any other register than R0, the contents of the register plus the value of the displacement are the determine number of bits to shift.

In many cases only the displacement is specified such as:

```
SLL  R5,10
```

In this case the second operand is shorthand for:

```
10(R0)
```

and thus the instruction means to shift the contents of R5 left 10 bit positions.

Shifting a binary number to the left has the effect of multiplying it by 2; shifting it 2 positions to the left multiplies by 4; 3 positions by 8 and so forth. Similarly, shifting a binary number to the right has the effect of dividing by 2, 4, 8, *etc.*

16.2.1 Logical Shift (SRL, SRDL, SLL, SLDL)

The logical shift instructions are:

```
SRL  - shift right logical (single)
SRDL - shift right double logical
```

```
SLL  – shift left logical (single)
SLDL – shift left double logical
```

In logical shifts, all bits participate. The values are treated as unsigned quantities. The Condition Code remains unchanged. Zeros are provided to replaced the shifted bits in both directions.

In the single shifts, only the low order 32 bits of the register specified as the first operand participate.

In the double shifts, the first operand must designate an even register of an even/odd pair. In double shifts, the low order 32 bits from the even register and the low order 32 bits from the odd register are treated as a single 64 bit entity.

16.2.2 Arithmetic (SRA, SRDA, SLA, SLDA)

The arithmetic shift instructions are:

```
SRA  – shift right arithmetic (single)
SRDA – shift right double arithmetic
SLA  – shift left arithmetic (single)
SLDA – shift left double arithmetic
```

The Condition Code is set:

```
CC=0 Result is 0
CC=1 Result is negative
CC=2 Result is positive
CC=3 Overflow
```

An overflow can occur only in *left* shifts when a bit unlike the sign bit is shifted into the sign bit position. During left shifts, zeros are supplied to replace the shifted bits. During *right* shifts, bits like the sign bit are provided to replace the shifted bits.

The first operands for single and double shifts are treated the same as for the logical shifts.

Table 37 shows all shift operations. The recently added versions are shaded.

16.3 Test Under Mask (TM)

The TM instruction is an SI instruction. Those bits in the byte in memory addressed by the first operand which correspond to bits with a value of 1 in the immediate operand are tested and the Condition Code is set.

1. If all the tested bits are 0, the Condition Code is set to 0.

2. If the tested bits are mixed 1s and 0s, the Condition Code is set to 1.

3. If all the tested bits are 1s, the Condition Code is set to 3.

For example, if a byte in memory at label L1 has the value:

```
0011 0101
```

The instruction:

```
TM  L1,B'11001010'
```

will set the Condition Code to 0 (all tested bits were 0s). The instruction:

```
TM L1,B'00110101'
```

will set the Condition Code to 3 (all tested bits were 1s). The instruction:

```
TM L1,B'00001111'
```

will set the Condition Code to 1 (tested bits were mixed).

OpCode	Type	1st Operand	2nd Operand	Result	Operation
SRL	RS	32 bit register	Address arithmetic	32 bit register	
SRDL	RS	2 32 bit registers	Address arithmetic	2 32 bit registers	
SLL	RS	32 bit register	Address arithmetic	32 bit register	
SLDL	RS	2 32 bit registers	Address arithmetic	2 32 bit registers	
SRA	RS	32 bit register	Address arithmetic	32 bit register	
SRDA	RS	2 32 bit registers	Address arithmetic	2 32 bit registers	Left or Right, Arithmetic or Logical, shifts of 63/64 bits.
SLA	RS	32 bit register	Address arithmetic	32 bit register	
SLDA	RS	2 32 bit registers	Address arithmetic	2 32 bit registers	
SLAG	RSY	64 bit register	Address arithmetic	64 bit register	
SLLG	RSY	64 bit register	Address arithmetic	64 bit register	
SRAG	RSY	64 bit register	Address arithmetic	64 bit register	
SRLG	RSY	64 bit register	Address arithmetic	64 bit register	

Table 37 Shift Instructions

See also the TMY instruction which is the same as the TM but uses the extended addressing facility (20 bit signed displacement).

There are some additional variations in the newer architecture that operate on 16 bits. These are the TMHH, TMHL, TMLH and TMLL instructions.

16.4 Test and Set (TS)

The TS (Test and Set) instruction was listed as an SI instruction in the original architecture but the immediate operand was always omitted. In the current architecture, it is listed as a format S instruction which is the same as an SI instruction with no immediate operand.

The instruction tests the leftmost (high order) bit of the byte in memory designated as the first operand. If the bit is 0, the Condition Code is set to 0. If the bit is 1, the Condition code is set to 1. Regardless of the result, the byte in memory is set to B'11111111' (FF_{16}).

The original purpose of this instruction was to provide an uninterruptible way in which to test if a resource is available and, if not, mark it as in use.

For example, consider the case where a byte is used to indicate that some block of memory is available for allocation. If the byte is all 0s, it is available. If it is 1s, it is in use and unavailable.

If you execute a TS on this byte and if the first bit of this byte is a zero, Condition Code will be 0 *and* the TS mark the byte as all 1s. On the other hand, if the block is allocated and the first bit of the byte is 1, the TS will set the Condition Code 1.

What this instruction avoids is the situation where one program tests a byte, sees a 0, but before it can set the byte, an interrupt occurs and another program gains control. Likewise this program tests the same byte, sees a 0 and sets the byte to 1s. When the first program regains control it believes that the byte is 0 and likewise marks it as 1s and now both programs believe they own the block of memory.

The TS instruction is uninterruptible - the testing and setting take place in one operation so the previous scenario is impossible.

16.5 Execute (EX)

A program is said to be reentrant if it does not modify its memory image during execution. If it does not, the memory image may be shared among multiple users simultaneously.

However, in the original architecture, there are cases where modification of the code image was desirable. For example, take the case of the length byte in an MVC instruction. To achieve a variable length move you could modify the MVC's length attribute with a Store Character instruction and then execute the MVC however this would render the program non-reentrant.

In an environment where the code for a program is shared among several users where each user has their own data areas but the actual executable code image is shared, you could have a situation where one user modifies an MVC but another user executed it. For example, user 1 modifies an MVC to a length of 10. User 1 is interrupted by the operating system. User 2 eventually next gets control. User 2 modifies the same MVC to a length of 20. User 2 is interrupted. User 1 gets control and executes the MVC which now has a 20 in it and not 10.

The purpose of the Execute instruction is to permit programs to make such modifications remain *reentrant*. The Execute instruction, in one, uninterruptible operation, makes a copy of an instruction, modifies it and executes it. The actual original instruction in memory is unchanged.

The EX instruction is an RX instruction. The first operand is a register whose low order byte contains information that will be used to modify the copy of the instruction to be executed. The second operand is the address of the instruction to be executed. The EX works as follows:

1. a copy of the instruction at the address specified as the second operand is made;

2. the low order byte of the register specified as the second operand is or'ed with the second byte of the copy of the instruction to be executed;

3. the copy of the instruction with the modified second byte is executed.

In all SS instructions the second byte is the length byte. In several, such as the MVC and CLC, the length is the entire byte. In others, such as AP, SP, MP, DP and so forth, the byte is divided into 2 four bit fields the first of which is the length of the first operand and the second the length of the second operand. In SI instructions, the second byte is the immediate operand. The EX is normally used in connection with SS and SI instructions.

Instructions to be executed by the EX instruction are ordinarily placed in a data area of your program as they are not directly executed. The EX instruction appears in the code where the instruction to be executed would have appeared.

Note that rather than simply replacing the second byte, the EX or's the low byte of the register with the instruction byte. In cases where the instruction to be executed was coded with a second byte all of whose bits are zero, this results, in effect, in replacement.

However, consider the situation where the first operand of an AP with a base register of has a fixed length, say 10, but the second operand has a variable length. By coding the first half of the instruction length byte with 9 (machine language length values are always 1 less than the real length) and coding the second 4 bit field as all zeros, it is possible to modify only the second field. In this situation, in the register designated as the first operand of the EX, the low order byte of the register will have all zeros in its high four bits and the length for the second operand in the low four bits. When the EX executes, the high four bits from the low byte of the register will leave the first operand length unchanged but the second operand length will become the low four bits from the register. For example:

1. R5 contains 00 00 00 05$_{16}$.
2. The instruction is: `FA 90 D0 20 D0 40` which in assembly language is: `AP 32(9,R13),64(0,R13)`
3. The AP instruction is located at label APL.
4. The EX is: `EX R5,APL`
5. The result to be executed is: `FA 95 D0 20 D0 40`

The 05$_{16}$ was or'ed with 90$_{16}$ yielding 95$_{16}$ as the effective length byte.

17. Decimal Arithmetic

The decimal instruction set consists of those instructions that operate on or support packed decimal (also known as BCD or binary coded decimal) data.

17.1 Zoned and Packed Decimal

Arithmetic on an IBM mainframe can be carried out in fixed point binary integer, packed decimal and floating point modes.

Initially, when numbers are read as character (EBCDIC) input (when using the z390 emulator, ASCII input is automatically converted to EBCDIC by the emulator.), they are in what is called zoned decimal format where the high order 4 bits of each byte contain a hexadecimal F_{16} called the zone and the low order 4 bits (called the digit) are the value of the character number in binary (0 through 9). For example, the internal hexadecimal EBCDIC for the printable number 1234 is:

> F1 F2 F3 F4$_{16}$

Arithmetic may not be performed on character representations of numbers. Instead, they must be converted to one of the numeric types: packed decimal, fixed point binary or floating point. Of these, conversion to packed decimal is the easiest.

A packed decimal number is a string of one or more bytes containing, in each half byte, a value (in binary) from 0 to 9 except for the last half byte. The last half byte contains the sign of the number. The hex codes C,A,F, and E mean the number is positive (CAFE) and the codes D and B mean it's negative (DB). Thus, the zoned decimal number 1234 (F1 F2 F3 F4$_1$) in packed format would be:

> 01 23 4F$_{16}$

In this format the zones have been eliminated and a sign appended. All packed decimal numbers occupy an integral number of bytes in memory. A leading zero is prepended as necessary.

Packed decimal numbers can be up to 16 bytes long and, therefore, can represent numbers up to 31 digits (2 digits per byte except for the last byte which has one digit and the sign). Packed decimal is especially useful for business applications where many digits of accuracy are required.

17.2 The PACK Instruction

The PACK instruction is used to convert from printable, zoned decimal character strings to packed decimal. As noted above, all zoned numeric characters have the same value of F_{16} for their zone (the high order 4 bits of each character). The low order portion of all zoned numeric characters (called the numeric part of a byte) is a 4 bit binary number whose value is between zero and nine. The PACK instruction, when applied to a string of zoned numbers, removes the zones from all bytes except the last and packs two numerics per byte. In the last byte (possibly the only byte), it swaps the numeric and zoned fields. The result is padded with leading zeros as needed to make an integral number of bytes. This is illustrated in Figure 57.

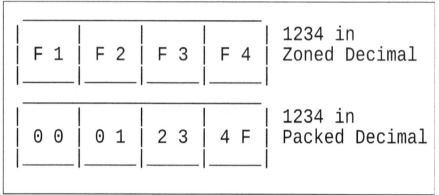

Figure 57 1234 in Zoned & Packed

In a PACK instruction, both operands are located in memory. The operands are processed one byte at a time from left to right. The second operand is the source and the result replaces the first operand. The Condition Code is unchanged.

Bytes from left to right of the source are read, the zone is removed and the digit portion stored in the next available half byte moving to the right in the target. The source and target may be of different lengths but the target must be long enough to hold the answer. If the source field is short and the target field long, the target will be padded to the left with leading zeros as needed.

The final byte of the source, however, is treated differently. In this case, the zone and digit parts of the source byte are reversed and placed in the last (right most) byte of the target. This always results in an F_{16} code in the sign position. Since F_{16} is one of the positive sign indicators in packed format, all numbers are initially positive until altered by the program. The positive sign can be changed to negative by executing an And Immediate instruction on the low order (rightmost) byte of the packed result with an immediate byte (mask) of X'FD'. This will preserve the high order four bits and alter the low order F_{16} to D_{16} thus making the number negative.

Once a number is in packed format, you may do arithmetic on it. While packed or decimal arithmetic is slower than binary arithmetic, it can handle more digits of accuracy and it does not need any further conversion.

17.3 Converting Packed Decimal to Binary

To convert a number from zoned decimal to fixed point binary, you first must pack the number (PACK is very fast), then perform a Convert to Binary instruction. In the original architecture, this was performed by the CVB instruction which converts a packed number to a 32 bit signed fixed point binary integer leaving the result in a register.

More recently, the similar CVBY instruction has been added which differs from the CVB in that it uses signed long displacements. Also added is the CVBG which likewise uses signed long displacements but the result occupies 64 bits. For the CVB and CVBY instructions, the second operand is an 8 byte packed decimal field while, for the CVBG, the second operand is a 16 byte packed decimal field.

The reverse, converting binary to packed, is done by the Convert to Decimal CVD instruction which uses a signed 32 bit source register. Also available are the CVDY and CDVG instructions which use long signed displacements and, in the case of the CVDG, the source is a 64 bit register. The instructions write either an 8 or 16 byte signed packed decimal number to memory for 32 and 64 bit register source operands respectively.

17.4 Decimal Instruction Set

The basic set of packed decimal arithmetic instructions are shown in Figure 58.

```
AP              Add Packed
CP              Compare Packed
DP              Divide Packed
ED              Edit
EDMK            Edit and Mark
MP              Multiply Packed
SP              Subtract Packed
SRP             Shift and Round Packed
TP              Test Packed
ZAP             Zero and Add Packed
```

Figure 58 Decimal Instructions

The example in Figure 59 illustrates some basic packed arithmetic operations. It reads in a set of numbers in zoned format, packs them, and adds them into an accumulator then prints the total.

The input file for the program in Figure 59 is shown at the end. The program in Figure 59 operates as follows:

1. Input lines consisting of a sign followed by 7 digits are read and echoed (lines 4 through 6).

2. The 7 digits are packed into the field NBR (line 7). The starting point in IN is offset by one to avoid the sign and the length is adjusted to 7 from 8.

3. The first character is inspected (line 8). If it is a plus sign, a branch is made to the label ADD. If it is not a plus sign nor a minus sign, a branch is made to ERR1.

4. If a minus sign is detected, the low order byte of NBR is And'ed with X'FD' which have the effect of altering the sign from F_{16} to D_{16} (line 12).

5. The packed number is tested for errors. If any, a branch is made to ERR1 (lines 13 and 14).

6. The positive or negative number is added to the accumulator ACC (line 15).

7. When there is no more input, a branch is made to ATEND which uses the ED instruction to unpack and format the answer which is printed (lines 26 and 27). The Edit (ED) instruction is covered in section 17.8 It unpacks and formats numbers based on a pattern which in this case is contained in RSLT.

Some sample input is shown at the end of the figure. The final result of execution is the number 3 preceded by seven blanks.

17.5 Add, Subtract, Zero and Add Positive (AP, SP, ZAP)

In these instructions the first operand is the target and the second is the source. The first operand must be large enough to contain the result or a Decimal Overflow occurs.

The AP adds two packed numbers and the SP subtracts two packed numbers. In the case of the ZAP (Zero and Add Packed), the target is zeroed before addition. In all, both operands are in memory.

The Condition Code will be zero if the result is zero; 1 if the result is less than zero; 2 if the result is greater than zero and 3 in the case of overflow.

```
1           PRINT      NOGEN
2    SUM    SUBENTRY
3
4    LOOP   XREAD      IN,L'IN
5           BC         B'0100',ATEND
6           XPRNT      IN,L'IN
7           PACK       NBR,IN+1(7)      * PACK THE NUMBER
8           CLI        IN,C'+'
9           BE         ADD
10          CLI        IN,C'-'
11          BNE        ERR1
12          NI         NBR+7,X'FD'      * make negative
13   ADD    TP         NBR
14          BNE        ERR2
15          AP         ACC,NBR          * ADD TO TOTAL
16          B          LOOP             * READ ANOTHER RECORD
17
18   * EOF - BRANCH HERE WHEN OUT OF RECORDS
19
20   ERR1   XPRNT      ERRM1,L'ERRM1
21          B          EXIT
22
23   ERR2   XPRNT      ERRM2,L'ERRM2
24          B          EXIT
25
26   ATEND  ED         RSLT,ACC         * UNPACK AND FORMAT RESULT
27          XPRNT      RSLT,L'RSLT
28   EXIT   SUBEXIT
29
30   IN     DS         CL8
31   NBR    DS         PL8
32   ACC    DC         PL4'0'
33   ERRM1  DC         C'SIGN ERROR'
34   ERRM2  DC         C'NUMBER ERROR'
35
36   RSLT   DC         X'4020202020202120' * EDIT PATTERN
37
38   END    ADD
Sample input data:

1
1234
-1234
2
```
                    Figure 59 Decimal Arithmetic Example

17.6 Multiply Packed (MP)

In the MP instruction, the multiplier (the second operand) is multiplied by the multiplicand (first operand) and the result is placed in the first operand. The multiplier may not be longer than 15 digits and must be shorter in length than the multiplicand. In order to prevent an overflow from occurring, the multiplicand must include at least as many leading bytes of zeros as the number of bytes in the multiplier. If this is not the case, a data exception occurs. The Condition Code is unchanged.

17.7 Divide Packed (DP)

In the DP instruction, the first operand is the dividend and the second operand is the divisor. The results are a quotient and a remainder which will replace the dividend. The divisor may not be longer than 15 digits.

The quotient occupies the leftmost bytes of the result. Its length is equal to the difference between the length of the dividend (L1) and the divisor (L2). The remainder occupies the remaining bytes of the first operand. A Decimal Divide exception occurs in the case of divide by zero or a quotient too large to fit in the digits available. The Condition Code is unchanged.

17.8 EDIT (ED)

Although there is an Unpack instruction (UNPK), the ED instruction is the preferred way to a convert packed decimal number to a zoned decimal, printable string. The first operand is a set of pattern codes that control the formatting process and the second operand is the packed number to be converted. The result replaces the first operand.

The first byte of the first operand pattern is called the *fill byte*. It will be placed in the leading bytes of the result in place of non-significant leading zeros.

Following the fill byte are a collection of *pattern* bytes and *message* bytes.

When the instruction begins the *significance indicator* is off. It stays off until a significant digit (*i.e.*, non-zero) is encountered or turned on by a pattern byte. When the significance indicator is off, zeros in the source are replaced by the fill byte. If the significance indicator is on, the source digit appears in the result even if it is zero.

There are two main pattern bytes: 20_{16} and 21_{16}. The first is called the *digit selector*. If encountered in the format, the next digit in the source field is selected. If the source digit is zero and the significance indicator is off, the fill byte replaces the digit selector. If the digit is non-zero or the significance indicator is on, the digit is converted to zoned decimal and replaces the digit selector. If a non-zero digit is selected, the significance indicator is turned on if not already on.

The pattern code 21_{16} is called the *significance starter*. It acts like the 20_{16} above except it turns the significance indicator on if not already on. Turning the significance indicator on affects the next digit, not the current digit.

Other characters in the pattern, such as commas and decimal points are only displayed if the significance indicator is on. Otherwise, they are replaced by the fill byte.

When the last digit of a number is selected, the sign is examined. If the sign is positive (*CAFE*), the significance indicator is turned off. If the sign is negative, it remains on or is turned on. The effect of this is to leave or replace trailing characters in the format. For example, the final characters in the format could be *(DB)* indicating a debit or negative balance. The *(DB)* will be replaced by the fill byte if the number is positive but remain in the result if the number is negative. (Note: you often see this in bank statements where a negative value is indicated at the end of the number). For example, the pattern (extra spaces added for readability):

```
40 20 20 20 6B 20 20 20 6B 20 21 20 4B 20 20 4D C4 C2 5D
```

40_{16} is a blank. $6B_{16}$ is a comma while $4B_{16}$ is a decimal point. $4D_{16}$ is an open parenthesis and $4D_{16}$ is a close parenthesis. $C4_{16}$ is the letter D and $C2_{16}$ is the letter B.

The fill character is blank. Until a nonzero character is encountered, blanks replace the selector bytes and the commas. However, just prior to the decimal point the significance indicator is forced on if not already on. This means that a zero immediately prior to the decimal point will be printed as well as the decimal point. The *(DB)* will be printed if the number is negative and converted to blanks if the number is positive. For example:

00 00 00 00 00 0C	becomes	0.00
00 00 00 00 00 0D	becomes	0.00 (DB)
00 00 00 00 10 0C	becomes	1.00
00 00 01 00 00 0C	becomes	1,000.00
00 10 00 00 00 0D	becomes	1,000,000.00 (DB)

17.9 Miscellaneous Decimal Related

17.10 Instructions

17.10.1 UNPACK (UNPK)

The UNPK instruction converts each packed decimal second operand to zoned format except for the last digit. Each digit in the source becomes a byte in the result with a leading F_{16} zone except in the case of the last digit, which becomes the digit in the final result byte but the zone is not F_{16} but the sign from the source. The UNPK is not as useful as the ED.

17.10.2 Move Numerics (MVN)

The right-most 4 bits of each source byte (second operand) are moved to the right-most 4 bits of the target operand (first operand). The zones are unchanged. The Condition Code is unchanged. Up to 256 bytes may participate.

17.10.3 Move Zones (MVZ)

The left-most 4 bits of each source byte (second operand) are moved to the left-most 4 bits of the target operand (first operand). The digits are unchanged. The Condition Code is unchanged. Up to 256 bytes may participate.

18. CSECTS, DSECTS and Base Registers

18.1 CSECT

Assembly language programs are comprised of one or more sections. There are three types of sections: control sections (CSECTs), common sections (COMs) and dummy sections (DSECTs). CSECTs contain ordinary code, dummy sections do not generate object code but are layouts or mappings of memory, and common sections are areas of memory common to multiple object modules.

A CSECT directive is used to begin or continue a control section. The label on the CSECT directive is the name of the section for linkage purposes. The START directive, used only at the beginning of an assembly program, is the equivalent of a CSECT. In a program with multiple CSECTs, the code for several sections may be intermingled in the source file. The CSECT directive is used to identify to which section different code sections belong.

```
FIRST       CSECT
              .
              .                some code for CSECT FIRST
              .
SECOND      CSECT
              .
              .                some code for CSECT SECOND
              .
TMPLT1      DSECT
              .
              .                some code for DSECT TMPLT1
              .
FIRST       CSECT
              .
              .                more code for CSECT FIRST
              .
SECOND      CSECT
              .
              .                more code for CSECT SECOND
              .
```

Figure 60 CSECT/DSECT Flow

In an assembly language program you may have several CSECTS and DSECTS (discussed below). These need not be contiguous. You may begin a CSECT and write some code then begin another, likewise write some code, interrupt that one and declare a DSECT, and then resume coding a previous CSECT. The assembler will gather all the pieces of each together into separate sections of you object module.

Figure 60 gives an example. Initially, we begin coding CSECT FIRST. This is interrupted by some code for CSECT SECOND which is interrupted by code for DSECT TMPLT1. We resume coding CSECT FIRST. This continues coding from where we left off. Likewise we next resume coding CSECT SECOND which will continue SECOND. The assembler will organize these into continuous blocks.

18.2 Base Register Addressing

As we have seen, in the original architecture, memory resident operands in RX, SI, SS and RS instructions are addressed by a combination of base register, index register and displacement in RX format, or displacement and base (in all others). To this list more recent versions of the architecture have added formats: RSL, RSY, RXE, RXF, RXY, S, SIY and SSE. In the original architecture and in most of the more recent instructions, base/displacement addressing of operands is the norm. However, formats RI, RIE, RIL and RSI have signed immediate operands that in some instructions are added to the current instruction address to form a memory address.

In formats RX, SI, SS, RS, RSL, RXE, RXF, S and SSE, the displacement is a 12 bit unsigned positive number. In RSY, RXY and SLY, the displacement is a 20 bit signed number in 2s complement.

When addressing a memory operand with base and displacement, the base register (any register between R1 and R15 but usually in the range R2 to R13) contains the address of a location in memory. The operand address is calculated by summing the displacement and the contents of the base and, optionally, the contents of an index register.

Displacements in the basic architecture are positive 12 bit numbers and thus can range from 0 to 4095. In some recent instructions, the displacements are 20 bit signed numbers that can range from +524,288 to -524,289. In the case of 20 bit displacements, a single base register is often adequate for an entire program. However, many legacy programs use the 12 bit displacement model and this usually means that a program must use more than one base register.

Ordinarily, at the beginning of an assembly language program the assembler is told which register will be the base register and then it is loaded with an address at or near the beginning of the program. From this point on, the assembler will calculate the addresses of labels as displacements from the point in the program whose address is contained in the base register.

18.3 Programs Longer than 4096 Bytes

One problem with the base-displacement addressing scheme used in the original architecture is that the maximum displacement from a base register is 4095 bytes. That is, the assembler cannot address a byte which is more than 4095 bytes from the address contained in the base register. When a byte is within this window of addressability we say that the label is *within using* of a base register.

Programs in the real world, however, are obviously longer than 4096 bytes. The base register addressability problem can be partly solved by having multiple base registers with the second pointing 4096 bytes beyond the first and so forth.

However, for large programs, there are usually not enough spare registers to allow very many to be pre-allocated as base registers so other techniques must be employed. One technique is that larger programs are organized as blocks of code where each block establishes its own base register on entry into the block. Thus, the same register or registers can be re-used.

18.4 Loading an Address - BALR / BASR

Loading a base register with the an address can be accomplished by either BALR or BASR instructions in which the second operand is specified as R0 (the BAL and BAS instructions will also load the current address into a register but they always branch). In BALR and BASR, no branch takes place because the second operand is R0. The first operand receives the address of the byte immediately following the BALR or BASR.

So, for example, if we want to establish R12 as a base register, we would first load it with the address of where we are in the program. Then we inform the assembler that R12 is a base register and where the contents of R12 are pointing. This could be accomplished with the following code fragment:

```
BASR R12,R0
USING *,R12
```

The above loads the address of the byte following the BASR into R12 then tells the assembler to use R12 as a base register. The format of the assembler directive USING is an address expression followed by one of more register designations. In this case the address expression is asterisk meaning *here*. The register is assumed to contain the address indicated by the address expression. If the USING specifies more than one register, they are assumed to contain the addresses 4096, 8192, and so forth beyond the value in the first register. Note that the USING follows the BALR/BASR. This is because the address loaded into the register specified as the first operand (R12) is the address of the byte immediately following the BALR/BASR. Hence, as the asterisk refers to the current address, the USING needs to be after the BALR. Had it been the other way around, the assembler would assume that the address in R12 was the address of the BALR/BASR.

You will also note there is a DROP directive. This discontinues use of a base register. The use of USING and DROP are assemble-time directives - they cover areas of code and are not run time states. That is, from the point or line in a program where a register is designated as a base register by USING until the point or line where it is dropped by a DROP (or the end of the program), the register may be used by the assembler to construct a base and displacement address. Outside that area, the register is not a base register.

When operands can be addressed with a valid base and displacement combination, they are said to be *in using*; if an operand is beyond the maximum 4095 byte displacement of any base register, the operand is said to be *out of using*.

18.5 Specifying More Than One Base Register

You tell the assembler to use multiple base registers by including more than one register in the USING statement as seen in Figure 61. The assembler assumes that each register has as its contents an address value 4096 higher than the previous register in the list. In a long program, the assembler will select the base register which is closest to a label.

As there are only fifteen register that can be used as base registers (R0 may not be a base register), most large programs frequently re-use base registers rather than using many registers at once. However, it is not unusual to have more than one base register available for addressing. In this case the programmer needs to be sure to load each register correctly. An example can be seen in Figure 61.

1	BALR	R12,R0
2	USING	*,R12,R11,R10
3	LA	R11,2048(R0,R12)
4	LA	R11,2048(R0,R11)
5	LA	R10,2048(R0,R11)
6	LA	R10,2048(R0,R10

Figure 61 Multiple Base Registers

The code in Figure 61 first loads R12 with the address of the byte immediately beyond the BALR. Then it tells the assembler that registers 12, 11 and 10 may be used as base registers. The assembler assumes that these registers are set to 4096 and 8192 bytes apart, respectively. The LA instruction is used to set R11 and R10 from the value in R12. Note that since the maximum displacement is 4095, two LAs are required to add 4096.

A simplified example of using multiple base registers local to blocks of code is given in Figure 62 where three base registers are used. In this example, the hexadecimal code generated for each line is shown to the right and the customary SUBENTRY macro has been replaced by a simpler form of entry code. Notes about this example:

1. The CSECT (line 3) tell the assembler the name of this module but generates no code.

2. By operating system convention, upon entry into a program, R15 always contains the address the first byte of the entry point, the beginning in this case.

3. The STM on line 5 saves the calling programs registers which are reloaded by the LM on line 15 prior to return.

4. On entry into a program, R14 contains the return address. Thus the BR on line 16 returns to the caller.

5. The USING on line 4 tells the assembler that it may use R15 as a base register and to assume that it contains the address of the current (*) byte. Since USING directives generate no code, the current byte is the first byte of the STM on the next line which is the first byte of the program and the one to which R15 is pointing.

6. On line 5 you can see that the STM used R15 (F_{16}) as the base register with a displacement of 008_{16} (highlighted)to address the label SAVE. Likewise, the XPRNT on line 8 used R15 as the base and a displacement of 060_{16} (highlighted) to address OUT1.

7. The BALR on line 9 loads the address of the byte following the BALR (first byte of the XPRNT) into R14 but does not branch because the second operand is R0.

8. The USING on line 10 tells the assembler that R14 is a base register and that its contents are the address of the first byte of the XPRNT on the following line. When you use a BALR or similar instruction to load an address, the USING is on the next line if it uses the * address form.

9. On line 11 there are two possible base registers: R15 and R14. The assembler chooses R14 (E_{16}) in the XPRNT with a displacement of $01E_{16}$ (highlighted).

10. Line 12, 13 and 14 repeat the pattern.

11. On line 15, the LM reloads the register but note that the base register selected is R15 with a displacement of 008_{16}. This is because R15 covers the area of your program beginning at line 4 and extending through the end and is available. Had there been a DROP prior to the STM, no base register would have been available.

While the loading of base registers is done at run-time, base register coverage is determined at assembly-time. One a base register has been established by a USING, is remains in effect until the end of the program or a DROP directive is encountered. When the assembler encounters a reference to a label, it looks to see which base registers are available that are currently valid for the label and then selects the base register (if more than one is available) which will produce the smallest displacement. In the original architecture, displacements may only be forward (positive). In some newer instructions, they may be negative.

1	000000			PRINT	NOGEN
2	000000			EQUREGS	
3	000000		DEMO	CSECT	
4	000000			USING	*,R15
5	000000	90ECF008		STM	R14,R12,SAVE
6	000004	47F0F044		B	L1
7	000008		SAVE	DS	15F
8	000044	E020F060000A	L1	XPRNT	OUT1,L'OUT1
9	00004A	05E0		BALR	R14,R0
10	00004C			USING	*,R14
11	00004C	E020E01E000A		XPRNT	OUT2,L'OUT2
12	000052	05D0		BALR	R13,R0
13	000054			USING	*,R13
14	000054	E020D020000A		XPRNT	OUT3,L'OUT3
15	00005A	98ECF008		LM	R14,R12,SAVE
16	00005E	07FE		BR	14
		D6E4E3F14040404			
17	000060	0	OUT1	DC	CL10'OUT1'
		D6E4E3F24040404			
18	00006A	0	OUT2	DC	CL10'OUT2'
		D6E4E3F34040404			
19	000074	0	OUT3	DC	CL10'OUT3'

Figure 62 Three Base Register Example

The program in Figure 63 similar but it shows the same base register, R14, being used more than once. This example is more typical of a program with many blocks of code each of which re-initializes a base register.

R15 is initially established as a base register and it remains in effect for the entire program. It is used in the XPRNT on line 8 with a displacement of 060_{16} (highlighted).

On lines 9 and 10, R14 becomes available and it is used in the XPRNT on line 11 with a displacement of $01E_{16}$ (highlighted).

On line 12, R14 is dropped as a base register but reinstated on lines 13 and 14, this time with a new contents (from the BALR on line 13). It is used in the XPRNT on line 15 with a displacement of 020_{16} (highlighted).

On line 16, the reference to SAVE is done with R15 and a displacement of 008_{16}. R15 remained a base for the entire program. It was used in lines 5, 6 and 8 as it was the only base register in effect when the code on these lines was assembled. R14 in both instances were not yet in effect. R15 is used in line 16 because is is the only base register currently in effect which was in effect when the label SAVE was seen.

1	000000			PRINT	NOGEN
2	000000			EQUREGS	
3	000000		DEMO	CSECT	
4	000000			USING	*,R15
5	000000	90ECF008		STM	R14,R12,SAVE
6	000004	47F0F044		B	L1
7	000008		SAVE	DS	15F
8	000044	E020F060000A	L1	XPRNT	OUT1,L'OUT1
9	00004A	05E0		BALR	R14,R0
10	00004C			USING	*,R14
11	00004C	E020E01E000A		XPRNT	OUT2,L'OUT2
12	000052	05D0		BALR	R13,R0
13	000054			USING	*,R13
14	000054	E020D020000A		XPRNT	OUT3,L'OUT3
15	00005A	98ECF008		LM	R14,R12,SAVE
16	00005E	07FE		BR	14
17	000060	D6E4E3F140404040	OUT1	DC	CL10'OUT1'
18	00006A	D6E4E3F240404040	OUT2	DC	CL10'OUT2'
19	000074	D6E4E3F340404040	OUT3	DC	CL10'OUT3'
20	00007E			END	

Figure 63 DROP example

18.6 DSECTs

A DSECT is a code section which contains ordinary assembly language statements but no object code is generated. They are mainly used as layouts to assist in writing programs.

For example, consider a program with an array structured phone directory. Each entry in the array consists of a 30 character name, a 30 character city, a two character state code, a 5 character zip code and a 10 character phone number for a total of 77 bytes for each entry. Assume the array is 77,000 bytes long, log enough for 1,000 entries. Figure 64 gives a code fragment to print each element of the array. It loops 1,000 times, until R3 becomes zero, by means of the BCT on line 9. Each XPRNT statement prints a part of the structure using displacements from the start of each array entry. R2 is a pointer that is advanced from the beginning of each array entry to the next.

Figure 65 shows the same code using a DSECT. In this example, the name of the current CSECT is PGM. Lines 1 through 6 define the DSECT which is named ID. Line 7 ends the DSECT and resumes the CSECT PGM (we interrupted the code for PGM on line 1).

```
1              LA       R2,ARRAY
2              L        R3,=F'1000'
3    LOOP      XPRNT    0(R2),30          * NAME
4              XPRNT    30(R2),30         * CITY
5              XPRNT    60(R2),2          * STATE
6              XPRNT    62(R2),5          * ZIP
7              XPRNT    67(R2),10         * PHONE
8              LA       R2,77(0,R2)       * INCR POINTER
9              BCT      R3,LOOP
```

Figure 64 Table without DSECT

The DSECT is a layout for an element in the array. It does not actually reserve memory in the object module.

On line 8 we load the address of the data array into R2 and on line 9 tell the assembler that any references to data described in the DSECT ID should be based on R2. Consequently, when we reference the labels from the DSECT in lines 11 through 15, the assembler generates code relative to R2 with displacements calculated from the beginning of the DSECT (NAME has a displacement of 0, CITY a displacement of 30, STATE a displacement of 60 and so on).

There are several obvious advantages to the DSECT approach not the least of which are readability. It should also be noted that, should the data structure change, say, to enlarge the name field, it need be done only in the DSECT itself and not in each of the XPRNT statements.

```
1    ID       DSECT
2    NAME     DS       CL30
3    CITY     DS       CL30
4    STATE    DS       CL2
5    ZIP      DS       CL5
6    PHONE    DS       CL10
7    PGM      CSECT
8             LA       R2,ARRAY
9             USING    ID,R2
10            L        R3,=F'1000'
11   LOOP     XPRNT    NAME,L'NAME      * NAME
12            XPRNT    CITY,L'CITY      * CITY
13            XPRNT    STATE,L'STATE    * STATE
14            XPRNT    ZIP,L'ZIP        * ZIP
15            XPRNT    PHONE,L'PHONE    * PHONE
16            LA       R2,77(0,R2)      * INCR POINTER
17            BCT      R3,LOOP
```

Figure 65 Table with DSECT

19. Subroutine Calls and Linkage

Linkage refers to the set of conventions used by an operating system whereby programs call one another, pass arguments, and return values. The IBM mainframe still uses many of the original linkage conventions established when the machine was introduced in 1964 although there have been additional modes added since then. For purposes of this text, we have mainly used the legacy linkage as embodied in the SUBENTRY and SUBEXIT macros provided by the z390 emulator. These macros follow the legacy 31 bit program linkage conventions. Depending on addressing mode and other language dependent conditions, such as calling programs written in C/C++, other linkage conventions may apply.

SUBENTRY saves the contents of the calling program's registers in the calling program's save area, creates a local save area to be used by any programs our program calls, and sets up a base register. SUBEXIT restores the calling program's registers and branches back to the calling program.

19.1 Linkage Registers

· On entry into a routine, several registers have predefined values as shown in Table 38.

```
R1      Address of a parameter list
R13     Address of save area in calling program
R14     Address of return point in calling program
R15     Address of entry point in called program

             Table 38 Linkage Registers
```

1. On entry to a routine, R1 points to a table of addresses in memory. Each address, in turn, points to an argument being passed to the subroutine.

2. On entry, R13 points to the address in the calling program of a 72 byte save area where the called program will store most of the calling programs registers. There are restore on exit from the called program.

3. R14 contains the return address. That is, when your program has finished, it should branch to the address contained in R14.

4. R15 contains the address of the entry point in the called program. Normally this is the address of the first instruction in the called program however some routines can have multiple entry points. In any event, R15 is the address of the first instruction to be executed upon entry into your routine. It is also provided by the calling program.

5. Upon entry into a program, it is the responsibility of the called program to save the calling programs registers and, upon exit, to restore them.

6. There are two places where a program saves registers. The first is in a save area provided by the calling program (pointed to by R13) and the second is in a system-provided linkage stack.

7. The ASC mode of the called program determines which method may be used. A primary mode program may use either the linkage stack or the calling program's save area while an AR mode program must use the linkage stack.

8. The save area provided by the calling program may be statically allocated in the calling program or it may be a dynamically allocated area. Save areas for programs operating in 31 or 24 bit addressing modes are 18 full words or 72 bytes in length.

19.2 Static Save Area

In the original linkage model, every program that may call another program has a local save area. Lowest level programs that call no other programs, do not need a local save area A save area, as shown in Table 39, is an 18 full word (72 byte) area (assumes 31 bit or 24 addressing mode) in which you save the contents of registers. It is also helpful for debugging by providing a linked list of pointers to previous save areas. Note: There are newer linkage models that permit the save area to be allocated on a system stack thus permitting recursion, multi-threading and so forth.

By convention, upon entry, R13 will contain the address of a save area in the calling program's data area. When your routine starts, it should immediately save the contents of all the general purpose registers (except R13) into the calling program's save area. Then you create a save area of your own and, after some cross linking, place the address of your program's save area in R13.

The z390 provides a macro named *SUBENTRY* to do the basic program entry tasks. This code saves the calling program's registers and sets up your local save area. An example of the code generated by the SUBENTRY macro as shown in Figure 66 SUBENTRY Code. The line numbers are from the assembler and the plus sign after each indicates that the code is from a macro expansion (non-macro code does not have a plus sign on the line number).

Offset	Word	Contents
0	Word 1	
4	Word 2	Addr of calling pgm save area
8	Word 3	Addr of called pgm save area
12	Word 4	Register 14
16	Word 5	Register 15
20	Word 6	Register 0
24	Word 7	Register 1
28	Word 8	Register 2
32	Word 9	Register 3
36	Word 10	Register 4
40	Word 11	Register 5
44	Word 12	Register 6
48	Word 13	Register 7
52	Word 14	Register 8
56	Word 15	Register 9
60	Word 16	Register 10
64	Word 17	Register 11
68	Word 18	Register 12

Table 39 Save Area

On line 3 the assembler is told that this is the start of a control section and that its name is ADD (from the label on the SUBENTRY). A CSECT is an assembler directive and does not generate code. It means control section.

On line 4 the STM (Store Multiple) causes registers R14, R15, R0, R1, ... R11, R12 to be saved in successive 4 byte full words beginning at the fourth full word in the calling program's (R13) save area. Word 4 begins at offset 12 from the start of the calling program's save area whose address is in R13 and thus the displacement of 12 past R13.

```
3+ADD          CSECT
4+             STM        14,12,12(13)
5+             BAL        15,104(15)
6+             DC         18F'0'
7+             DC         CL8'ADD'
8+             DC         CL8'09/14/10'
9+             DC         CL8'20.33'
10+            ST         15,8(13)
11+            ST         13,4(15)
12+            LR         13,15
13+            USING      ADD+8,13
```

Figure 66 SUBENTRY Code

The next instruction, the BAL (Branch and Link), does two things: it causes a branch to the ST (Store) instruction on line 10 and it resets the contents of R15 to point to the first byte of the local 18 full word save area immediately following it. This is the current program's save area. Note that it is statically (*i.e.*, not dynamically) allocated.

The branch address in line 5 is calculated by adding the contents of R15 and 104, the displacement which is sufficient to branch around the save area and the fixed length program name information. The ST instruction at line 10 is 104 bytes from the beginning STM.

R15 receives the address of the first byte of the save area (because of the BAL) but not until after the branch address is calculated. The BAL first calculates the branch target address. Then it loads into the first operand, R15, the updated address portion of the PSW, that is, the address of the byte immediately following the BAL. Finally, it branches.

As an instruction executes, the address portion of the PSW always contains the address of the byte immediately following the instruction. In most cases, this is the address of the next instruction. In this case, however, it is the address of our program's save area.

At line 10, the ST instruction stores the address of our save area into the third word of the calling program's save area then stores the address of the calling program's save area in the second word of our save area. Thus, the calling program's save area points to ours and ours points to the calling program's save area.

The contents of R15 (now the address of our save area) are copied to R13 and the assembler is told to use R13 as a base register and to assume that it is pointing at the 8th byte of the program (the 1st byte of the save area) which it is.

You will note that after the 18 word save area there are character fields containing the name of the CSECT and the date and time when it was assembled.

Happily all this is done by the SUBENTRY macro. Likewise, the SUBEXIT macro reloads the calling program's registers and returns to the address originally provided in R14.

19.3 Linking Reentrant and Recursive Programs

While much, if not most, legacy code is written with static save areas and linkage as discussed above, there are problems with this approach. These include problems with programs calling themselves either directly or indirectly (recursion), and issues

---

relating to reentrancy. In both these cases, static save areas are not adequate.

Programs can be classified as either serially reusable, reentrant or neither. In reusable programs, a copy of a program loaded in memory may be used by only one user at a time but, upon completion, the original state of the program's data is restored and another used may use the code.

A reentrant routine is one which may have more than one concurrent users. In order to allow this, it must be pure, unchanging code and data. Any code or data subject to modification must not be part of the shared image. It must belong to individual users.

For example, the program code for an editor may be used by several users concurrently. It is much more efficient to have only one copy of the program reside in memory rather than a copy for each user. The program is shared among several users. But in order for this to work, each user must have their own data areas and registers. The program itself may contain only code and constants. If the program contained alterable data, it would eventually occur that:

1. One user executing the program would set a data value and be interrupted,

2. Another user would gain control and set the same data but to a different value and become interrupted,

3. The first use gain control and use that data value actually set by the other user.

To avoid this, we write programs where the code and data is unchanging. The hardware even supports this with the Execute instruction which permits reentrant compliant temporary modification of, among other things, the length byte in SS instructions.

In a multi-user system, each user has their own privately allocated data area pointed to by their registers. When an operating system switches between users, the currently executing user's set of general purpose registers, floating point registers and PSW and other per user information are saved and, ultimately, restored when the user gains control again.

When a code module is shared among multiple users, it is using a particular user's registers to address that user's private data area. When another user gains control, the program uses that user's registers to access that user's data area.

Thus, for example, the code for the telephone table lookup shown in Figure 65 bases all its data accesses on the contents of register 2 which is the base for the DSECT ID. Similarly, if a reentrant program were to make all its data references within a DSECT which itself is based on a user supplied base register, the program would use different data areas for different users. The program itself would have no local data other than constants.

A program which only modifies the contents of its registers and data pointed to by the registers in the user's private data area does not violate reentrancy rules. Each user has their own set of registers and their own private (unshared) data area.

Even if a program is reentrant and each user has their own data area, there is still a problem when a program calls itself (recursive call) if it uses a statically allocated (legacy) save area.

If a program calls itself, the second call will overwrite the statically allocated save area. This is also true if a program indirectly calls itself. Consequently, we need a mechanism to stack multiple save areas for the same function.

One approach to is to have the called routine dynamically allocate a new save area each time it is called and free it upon ultimate return. This is usually done with the GETMAIN or STORAGE system macros.

Another approach is to use the system stack. The original IBM 360 architecture did not provide for system supported stacks. It is rumored that the engineers thought this feature was more characteristic of a mini-computer. Nonetheless, the feature was ultimately introduced in 1989 – 25 years later! The system stack and several semi-privileged instructions support recursive calls.

19.3.1 Chained Dynamically Allocated Save Areas

As noted, programs that are to be recursively called need to be reentrant so that successive calls do not use or alter previous calls' intermediate results if they are stored in. For example, the calculation of factorials is often done as a series of recursive calls. Each instance waits for the return of one or more deeper invocations. Each invocation stores local values as needed to complete its evaluation level prior to making a return.

An example of factorial in C is given in Figure 67Figure 1 where, on line 12, each invocation waits for lower level invocations to return and, ultimately, their result be multiplied by a current value of i. The variable i must be local to each invocation and not shared.

On way to implement this program is to use a chain of save areas dynamically allocated by the GETMAIN or STORAGE macros.

Each invocation of the reentrant program results in the allocation of an area of memory for its save area and any other local data needed for each recursion. Since the address of the allocated memory returned by the macros resides in a register, it will be restored when lower levels return and restore the previous level's registers.

```
1   #include <stdio.h>
2
3   int main() {
4
5       printf("factorial of 5 = %d\n",fact(5));
6       return 0;
7       }
8
9   int fact(int i) {
10
11      if (i==1) return 1;
12      return i*fact(i-1);
13      }
```

Figure 67 Factorial in C

When a routine calls itself, on entry, it allocates a new area and stores the calling program's registers in the calling program's save area which itself is allocated storage. When a function returns, if frees its area and reloads the calling programs registers. This creates, in effect, a linked list of save areas and associated data areas which behave like a stack.

19.3.1.1 Save Area Example Using GETMAIN

Figure 68 give an example of calculating factorials in a recursive, reentrant procedure using GETMAIN. It is based on the code in Figure 67.

The MAIN program (lines 3 through 23) has standard, static save area linkage with it's parent by means of SUBENTRY on line 3 and SUBEXIT on line 16. It stores the number whose factorial is to be calculated at the label N (line 20) and places the address of N at the label PARMS (an A-type address constant). It loads the address of the parameter list into R1 on line 7. Legacy linkage conventions say that R1 should contain the address of the first word of a table of addresses. Each address in the table is the address of a parameter being passed to the subroutine. In this case, there is only one parameter and only one address in the table.

A standard call is made to the function FACT on lines 9 and 10. Upon return, the result is in N and it is printed and the program terminates with a return code (in R15) of zero (lines 12 through 15).

The subroutine FACT is on lines 32 through 93. It repeatedly calls itself passing N-1 each time until N is one at which time it returns (see line 12 in Figure 67). Since the program calls itself, it cannot use a static save area. It must allocate a new save area at each entry and delete it upon exit.

Upon entry, FACT performs the usual Store Multiple (line 33) to save the calling program's registers in the calling program's save area pointed to by R13 according to the traditional linkage convention. Lines 34 and 35 establish a local base register (R12).

Now things deviate from the usual entry sequence. First, we preserve R1, the contents of which are a pointer to the parameter list, by copying it to R3. This is necessary since the GETMAIN on line 41 returns an address in R1 of the memory allocated.

```
1              PRINT    NOGEN

2              EQUREGS

3    MAIN      SUBENTRY                      * LEGACY LINKAGE

4

5              LA       R5,5                 * FIND FACTORIAL OF 5

6              ST       R5,N                 * SAVE IN MEMORY

7              LA       R1,PARMS             * ADDRESS OF PARM LIST

8

9              L        R15,=V(FACT)         * CALL FUNCTION

10             BASR     R14,R15

11

12             L        R1,N                 * LOAD ANSVER

13             XDECO    R1,OUT               * CVT TO DEC & PRINT

14             XPRNT    MSG,L'MSG+L'OUT

15             SR       R15,R15              * RETURN CODE

16             SUBEXIT                       * LEGACY REGURN

17             LTORG

18

19   PARMS     DC       A(N)                 * PARM LIST

20   N         DS       F
                        C'FACTORIAL   5
21   MSG       DC       ='

22   OUT       DS       CL12

23

24   *

25   * DSECT TO ADDRESS GETMAIN ALLOCATIONS

26   *

27   AUTO      DSECT

28   SAVE      DS       18F                  * SAVE AREA
```

```
29 PARM    DS       F                    * PARM LIST
30 N1      DS       F                    * DATA
31
32 FACT    CSECT
33         STM      R14,R12,12(R13)      * SAVE REGS
34         BALR     R12,R0               * EST BASE REG
35         USING    *,R12                * EST BASE REG
36
37         LR       R3,R1                * PRESERVE R1
38 *                                     * ADDR OF PARM LIST
39 *                                     * GETMAIN WILL ALTER R1
40
41         GETMAIN  RU,LV=80             * GET 80 BYTES
42 *                                     * ALTERS R1 and R0
43         ST       R1,8(R13)            * PARENT -> US
44         ST       R13,4(R1)            * WE -> PARENT SAVE AREA
45         LR       R13,R1               * ALLOC AREA NOW OUR SAVE
46         USING    AUTO,R13             * POINT DSECT AT ALLOC MEM
47         LR       R1,R3                * RESTORE R1
48
49         L        R5,0(0,R1)
50         L        R5,0(0,R5)           * 1ST PARM -> R5
51         XDECO    R5,OT1
52         XPRNT    MSG1,L'OT1+L'MS
                    G1
53         C        R5,=F'1'             * END OF RECURSION?
54         BNE      RECURS               * NO
55         L        R2,0(0,R1)           * ADDR 1ST PARM -> R2
56         ST       R5,0(0,R2)           * STORE 1 in 1ST PARM
57
58 EXIT    LR       R1,R13               * ADDR ALLOC MEM
59         L        R13,4(R13)           * ADD SAVE AREA ABOVE
60         FREEMAIN RU,A=(1),LV=80       * RELEASE MEM
61         LM       R14,R12,12(R13)      * RESTORE REGS
62         BR       14                   * RETURN
63
64 RECURS  LR       R6,R5                * COPY PARM -> R6
65         S        R6,=F'1'             * DECREMENT
66         ST       R6,N1                * STORE AS OUR PARM
67         LA       R7,N1                * ADDR OF PARM
68         ST       R7,PARM              * STORE ADDR TO PARM LIST
69         LR       R3,R1                * PRESERVE PARENT PARM
70         LA       R1,PARM              * R1 -> PARM LIST
71
```

```
72            L       R15,=V(FACT)      * RECURSE
73            BASR    R14,R15
74
75            LR      R1,R3             * RESTORE
76
77            SR      R6,R6             * EVEN REG MULT
78            L       R7,N1             * ODD REG MULT
79            MR      R6,R5
80            L       R2,0(0,R1)        * ADDR OF PARM
81   *                                  * IN PARENT
82            ST      R7,0(0,R2)        * RSLT STORED
83
84            XDECO   R7,OT2
                      MSG2,L'MSG2+L'O
85            XPRNT   T2
86            B       EXIT
87
                      C'ENTRY VALUE =
88  MSG1     DC       '
89  OT1      DS       CL12
                      C'RTRND VALUE =
90  MSG2     DC       '
91  OT2      DS       CL12
92  RMSG     DC       C'RETURN'
93           LTORG
94           END
Output:
ENTRY VALUE =             5
ENTRY VALUE =             4
ENTRY VALUE =             3
ENTRY VALUE =             2
ENTRY VALUE =             1
RTRND VALUE =             2
RTRND VALUE =             6
RTRND VALUE =            24
RTRND VALUE =           120
FACTORIAL  5 =          120
```

Figure 68 GETMAIN Based Linkage

The GETMAIN allocates 80 bytes. The first 72 bytes will be for our local save area and the final two words will be for our parameter list and local copy of the factorial parameter (N from the original invocation). Lines 43 and 45 store the address of our save area (R1) in the parent save area and the address of the parent save area in our save area.

Next we then copy the address from R1 to R13 as this is now our save area. It is also the address of the first byte of the allocated area which we will need when we exit and free the storage (FREEMAIN). Now we have a dynamically allocated local save area and two dynamically allocate local variables.

On line 46 we tell the assembler that references to labels in the DSECT AUTO should be calculated relative to R13. That is, R13 is the base register for AUTO. Note that the labels in AUTO correspond to an 18 byte save area (SAVE) and two full word variables PARMS and N1. The DSECT makes it more convenient to reference items in dynamically allocated memory areas.

Next, R1 is restored from R3 (line 47). The address of the parameter list is loaded into R5 and then the value of the single parameter is loaded into R5 (lines 49 and 50).The value of the parameter is printed and compared with one. If not one, a branch is made to RECURS. If it is one, the lowest level of recursion has been achieved and the value of one needs to be returned. The address of the parameter in the calling program is loaded into R2 and the value in R5 (1) is stored at that location (lines 55 and 56).

The exit sequence is entered (lines 58 through 62). The address of the allocated area (in R13) is copied to R1and the address of the calling program's save area is loaded into R13. The FREEMAIN macro is executed. It frees the 80 bytes of memory pointed to by R1. The caller's registers are restored and return is made to the calling program.

At RECURS, The value of the parameter (in R5) is copied to R6 and decremented. This value is then saved in local, dynamically allocated memory at N1 and its address is stored in the local parameter list (PARMS). The address of the parameter list is loaded into R1 (lines 64 through 70).

On lines 72 and 73 the function recursively calls itself passing *via* R1 the address of the address of the decremented parameter. Upon entry, FACT will again allocate a new save and data area while the previous save and data area remains waiting for return. Lines 75 through 86 are executed when FACT returns. They multiply the previous value of N contained in R5 with the value returned in N1. Note that R5 was restored, along with other registers, when the function returned. The result of the Multiply Register is in R7 and this is stored in the calling program's version of N. The function now returns as discussed above.

19.3.2 System Stack Based Linkage

The original IBM 360 included neither hardware stack support nor separate instruction and data address spaces. In more recent versions, these have been added to some extent.

The Linkage Stack, introduced in 1989, is a system provided means to save registers and other system state information. The instructions that use the Linkage Stack are shown in Figure 69.

The Linkage Stack must be used for AR (access register) Address Space Control (ASC) programs. In primary mode, the CPU uses the general purpose registers to calculate an address while in AR mode, the contents of access registers as well as the general purpose registers are used. This text deals only with primary ASC mode programming. AR Mode is for multiple address spaces. It is optional for non-AR (primary) ASC programs.

When the Branch and Stack (BAKR) and Program Call (PC) instructions execute, they save the required registers and status on the system stack. When the Program Return (PR) is executed, it restores the registers and status. The BAKR, among other things, stores general purpose registers 2 through 14 while the PR instruction restores them and branches to the return address.

Instruction	Mnemonic	Type
Branch and Stack	BAKR	RRE
Extract Stacked Registers	EREG/EREGG	RRE
Extract Stacked State	ESTA	RRE
Modify Stacked State	MSTA	RRE
Program Call	PC	S
Program Return	PR	E
Test Access	TAR	RRE

Figure 69 Stack Linkage Instructions

19.3.2.1 System Stack Linkage Example

Figure 70 shows the factorial program calculated using the system stack. The instructions used access the stack are Branch and Stack Register (BAKR) and Program Return (PR).

The BAKR instruction stores the general purpose registers and access registers (used to access alternate virtual memory data spaces when the program is in AR mode) on the linkage stack. The first operand contains the return address. A branch is made to the second operand unless it is zero.

The PR instruction restores the calling program's access registers and general purpose registers 2 – 14, removes the entry from the linkage stack, and returns control to the calling program. Note that only general purpose and access registers 2 through 14 are restored.

The program in Figure 70 function is very similar to that in Figure 69 except that *all* intermediate and final results are stored in registers, not memory. Thus, the program is reentrant. Because of the usage of the system stack, it is also recursive.

The number whose factorial is to be calculated (5) is loaded into R5 in line 8 and the FACT subroutine is called in lines 10 and 11. Upon return, the value is R1, the answer, is printed. FACT receives its argument in R5 and returns its result in R1.

On entry, FACT performs a Branch and Stack Register thereby storing the calling programs registers. It establishes a base register and tests if the value passed in R5 is one. If not, it branches to RECURS. If yes, the contents of R5 (1) are copied to R1 and the Program Return (PR) instruction is performed. Note that PR does not alter R1.

```
1              PRINT    NOGEN
2              EQUREGS
3     MAIN     CSECT
4              BAKR     R14,0          * STACK CALLERS REGS
5              BASR     R12,0          * GET ABS ADDR
6              USING    *,R12          * EST BASE REG
7
8              L        R5,=F'5'       * FACTORIAL TO CALC
9
10             L        R15,=V(FACT)   * CALL FCN
11             BASR     R14,R15        * CALL FCN
12
13             XDECO    R1,OUT
14             XPRNT    MSG,L'MSG+L'OUT
15             SR       R15,R15        * RETURN CODE ZERO
16             PR
17
18             LTORG
19    MSG      DC       C' 5 FACTORIAL = '
20    OUT      DS       CL12
21
22    FACT     CSECT
23             BAKR     R14,0          * STACK CALLERS REGS
24             BASR     R12,0          * GET ABS ADDR
25             USING    *,R12          * EST BASE REG
26
27             C        R5,=F'1'       * DONE?
28             BNE      RECURS         * NO
29             LR       R1,R5          * ANS -> R1
```

```
30            PR
31
      RECUR
32  S     LR      R6,R5              * SAVE CRNT FACTOR
33        S       R5,=F'1'           * DECR FOR NEXT LEVEL
34        L       R15,=V(FACT)       * RECURSE
35        BASR    R14,R15
36        SR      R4,R4              * GET READY TO MULT
37        LR      R5,R6              * MULTIPLICAND
38        MR      R4,R1              * R1 RETRND FROM FCN
39        LR      R1,R5              * COPY ANS TO R1 FOR RETRN
40        PR                         * RESTORE REGS AND RETURN
41
42        LTORG
43        END
Output:
  5 FACTORIAL =         120
```

Figure 70 System Stack Based Linkage

At RECURS the program saves the incoming of R5 to R6,
decrements R5 and calls itself. Upon return (lines 36 through
40), it multiplies the contents of R4/R5 by R1 (the value
returned), copies the result to R1 and returns.

20. Debugging (XDUMP, SNAP)

A *dump* is a snapshot, usually in hexadecimal, of the contents of memory, the registers, the PSW and other information relating to the state of the machine at a given instant. The memory area shown by the dump can either be that of a currently running program or larger. In the early days of computing, dumps were produced on paper and could run to thousands of pages. Now they are written to a file.

A dump is ordinarily produced when a program encounters a run time exception or interrupt. Alternatively, a programmer can explicitly request a dump with either the ASSIST XDUMP macro or the system macro SNAP.

In the case of a dump resulting from an error, the program terminates. When a programmer requests a dump, it is usually for diagnostic reasons and the program may or may not terminate, at the programmer's option.

For example, if the program from Figure 47 were modified to include the XDUMP as shown in Figure 71, the result is the text shown in Figure 72 (long lines truncated).

The contents of a dump consist of one or more of the following:

1. The contents of the 16 64-bit general purpose registers R0 through RF (R0 through R15);

2. The contents of the 16 64-bit floating point registers F0 through FF (F0 through F15);

3. The contents of memory beginning at location 00000000_{16} through location $000FFFFF_{16}$.

4. The PSW.

5. A save area trace back.

The contents of the general purpose and floating point registers are displayed as 16 hexadecimal digits (corresponding to 8 bytes). Normally, there are four registers displayed per line. For example, the first line for the general purpose registers displays R0, R1, R2 and R3 while the last line displays the contents of registers RC (R12), RD (R13), RE (R14) and RF (R15). A similar pattern is shown for the floating point registers (F0 through FF).

The z390 emulator pre-initializes each byte of each register to $F4_{16}$, thus the high order 32 bits of the registers may be $F4_{16}$ if the program only uses 32 bit instructions. The low order 32 bits of a register will be $F4_{16}$ unless the register was used in the course of the program.

20.1 XDUMP

XDUMP is part of the ASSIST package. It dumps the general purpose and floating point registers and either all or a portion of the user memory area. The entire user memory area is written if the XDUMP macro has no arguments while a limited area is written if the user specifies two operands giving the start and length of the memory area to dump. In both cases, the contents of the registers are displayed. In the z390 emulator, the output appears on the user's console and is also written to the .LOG file for the program. The length, if present, consists of a constant or a register surrounded by parentheses.

```
XDUMP * REGS AND ALL MEMORY WRITTEN
XDUMP  BEGIN,LENGTH * REGS & SOME MEMORY WRITTEN
```

20.2 SNAP

SNAP is a system macro generally available on most systems. It is similar to the XDUMP macro but has additional optional operand options:

1. ID= is optional. If given, the number provided after the equals sign will appear in the written output to identify which SNAP in the program wrote same.

2. PDATA=(...) indicates optional items to display in a comma list. Some of these are:

   2.1. REGS - all registers displayed;

   2.2. GPR – only the general purpose registers displayed;

   2.3. FPR – only the floating point registers displayed;

   2.4. CB – all control blocks;

   2.5. DCB - DDNAME, DCB, AND DSNAME'S

3. STORAGE=(BEGIN,END) where BEGIN and END are the addresses of the starting and ending points of the memory area to be displayed (usually labels).

4. ID=*nbr* – a programmer supplied number that identifies the SNAP output.

Example:

```
SNAP PDATA=(GPR),STORAGE=(LAB1,LAB2)
```

20.3 Dump Format

The format of the output of both the SNAP and XDUMP are similar. The program in Figure 71 produced the XDUMP shown in Figure 72.

In Figure 71 we initially see the 16 general purpose registers R0 through RF (register identifiers are in hexadecimal), four 8 byte registers per line. Next, you will see the 16 floating point registers designated as F0 through FF. Note that the z390 emulator initializes all registers to $F4_{16}$ by default. This would not be the case in a real system.

Next we see the contents of memory shown in rows of 32 hexadecimal digits grouped into four fields of 8 digits each. Each group of 8 digits corresponds to one word (4 bytes) of memory. They are separated from one another by a blank to improve readability. Each line, therefore, displays 16 bytes of memory.

At the beginning of each row is the address of the first byte in the row. On the right hand side is an attempted conversion of each byte in the row to a printable character. Where there is no printable character for a byte code, a period is printed. Where the byte code has a printable equivalent, it is shown. In most cases, the printable equivalents are not meaningful.

Thus, the following line:

```
00002600 *F0F961F1 F461F1F0 00000000 00000000* *09/14/10........*
```

means that it is the dump of the 16 memory locations beginning at 2600_{16} through $260F_{16}$ inclusive (16 bytes of data). Because each line has 10_{16} (16_{10}) bytes of data, the address on the next line will be incremented by 10_{16}.

000000		(1/1)1	PRINT	GEN
000000		(1/2)2 ADD	SUBENTRY	
000000		(2/77)3+ADD	CSECT	
000000	90ECD00C	(2/167)4+	STM	14,12,12(13)
000004	45FF0068	(2/168)5+	BAL	15,104(15)
	00000000000000			
000008	00	(2/169)6+	DC	18F'0'
	C1C4C440404040			
000050	40	(2/170)7+	DC	CL8'ADD'
	F0F961F1F461F1			
000058	F0	(2/171)8+	DC	CL8'09/14/10'
	F2F04BF3F34040			
000060	40	(2/172)9+	DC	CL8'20.33'
000068	50FD0008	(2/173)10+	ST	15,8(13)
00006C	50DF0004	(2/174)11+	ST	13,4(15)
000070	18DF	(2/175)12+	LR	13,15

```
000072                            (2/188)13+    USING    ADD+8,13
000072                            (1/3)15       EQUREGS
                    00000
000072              0             (3/41)16+R0   EQU  0
                    00000
000072              1             (3/41)17+R1   EQU  1
                    00000
000072              2             (3/41)18+R2   EQU  2
                    00000
000072              3             (3/41)19+R3   EQU  3
                    00000
000072              4             (3/41)20+R4   EQU  4
                    00000
000072              5             (3/41)21+R5   EQU  5
                    00000
000072              6             (3/41)22+R6   EQU  6
                    00000
000072              7             (3/41)23+R7   EQU  7
                    00000
000072              8             (3/41)24+R8   EQU  8
                    00000
000072              9             (3/41)25+R9   EQU  9
                    00000
000072              A             (3/41)26+R10  EQU  10
                    00000
000072              B             (3/41)27+R11  EQU  11
                    00000
000072              C             (3/41)28+R12  EQU  12
                    00000
000072              D             (3/41)29+R13  EQU  13
                    00000
000072              E             (3/41)30+R14  EQU  14
                    00000
000072              F             (3/41)31+R15  EQU  15
000072  1B22                      (1/4)33       SR       R2,R2  * zero
000074  5A20D0B8          0000C0  (1/5)34       A        R2,ONE
000078  5A20D0BC          0000C4  (1/6)35       A        R2,TWO
00007C  5A20D0C0          0000C8  (1/7)36       A        R2,THREE
000080  5A20D0C4          0000CC  (1/8)37       A        R2,FOUR
000084  5A20D0C8          0000D0  (1/9)38       A        R2,FIVE
000088  E020D0A8000E      0000B0  (1/10)39      XPRNT    MSG,L'MSG
00008E  5220D0CC          0000D4  (1/11)40      XDECO    R2,DBL
000092  E020D0CC000C      0000D4  (1/12)41      XPRNT    DBL,L'DBL
000098  E06000000000              (1/13)42      XDUMP
00009E                            (1/14)43      SUBEXIT
00009E  41F00000                  (4/33)44+     LA       15,0
0000A2  58D0D004                  (4/50)45+     L        13,4(,13)
0000A6  58E0D00C                  (4/51)46+     L        14,12(,13)
0000AA  982CD01C                  (4/52)47+     LM       2,12,28(13)
0000AE  07FE                      (4/53)48+     BR       14
        C1848489958740
0000B0  D5                        (1/15)50 MSG  DC       C'Adding Numbers'
0000C0  00000001                  (1/16)51 ONE  DC       F'1'
0000C4  00000002                  (1/17)52 TWO  DC       F'2'
                                  (1/18)53
0000C8  00000003        THREE     DC       F'3'
0000CC  00000004                  (1/19)54      DC       F'4'
```

```
                                        FOUR
                                        (1/20)55
0000D0  00000005                        FIVE            DC      F'5'

0000D4                                  (1/21)56 DBL    DS      CL12

0000E0                                  (1/22)57        END
```

Figure 71 Add Program Details

On the far right column is the attempted character interpretation of the bytes. It tells us that the first eight bytes of the line's content correspond to the characters: *09/14/10* which appears to be a date. The remaining 8 bytes did not have printable equivalents. This is indicated by the periods.

Comparing the code from Figure 71 with the dump in Figure 72, we can see that the program's first executable instruction (line 4) is the Store Multiple RS instruction:

STM   14,12,12(13)

which corresponds to the machine code:

90ECD00C

Which corresponds to the RS format (See Figure 12):

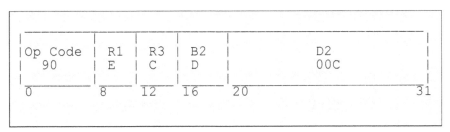

Where the opcode is 90_{16}, E_{16} (R14) is in the R1 field, C_{16} (R12) is in the R3 field, D_{16} (R13) is in the B2 field and $00C_{16}$ is in the D2 field.

If you look in the dump at address 8000_{16} you will see the same code for the STM instruction. Location 8000_{16} is the first byte of the program. In fact, because of the emulator, all programs will appear to begin at location 8000_{16}.

Moving on, the next instruction following the STM is:

    BAL   15,104(15)

which is the Branch and Link RX instruction and translates into the machine language:

    45FF0068

Where 45_{16} is the opcode, F_{16} (R15) is the R1 field, F_{16} (R15) is the B2 field (base register), 0 (R0) is the X2 (index register) field and 068_{16} is the D2 field.

In the memory dump area, the presence of "........" in the address column means the missing lines are the same as the line above.

Looking at the general purpose registers you can see the contents of the base register, R13, are 80008008_{16}. The high order bit is 1 (hence the leading 8) and only the lower 31 bits are used for addressing. This corresponds to the address of the start of the save area. Notice that R14 has the return address, 2018_{16} and that R15 has the same contents as R13, as expected.

Note that R2 has 15_{10} (F_{16}) in it which is the answer from the calculations.

```
Adding Numbers
        15
R0-R3 F4F4F4F480008000 F4F4F4F400002300 F4F4F4F40000000F F4F4F4F4F4F4F4F4
R4-R7 F4F4F4F4F4F4F4F4 F4F4F4F4F4F4F4F4 F4F4F4F4F4F4F4F4 F4F4F4F4F4F4F4F4
R8-RB F4F4F4F4F4F4F4F4 F4F4F4F4F4F4F4F4 F4F4F4F4F4F4F4F4 F4F4F4F4F4F4F4F4
RC-RF F4F4F4F4F4F4F4F4 F4F4F4F480008008 F4F4F4F400002018 F4F4F4F480008008
F0-F3 F4F4F4F4F4F4F4F4 F4F4F4F4F4F4F4F4 F4F4F4F4F4F4F4F4 F4F4F4F4F4F4F4F4
F4-F7 F4F4F4F4F4F4F4F4 F4F4F4F4F4F4F4F4 F4F4F4F4F4F4F4F4 F4F4F4F4F4F4F4F4
F8-FB F4F4F4F4F4F4F4F4 F4F4F4F4F4F4F4F4 F4F4F4F4F4F4F4F4 F4F4F4F4F4F4F4F4
FC-FF F4F4F4F4F4F4F4F4 F4F4F4F4F4F4F4F4 F4F4F4F4F4F4F4F4 F4F4F4F4F4F4F4F4
00000000 *00000000 00000000 00000000 00000000* *................*
00000010 *00002000 00000000 00000000 00000000* *..?.............*
00000020 *00000000 00000000 00000000 00000000* *................*
........
00000040 *00000000 00000000 00000000 00002000* *...............?.*
00000050 *00000000 00000000 00000000 00000000* *................*
........
00002000 *859999F1 40404040 40404040 40404040* *err1            *
00002010 *00008108 00000000 0A030000 00000000* *..a?....?.......*
00002020 *00000000 00000000 00000000 00000000* *................*
........
00002070 *00000000 9B000000 00000000 00000000* *....‖...........*
00002080 *00000000 00000000 00000000 00000000* *................*
........
000020D0 *000080E0 00000000 00000000 00000000* *..+\............*
000020E0 *00000000 00000000 00000000 00000000* *................*
........
00002100 *00000000 00000000 80008008 00002018* *.........+.+?..?.*
00002110 *80008000 80008000 00002300 F4F4F4F4* *+.+.+.+...?.4444*
00002120 *F4F4F4F4 F4F4F4F4 F4F4F4F4 F4F4F4F4* *4444444444444444*
........
00002140 *F4F4F4F4 F4F4F4F4 00000000 00000000* *44444444........*
00002150 *00000000 00000000 00000000 00000000* *................*
........
00002300 *00002304 00000000 00000000 00000000* *..??............*
00002310 *00000000 00000000 00000000 00000000* *................*
........
00002600 *F0F961F1 F461F1F0 00000000 00000000* *09/14/10........*
00002610 *00000000 00000000 859999F1 40404040* *........err1    *
00002620 *00000000 00000000 00000000 00000000* *................*
........
00008000 *90ECD00C 45FF0068 00000000 00002100* *░r}.ß?.‖......?.*
00008010 *00000000 00000000 00000000 00000000* *................*
........
00008050 *C1C4C440 40404040 F0F961F1 F461F1F0* *ADD     09/14/10*
00008060 *F1F74BF5 F2404040 50FD0008 50DF0004* *17.52   &⌐.?& .?*
00008070 *18DF1B22 5A20D0B8 5A20D0BC 5A20D0C0* *. ??!?}ᴶ!?}»!?}{*
00008080 *5A20D0C4 5A20D0C8 E020D0A8 000E5220* *!?}D!?}H\?}y..Ω?*
00008090 *D0CCE020 D0CC000C E0600000 000041F0* *}+\?}+..\-....á0*
000080A0 *000058D0 D00458E0 D00C982C D01C07FE* *..∞}}?∞\}.q?}.Ω⌐*
000080B0 *C1848489 958740D5 A4948285 99A2F6R6* *Adding Numbers66*
000080C0 *00000001 00000002 00000003 00000004* *...............?*
000080D0 *00000005 40404040 40404040 4040F1F5* *....          15*
```

```
000080E0 *00000000 000F7F20 859999F1 4BF3F9F0* *......"?errl.390*
000080F0 *80008000 F5F5F5F5 01F5F5F5 F5F5F5F5* *+.+.5555.5555555*
00008100 *80008000 000000E0 00000000 000F7EF8* *+.+....\......=8*
00008110 *F5F5F5F5 F5F5F5F5 F5F5F5F5 F5F5F5F5* *5555555555555555*
........
000FFFF0 *F5F5F5F5 F5F5F5F5 F5F5F5F5 F5F5F5F5* *5555555555555555*
17:52:05 errl      EZ390 ENDED   RC= 0 SEC= 0 MEM(MB)= 21 IO=79
```

Figure 72 XDUMP Format

The 12 bytes beginning at label DBL can be seen to start at byte
$80D4_{16}$. This can be deduced from the location counter address
from the assembler for DBL which is $D4_{16}$. Since the program is
loaded at location 8000_{16}, the label DBL is , therefore, at $80D4_{16}$.

The full words for labels ONE, TWO, THREE, FOUR and FIVE
can be seen at $80C0_{16}$, $80C4_{16}$, $80C8_{16}$, $80CC_{16}$ and $80D0_{16}$. The
body of the program begins with the SR at 8072_{16} followed by the
Add instructions.

If your program fails, you will normally be given the address
contents from the PSW at the time of the failure. As the PSW is
always updated, that is, pointing at the next instruction, the
actual error is normally at the instruction preceding the address
in the PSW. Using the dump and the assembler listing, it should
be easy to locate where the error took place and determine how
it was caused.

21. System Input/Output Macros

Operating system provided input/output macros will vary according the operating system and data access method. The IBM architecture has many legacy access methods. Among these are:

1. VSAM – Virtual Storage Access Method

2. BISAM/QISAM – Basic and Queued Indexed Sequential access Method

3. BPAM – Basic Partitioned Access Method

4. BDAM – Basic Direct Access Method

5. BSAM/QSAM – Basic/Queued Sequential Access Method

Common to all methods is the concept of the Data Control Block (DCB) created by a macro of the same name which establishes a table of data concerning the data set (file) to be accessed. Anther table building macro is the Data Event Control Block (DECB) used, depending on the access method, to synchronize asynchronous I/O.

21.1 Console Input/Output

In addition to the access methods listed above, there are also macros for console input/output. These were designed to permit programs to communicate directly with the system operator at the system console.

You may read and write directly to the console (in the z390 emulator, the console is your screen) using the WTO and WTOR macros. Here we demonstrate the WTO and WTOR macros which are normally available in the IBM assembler.

The WTO macro can be used to write a constant string to the console (your command prompt window in the emulator) or it can be used to write a memory resident string. The simplest form is:

WTO 'STRING TO BE WRITTEN'

The above will write the contents within the quote marks (up to 119 characters) to the console window. Alternatively, you can write a string stored in memory to the console with:

```
WTO MF=(E,MSG)
```

where MSG refers to a data area such as the following:

```
MSG     DC AL2(MSGEND-*,0)
```

```
MSG1    DS CL20
MSGEND EQU *
```

The first line, MSG, consists of 2 half words. The first halfword contains the length of the string to be written (including the half words themselves). The second halfword contains a zero. This is then followed by the data area containing the string to be written, in this case a string of length 20 whose contents will be set from somewhere else in the program.

The symbol MSGEND has as its value the location counter of point in your program where the symbol occurs. This value is used in the line with label MSG. The value of the first half word at MSG is the difference between the location counter value for MSG and the location counter value after MSG1. Remember, * means the current location counter value as was seen with USING so MSGEND-* is the difference or, in this case, the length, of the message including the initial halfwords.

```
1                   PRINT       NOGEN

2                   EQUREGS

3     WTO           SUBENTRY

4

5                   WTO         'CONSOLE READ/WRITE'

6

7                   WTOR        'ENTER A STRING',STRING,20,EV

8                   WAIT        ECB=EV      * PAUSE

9                   WTO         MF=(E,MSG)

10

11                  SUBEXIT

12

13    MSG           DC          AL2(STREND-*,0),C'YOU TYPED '

14    STRING        DS          CL20

15    STREND        EQU         *

16

17    EV            DC          F'0'    * ECB

18

19                  END         WTO
```

Figure 73 Console I/O

WTOR is a related macro which both writes a message and receives a reply. Its parameters are the message to be written, an area in memory to receive a reply, an optional input length, and an event control block (ECB) (A full word in memory initially set to zero). If the input length is omitted, it will be determined from the implied length of the area to receive the input. The macro is followed by a line with the WAIT macro with the ECB from the WTOR. This pauses the program until a reply has been entered.

If the WAIT is not issued, the program will continue executing without waiting for the reply.

The example in Figure 73 shows how a message is written by the simple form of the WTO macro. Next, another message is written by the WTOR macro and the program waits for a reply. The reply is then printed using the extended form of the WTO.

21.2 QSAM

File access macros include OPEN, CLOSE, GET, PUT, READ, WRITE and others. For the most part, these are operating system specific and beyond the scope of this book but we present a brief example with one of the simpler methods, QSAM.

Input/output operations on a mainframe traditionally have been record oriented. Access to files is usually by means of system provided input/output macros. In the examples up to this point we have used the ASSIST pseudo-macros as they simplify the process for novice users. In this section, however, we introduce several simple QSAM (Queued Sequential Access Method) macros. Most systems will probably not have the ASSIST package and QSAM is one of the basic access methods supported by most IBM operating systems.

21.2.1 Data Control Block (DCB)

In order to perform either input or output it is first necessary to define a DCB (Data Control Block). The DCB is a table built partly by the user and partly by the system. It defines the file being operated upon. The DCB has many options, only a few are shown here. A DCB is constructed by the DCB macro.

Once a DCB has been constructed, a file is *opened* with the OPEN system macro. The OPEN macro connects your program's DCB with the file being accessed. The OPEN and the DCB specify if the file is being opened for input, output or both.

Once a file is open, you may access the file with several macros. Among these are GET and PUT (there are others). When file processing is finished, you should issue a CLOSE macro to finalize the output, free memory buffers, and disconnect from the file.

```
LRECL=34          logical record length of 34 bytes

RECFM=FT          fixed length records, ASCII/EBCDIC conversion

MACRF=GM          the GET file access macro will be used

MACRF=PM          the PUT file access macro will be used

EODAD=ATEND       branch to label ATEND on end of input data

DDNAME=IN         DDNAME name to be opened and read

DDNAME=OUT        DDNAME name to be opened and written
```

In the example in Figure 74, 34 byte long input records are read from one file and written to another. The input DCB is named INDCB and the output DCB is named OUTDCB. The DCB parameters used in Figure 74 mean the following:

The LRECL determines the size of the input or output records.

The RECFM parameter tells the system that the input and output files will consist of fixed length records. The MACRF parameter tells the system that the GET or PUT macros will be used for actual input and output and the data will be moved from/to the file buffers rather than being operated on while still in the buffers.

For input operations, the EODAD parameter tells the system the label to branch to upon encountering the end of file. This parameter is not used for output DCBs.

Finally, the DDNAME is used to link the program's DCB to an actual file. In the z390 emulator running on a Windows based PC, this will be the name of an *environment variable* set by the user which will contain the actual file name to be used. For example, to the Windows Command Prompt window, type:

```
set IN=IN.DAT
set OUT=OUT.DAT
```

When the assembly language program runs, it will read from the file IN.DAT and write to the file OUT.DAT. You can see the complete list of environment variables by typing the command *set* by itself. You can delete an environment variable by entering a *set* command equating variable with nothing such as:

```
set IN=
```

The selection of the DDNAMEs IN and OUT was arbitrary. You may use any names that the system accepts.

21.2.2 OPEN Macro

In the program in Figure 74, after the usual initialization, the DCBs are opened by the OPEN macro for OUTPUT and INPUT, respectively. They could have also been opened individually with code such as:

```
OPEN OUTDCB,OUTPUT
OPEN INDCB,INPUT
```

21.2.3 GET/PUT

Next the program in Figure 74 enters a three line infinite loop consisting of the GET and PUT macros and the unconditional branch (mask of B'1111'). The GET macro reads from the file

---

associated with INDCB into the data area REC and the PUT macro writes from the data area to the output file associated with OUTDCB.

When the GET encounters the end of file, the GET macro executes a branch to the label ATEND as specified by the EODAD=ATEND parameter in the INDCB. The CLOSE macro at ATEND flushes the buffers and disconnects from the output file. Failure to CLOSE an output file will may result in the loss of about 2 lines of data. The file OUT.DAT will be an identical copy of the input file.

```
1               PRINT   NOGEN
2               EQUREGS
3   COPY        SUBENTRY
4
5               OPEN    (OUTDCB,(OUTPUT),INDCB,(INPUT))
6
7               WTO     '*** FILES OPEN ***'
8
9   LOOP        GET     INDCB,REC              * read a record
10              PUT     OUTDCB,REC             * write the record
11              B       LOOP                   * loop
12  *
13  *     EOJ  processing
14  *
15  ATEND       CLOSE   OUTDCB
16              SUBEXIT
17  *
    *
    File
18  DCB's
19  *
20  OUTDCB      DCB     LRECL=80,RECFM=FT,MACRF=PM,DDNAME=OUT
21
22  INDCB       DCB     LRECL=80,RECFM=FT,MACRF=GM,EODAD=ATEND,DDNAME=IN
23  *
    *
    INPUT
24  RECORD
25  *
26  REC         DS      CL80
```
Figure 74 QSAM Input/Output

22. Macros

Macros are code fragments stored in a library that are processed and inserted into your program when you reference them. When placed in your program, internal macro statements may tailor the macro to your particular needs. Macros are serviced by a pre-processor which reads your program and scans for any macro references before the program is passed to the assembler. The macro pre-processor has its own language which is used to tailor the macro code to your needs. The macro language, distinct from the host assembly language, includes variables, data types, IF statements, GOTOs and so forth.

While macro pre-processors are nearly universally available in assembly languages, they are also widely used in many high level languages such as PL/I, C/C++ and others. The GNU M4 macro pre-processor is generic and used in many applications. This chapter presents an overview of the IBM assembly language macro pre-processor language along with examples.

To the casual observer, macros in an assembly language program look like ordinary instructions. They have an optional label, an opcode (the name of the macro) and zero or more operands.

When you assemble your program it is first read by the macro pre-processor. The output of the pre-processor is submitted to the actual assembler. While reading your program, when the pre-processor encounters an opcode that is not a machine instruction opcode or assembly language directive, it checks the macro library to see if there is a macro with the same name. If there is, it inserts it into you program at the place where the reference occurred. The source program label and operands on the macro reference, if any, are made available to the macro. These will be used as labels, operands and parameters in the process of *macro expansion*.

During macro expansion, the pre-processor examines each line of code in the macro. If a line contains no pre-processor code, the line is normally copied to the output file which will ultimately be seen by the assembler. Any macro language statements found in a line of code will be processed and the resulting modified or generated code is inserted into the output file.

22.1 ADD Macro

By way of example we start with a very simple macro to add the contents of two user specified registers and place the result in a third. The macro is shown in Figure 75. The key features of any macro are:

```
1                       MACRO
2        &LAB           ADD            &R1,&R2,&R3
3        &LAB           LR             &R1,&R2
4                       AR             &R1,&R3
5                       MEND
```

Figure 75 ADD Macro

1. The first line contains the word MACRO

2. The second line is the prototype giving the name of the macro, a macro symbol to receive a label, if any and macro symbols to receive operands, if any.

3. The body of the macro consisting of model statements.

4. the keyword MEND (macro end).

In Figure 75, line 2 is the prototype. The symbol in the label position, &LAB, is a symbolic parameter that will receive a source program label, if present. When the macro is expanded (inserted) into your program, this label will normally appear on one of the statements written to the output file. The name of this macro is ADD. This name must not conflict with machine instructions mnemonics, assembly language directives or other macro names. Finally, zero or more symbolic parameter operands which will contain values from the user program's macro invocation.

```
1                PRINT            GEN
2                EQUREGS
3        MAC1     SUBENTRY
4                L                R3,=F'5'
5                L                R5,=F'10'
6        L1       ADD              R1,R3,R5
7                XDECO            R1,OUT
8                XPRNT            OUT,L'OUT
9                SUBEXIT
10               LTORG
11       OUT      DS               CL12
12               END
```

Figure 76 Invoking the ADD Macro

Figure 76 shows an assembly language program that invokes the ADD macro (line 6). When the pre-processor sees the ADD macro, it reads the macro from the macro library and prepares to insert it into the program at this point. The label L1 from the macro invocation becomes the value of the macro symbol &LAB1 and the values R1, R3 and R5 from the source program become the values of &R1, &R2 and &R3, respectively. Macro symbols begin with the ampersand character. The pre-processor will look for all instances of &LAB1, &R1, &R2, and &R3 in the macro and replace any symbol found with the value passed for that symbol in the invocation. In the z390 emulator, macros can be files in the current directory or a library directory with the .MAC file extension.

1		PRINT	GEN
2		EQUREGS	
3	MAC1	SUBENTRY	
4		L	R3,=F'5'
5		L	R5,=F'10'
6	L1	ADD	R1,R3,R5
7	+L1	LR	R1,R3
8	+	AR	R1,R5
9		XDECO	R1,OUT
10		XPRNT	OUT,L'OUT
11		SUBEXIT	
12		LTORG	
13	OUT	DS	CL12
14		END	

Figure 77 Macro Expansion

The net result is shown in Figure 77. Note the PRINT GEN directive was used to display the macro expansions. In this figure, the expansions for EQUREGS, SUBENTRY and SUBEXIT were removed so only the expansion for ADD remains visible. As can be seen, lines of code in the macro that contained symbolic parameters have had those symbols replaced with the values supplied in the macro invocation.

22.2 Set and Sequence Symbols

In addition to symbolic parameters, the macro language has variables, called *set symbols,* and labels, called *sequence symbols*. These are visible only to the pre-processor. They, as is the case with all pre-processor statements, do not appear in the pre-processor file passed to the assembler.

Set symbols can either be local to an individual macro expansion or global and known to all other macros in an assembly. They can be declared as arithmetic, Boolean or character string, either as simple variables or one-dimensional arrays. All set symbols begin with an ampersand. There are also some pre-defined system set symbols.

The macro statements LCLA, LCLB and LCLC are used to declare local arithmetic, Boolean and character string set symbols, respectively. The macro statements GBLA, GBLB and GBLC are used to declare global arithmetic, Boolean and character string set symbols.

A local set symbol is created when a macro is invoked and deleted when the macro expansion is finished. Its name and value are not known to other macros. A global set symbol is accessible by all macros and provides a means by which to pass information from one macro to another.

A *sequence symbol* is a pre-processor label. It appears at the beginning of the line and is always preceded by a decimal point in column one. It can appear on ordinary assembly language code as well as pre-processor statements. In many cases, where logic would dictate that a sequence symbol should be attached to an assembly language statement but where the assembly language statement already has an assembly language label, the sequence symbol will appear on an ANOP statement that immediately before the assembly language statement. ANOP statements do nothing other than support placement of sequence symbols.

22.3 SETA, SETB and SETC

The SETA, SETB and SETC statements are the pre-processor's assignment statements and are used to assign arithmetic, Boolean and characters string values, respectively. In these assignment statements a set symbol appears on the left in the label position and an expression appearing on the right in the operand position. The expression is evaluated and the result is assigned to the set symbol.

The arithmetic assignment statement, SETA, accepts expressions involving the operators +, -, * and / and parentheses. Expressions obey the ordinary rules of precedence. Set symbols, constants and values derived from the macro parameters and their attributes may participate in expressions.

The Boolean assignment statement, SETB, accepts expressions containing the logical operators AND, OR and NOT which operate on truth-valued expressions and other Boolean set symbols. Truth valued expressions may contain relational sub-expressions involving the operators EQ (equal), NE (not equal), LT (less than), GT (greater than), LE (less than or equal), and GE (greater than or equal).

The character assignment statement, SETC, accepts expressions involving character strings, set symbols, parameters, attributes of parameters, the concatenation operator (.), and a substring operator.

22.4 Type Attribute

The type operator is coded as the letter capital T followed by a single quote and it applies to a macro argument. The type operator yields a character indicating the type of the original argument from the source program. For example, if &ARG is an argument to the macro, T'&ARG yields the type of the invoking macro parameter. Some examples of the codes returned by the type operator are shown in Figure 78.

```
A A-type address constant or symbol
C character constant or symbol
D long floating point constant or symbol
E short floating point constant or symbol
F full word fixed point constant or symbol
H half word constant or symbol
I machine instruction
J CSECT statement
M macro call
O omitted operand
P packed decimal constant or symbol
X hexadecimal constant

              Figure 78 Type Codes
```

22.5 AIF, AGO and ANOP

The macro language has an IF statement (AIF) and a GOTO statement (AGO) as well as a NO-OP statement (ANOP). If the expression in the AIF statement is true, a branch is made to the sequence symbol that appears at the end of the AIF. The AGO is an unconditional GOTO and its operand is a sequence symbol. As noted above, the ANOP is used mainly as a place holder in order to allow a sequence symbol to appear in the code at a given point when the line it logically belongs to already has an assembly language label. ANOPs do nothing.

22.6 MNOTE and MEXIT

The MNOTE statement inserts an error message and error level into the output of the assembler and the MEXIT terminates macro expansion.

22.7 &SYSNDX and &SYSECT

&SYSNDX and &SYSECT are built-in system variables. $SYSECT contains the name of the current CSECT. It can be useful for resuming the CSECT if, for example, the macro defines a DSECT.

&SYSNDX is a number unique to the current macro invocation. As it is not unusual for some macros to be invoked several times in a given program and, likewise, not unusual for a macro to have internal assembly language labels, there must be a mechanism to prevent the assembly language labels from multiple invocations from conflicting with one another as duplicate labels. $SYSNDX solves this problem.

To do this, when you define a label inside a macro, suffix its name with &SYSNDX. The system will append a number to the label that is unique to this invocation. For example, if you assembly language program needs to use an internal label named AA, write AA&SYSNDX.

Figure 79 has an example. In this figure we have written an entry linkage macro named ENTRY. The only parameter to the macro is the label &PGM which, in the expanded code, is placed on the CSECT statement (line 4). On lines 6 and 7 R12 is loaded with address of the byte immediately following the BALR (no branch takes place because the second operand is R0). R12 is established as the base register. The symbol * means 'the current address' which is the address of the byte immediately following the BALR which in fact corresponds to the contents of R12 during execution.

```
1                       PRINT       GEN
2                       MACRO
3       &PGM            ENTRY
4       &PGM            CSECT
5                       STM         R14,R12,12(R13)
6                       BALR        R12,R0
7                       USING       *,R12
8                       B           BB&SYSNDX
9       AA&SYSNDX       DS          18F
10      BB&SYSNDX       LA          R14,AA&SYSNDX
11                      ST          R14,8(R13)
12                      ST          R13,4(R14)
13                      LR          R13,R14
14                      MEND
15
16                      EQUREGS
17      PGM1            ENTRY
18                      L           R6,=F'1'
19                      A           R6,=F'1'
20                      XDECO       R6,OUT
21                      XPRNT       OUT,L'OUT
22                      SUBEXIT
23                      LTORG
24      OUT             DS          CL12
25                      END
```

Figure 79 &SYSNDX Example

We use two labels in the macro on lines 9 and 10. Since the macro might be invoked several times in a program, these must be unique. We accomplish this with &SYSNDX. The &SYSNDX portion is substituted by the pre-processor with a numeric value unique to each invocation at each place where the labels AA&SYSNDX or BB&SYNDX are used as seen in Figure 80. In this fragment of a listing file you can see the ENTRY macro expansion on lines 2 through 11. Note that all instances of AA&SYNDX have been replaced by AA0002 and all instances of BB&SYSNDX have been replaced by BB00002.

```
1       PGM1        ENTRY
2       +PGM1       CSECT
3       +           STM         R14,R12,12(R13)
4       +           BALR        R12,R0
5       +           USING       *,R12
6       +           B           BB0002
7       +AA0002     DS          18F
8       +BB0002     LA          R14,AA0002
9       +           ST          R14,8(R13)
10      +           ST          R13,4(R14)
11      +           LR          R13,R14

          ..
```

Figure 80 &SYSNDX Expansion

22.8 Example EQUREGS Macro

The purpose of the EQUREGS macro is to generate sixteen lines of the form:

```
        R0  EQU  0
        R1  EQU  1
        R2  EQU  2
          ...
```

We could do this with 16 EQU statements or, as shown in Figure 81, as a macro. On line 3 we declare a local arithmetic set symbol &R and, on line 4, initialize it to zero. Lines 5 through 8 constitute a loop. Line 6 is the only line that generates code for the assembler. The lines it generates have a label constructed by the concatenation of the letter R with the numeric value of the set symbol &R followed by blanks, the string EQU and the value of &R. Thus, each time line 6 is processed by the pre-processor, another EQU statement is generated into the user's program.

The first EQU generated is for &R with a value of zero. In line 7, however, &R is incremented. On line 8 we test if the value in &R is less than 16 and, if it is, we branch to the sequence symbol *loop* and the next EQU is generated. When sixteen have been produced, the AIF does not branch and the macro ends.

1		MACRO	
2		EQUREGS	
3		LCLA	&R
4	&R	SETA	0
5	.loop	ANOP	
6	R&R	EQU	&R
7	&R	SETA	&R+1
8		AIF	(&R LT 16).loop
9		MEND	

Figure 81 EQUREGS Macro

Note that the sequence symbol *loop* appears on an ANOP instruction. This is because line 6, the logical loop point, already has a label. ANOPs do nothing but they permit sequence symbols to appear where we want them to.

23. Programming Examples

The following sections present several short programs that illustrate assembly language code in use.

23.1 Simple Calculator

The program in Figure 82 is a simple calculator application that reads in lines, extracts two signed fixed point numbers, and an operation code. The it performs the operation and prints the result. The program functions as follows:

1. Line 7 and 8 read a line of input and branch to EXIT when there is no more.

2. Line 9 echoes the input to the output file. The start of the output record is INP but the length is the sum of the lengths of INP and IN. IN is the field immediately following INP. Consequently, the XPRNT begins at INP and prints the bytes in INP and IN, inclusive, as they are contiguous.

3. The address of the input line is loaded into R1 and the output field is blanked on lines 10 through 12.

4. The first number from the input is found and converted from zoned decimal to fixed point binary in line 18. If a properly formatted number is not found, a branch is made to print an error message and the program terminates. R1 is advanced by XDECI to point to the blank following the number scanned. The number scanned is written in zoned format to the output field OUT. Lines 14 through 20 process the second number in the same manner except that the zoned decimal version of the number is written to the output field OUT plus 12 since the first 12 bytes are for the first number – positions 0 through 11.

5. Lines 22 through 27 scan for the first non-blank character following the second number. R1 initially is the address of the blank immediately following the second number. It is incremented until a non-blank is found or it exceeds the length of the input string. LIM is the address of the byte immediately after the input sting IN. Note that it is declared with an address data type with the value of * (line 85). The * means the current address.

6. Lines 29 and 30 copy the operator and the characters => to the output field.

7. Lines 32 through 72 perform the calculation based on the operator, convert the result to zoned decimal and print it. Note that the result is placed in the output field displaced by 29 bytes.

```
 1                 TITLE     'CALCULATOR'
 2                 PRINT     NOGEN
 3
 4     CALC        SUBENTRY
 5                 EQUREGS
 6
 7     LOOP        XREAD     IN,40
 8                 BC        B'0100',EXIT
 9                 XPRNT     INP,L'INP+L'IN
10                 LA        R1,IN
11                 MVI       OUT,C' '
12                 MVC       OUT+1(L'OUT-1),OUT
13
14                 XDECI     R3,0(R0,R1) * FIRST OPND
15                 BC        B'001',ERR1
16                 XDECO     R3,OUT
17
18                 XDECI     R4,0(0,R1) * SECOND OPND
19                 BC        B'001',ERR2
20                 XDECO     R4,OUT+12
21
22     L5          CLI       0(R1),C' ' * FIND OPR
23                 BNE       L6
24                 LA        R1,1(R0,R1)
25                 C         R1,LIM
26                 BH        ERR4
27                 B         L5
28
29     L6          MVC       OUT+27(1),0(R1)
30                 MVC       OUT+27(2),=C'->'
31
32                 CLI       0(R1),C'+'
33                 BNE       SUB
34
35     ADD         AR        R3,R4
36                 XDECO     R3,OUT+29
37                 XPRNT     OUT,L'OUT
38                 B         LOOP
39
40     SUB         CLI       0(R1),C'-'
41                 BNE       MULT
42
43                 SR        R3,R4
44                 XDECO     R3,OUT+29
```

```
45              XPRNT       OUT,L'OUT
46              B           LOOP
47
48    MULT      CLI         0(R1),C'*'
49              BNE         DIV
50
51              MR          R2,R4
52              XDECO       R3,OUT+29
53              XPRNT       OUT,L'OUT
54              B           LOOP
55
56    DIV       CLI         0(R1),C'/'
57              BNE         MOD
58              LR          R2,R3
59              SRDA        R2,32
60              DR          R2,R4
61              XDECO       R3,OUT+29
62              XPRNT       OUT,L'OUT
63              B           LOOP
64
65    MOD       CLI         0(R1),C'%'
66              BNE         ERR3
67              LR          R2,R3
68              SRDA        R2,32
69              DR          R2,R4
70              XDECO       R2,OUT+29
71              XPRNT       OUT,L'OUT
72              B           LOOP
73
74    ERR1      XPRNT       ERRMSG1,L'ERRMSG1
75              B           EXIT
76    ERR2      XPRNT       ERRMSG2,L'ERRMSG2
77              B           EXIT
78    ERR3      XPRNT       ERRMSG3,L'ERRMSG3
79              B           EXIT
80    ERR4      XPRNT       ERRMSG4,L'ERRMSG4
81
82    EXIT      SUBEXIT
83    INP       DC          C'INPUT = '
84    IN        DS          CL40
85    LIM       DC          A(*)
86    OUT       DS          CL50
87
88    * ERROR
```

```
        MSGS
89
90    ERRMSG1    DC         C'FIRST OPERAND INPUT ERROR'
91    ERRMSG2    DC         C'SECOND OPERAND INPUT ERROR'
92    ERRMSG3    DC         C'OPERATOR ERROR'
93    ERRMSG4    DC         C'OPERATOR NOT FOUND'
94
95               END
Example output:
INPUT = 22 33 +
            22          33   ->            55
INPUT = 22 33 -
            22          33   ->           -11
INPUT = 22 33 *
            22          33   ->           726
INPUT = 22 33 /
            22          33   ->             0
INPUT = 22 33 %
22               33   ->         22
```

Figure 82 Calculator Program

23.2 Printing Bit Strings

Figure 83 gives an example of printing a bit strings for the powers of two from 0 to 20. It also illustrates calling a subroutine and passing arguments.

The main body of the program is the CSECT BIN (recall that the SUBENTRY macro includes a CSECT statement whose label is the same as that placed on the SUBENTRY itself) that extends from lines 4 through 21. We will refer to this as our main program. The subroutine is the CSECT BPRNT is contained on lines 25 through 53. The main program generates the binary powers and the subroutine converts the bits to EBCDIC zoned decimal 0s and 1s which the main program prints.

The main program BIN operates as follows:

1. The value of 2^0 is loaded into R6 on line 6 and R2 is zeroed on line 7.

2. Lines 8 through 16 are the main loop.

3. The decimal value of the power of two contained in R6 is written to the output field at OUT.

4. The address of the parameter list of loaded into R1 on line 9. The parameter list consists of one item: the address of the output field OUT. The value to be converted is passed in R6.

5. The address of the subroutine is loaded into R15 on line 10 and a branch is made to the subroutine on line 11 with the return address, the address of the instruction following the BASR, loaded into R14.

6. Upon return, the result is printed on line 12.

7. The value in R6 is shifted one position to the left effectively multiplying the value by two and raising it to the next power.

8. The counter in R2 is incremented and compared to 31. If less than, the loop repeats.

The subroutine receives a number in R6. This number 31 zeros and one bit with a value of one. The subroutine looks at each bit of R6 fro low order to high order. Based on what it finds, it sets the output string:

1. On entry to BPRNT, SUBENTRY saves the registers which will be restored on exit.

2. R1 points to the first (and only) word in the parameter list. The load on line 29 loads the value stored in the parameter list, the address of OUT, into R3 which is incremented in line 30 by 13 to point to the place after the decimal number already in OUT where we will place the printable bit string.

3. We place a character 0 at the location pointed to by R3 and then propagate it across the remainder of the output field (31 positions). Now the output field contains the printable decimal power of two followed by a blank and then 32 zeros.

4. We initialize R5 with 31 (line 36) and the low byte of R2 with a character one. R5 will be a counter which we will decrement. The low byte of R2 will be stored into the output string as needed.

5. Lines 39 through 46 are a loop which inspects each bit in R6 (passed from the main program) and, if it is one, store a character one into the corresponding position of the 32 digit binary output string thus changing the 0 already there to 1.

6. The value in R6 is always 31 zeros and one bit with the value one. This value is copied to R4 and ANDed with MASK which forces the leading 31 bits to zero. Only the 32nd bit is untouched. The AND sets the condition code to reflect the result. If the result is all zeros, the last bit must have been zero. If the result is not zero, the last bit must have been a 1. If the last bit was a 1, on line 42, we store a character 1 at the position in the output pointed to by the sum of R5 and R3. R3 is the address of the portion of OUT where the bit string begins. R5 is our counter, a

number that we decrement from 31. Thus, the sum of the contents of R3 and R5 are the address of the position in the output string whose bit we are examining. As R5 decrements, we will move to positions to the left. We begin at the rightmost.

7. On line 43 we shift the value in R6 to the right by one. This exposes the next higher order bit in R6 to our AND mask. We decrement R5 and test to see if it is zero. If greater than or equal, we branch to LOOP1 and repeat for the next bit.

```
                            'PRINT BIT
1              TITLE        STRINGS
2              PRINT        NOGEN
3
4   BIN        SUBENTRY
5              EQUREGS
6              L            R6,ONE            * INIT R6
7              SR           R2,R2             * COUNTER
8   LOOP       XDECO        R6,OUT            * CVT R6 TO DECIMAL
9              LA           R1,PARMTAB        * ADDR OF PARAMETER TABLE
10             L            R15,=V(BPRNT)     * ADDR OF SUB
11             BASR         R14,R15           * CALL SUB
12             XPRNT        OUT,L'OUT         * PRINT RSLT
13             SLL          R6,1              * SHIFT BIT LEFT
14             A            R2,=F'1'          * INC COUNTER
15             C            R2,=F'31'         * DONE?
16             BL           LOOP              * NOPE
17             SUBEXIT
18  ONE        DC           F'1'
19  OUT        DC           CL45' '
20  PARMTAB    DC           A(OUT)
21             LTORG
22  *
23  * SUB TO PRINT BIT STRINGS
24  *
25  BPRNT      SUBENTRY
26  *
27  * INITIALIZE 2ND PART OF OUT
28  *
29             L            R3,0(0,R1)        * ADDRESS OF OUT
30             LA           R3,13(0,R3)       * OUT+13
31             MVI          0(R3),C'0'        * SEED CHARACTER
32             MVC          1(31,R3),0(R3)    * RIPPLE MOVE
33  *
34  * INITALIZE REGISTERS
35  *
```

```
36          LA      R5,31(0,0)          * COUNT
37          IC      R2,CONE             * LOAD CHAR 1
38  *
39  LOOP1   LR      R4,R6               * COPY TO R4
40          N       R4,MASK             * AND WITH MASK
41          BZ      L1                  * LEAVE 0 IN OUT STR
42          STC     R2,0(R5,R3)         * PUT 1 IN OUT STR
43  L1      SRL     R6,1                * SHIFT RIGHT
44          S       R5,ONE1             * DEC COUNTER
45          C       R5,ZERO             * AT ZERO?
46          BNL     LOOP1               * NOPE
                                        * SAY G'NITE
47          SUBEXIT GRACIE
48  CONE    DC      C'1'
49  ONE1    DC      F'1'
50  N32     DC      F'32'
51  ZERO    DC      F'0'
52          DS      0F
53  MASK    DC      X'00000001'
54          END
```

Output

```
     1 00000000000000000000000000000001

     2 00000000000000000000000000000010

     4 00000000000000000000000000000100

     8 00000000000000000000000000001000
    16 00000000000000000000000000010000
    32 00000000000000000000000000100000
    64 00000000000000000000000001000000
   128 00000000000000000000000010000000
   256 00000000000000000000000100000000
   512 00000000000000000000001000000000
  1024 00000000000000000000010000000000
  2048 00000000000000000000100000000000
  4096 00000000000000000001000000000000
  8192 00000000000000000010000000000000
 16384 00000000000000000100000000000000
 32768 00000000000000001000000000000000
 65536 00000000000000010000000000000000
131072 00000000000000100000000000000000
262144 00000000000001000000000000000000
524288 00000000000010000000000000000000
```

211

```
 1048576  00000000000100000000000000000000000
 2097152  00000000001000000000000000000000000
 4194304  00000000010000000000000000000000000
 8388608  00000000100000000000000000000000000
16777216  00000001000000000000000000000000000
33554432  00000010000000000000000000000000000
67108864  00000100000000000000000000000000000
134217728 00001000000000000000000000000000000
268435456 00010000000000000000000000000000000
536870912 00100000000000000000000000000000000
1073741824 01000000000000000000000000000000000
```

Figure 83 Bit String Printing

23.3 Random Numbers

Many random number generator programs operate on a formula similar to:

```
x = ( a * x + b) % N
```

where x is initially a seed value, a and b are constants and N is usually a power of 2. The values of a and b determine the overall performance of the program. Each iteration of the formula produces a new random number until the sequence repeats. The % operator means modulo.

```
1    #include <stdio.h>
2
3    int main() {
4
5        unsigned int i, a, b, x, N;
6
7    a=214013;
8    b=2531011;
9    N=32768;
10       x=79; // seed
11
12       for (i=1; i<1000; i++) {
13               x = ( a * x + b ) % N;
14               printf("%d\n",x);
15               }
16       }
```

Figure 84 Random Numbers in C

Observe that, if N is a power of 2, then the modulo operation can be performed as a shift rather than as a real division operation. For example, if N is 32768 or 2^{15} a *divide* by 32768 can be accomplished by a right shift of 15 bits. The result will be the quotient. The *remainder*, however, will be the bits shifted out of the register, that is, the low order 15 bits of the original number.

Thus, we can obtain modulo 32768 on a binary number by zeroing out all bits but the lower 15. This can be accomplished by the And instruction with an appropriate mask. For example, in a 32 bit word, the mask to obtain modulo 32768 is:

```
X'00007FFF'
```

whose lower 16 bits are:

```
B'0111111111111111'
```

Figure 84 contains a short C program to generate 1000 random numbers with this technique. The values for a and b are 214013 and 2531011, respectively.

```
1                    PRINT       NOGEN
2                    EQUREGS
3    RAND            SUBENTRY
4
                                 'RANDOM
5                    WTO         NUMBERS'
6
                                             * LOAD R2
7                    LA          R2,8(0,0)    WITH 8
8
9
                                             * LOAD SEED
10   LOOP            L           R5,X         OR LAST VALUE
11                   M           R4,A         * MULT BY A
12
                                             * ADD
13                   AL          R5,B         (LOGICAL) B
                                             * MODULO
14                   N           R5,MASK      32768
                                             * STORE
15                   ST          R5,X         RESULT
                                             * PRINT
16                   XDECO       R5,OUT       RESULT
17                   XPRNT       OUT,12
                                             * DECR R2,
18                   BCT         R2,LOOP      BRANCH IF > 0
19
20                   SUBEXIT
21
22   A               DC          F'214013'
23   B               DC          F'2531011'
24   X               DC          F'79'
25   MASK            DC          X'00007FFF'
26   OUT             DS          CL12
27
28                   END         RAND
```

```
Output:
RANDOM NUMBERS
        6614
       10561
       26368
       27075
       11642
       32341
       14276
        1911
```

Figure 85 Random Number Generator

The assembly language equivalent of the program in Figure 84 can be seen in Figure 85. Note that the multiply instruction on line 11 addresses the even register of the even/odd pair.

Note the Add Logical instruction on line 13. This causes the number to be treated as an unsigned quantity for purposes of addition so no overflow error is possible. The Multiply instruction, on the other hand, has a 64 bit result but we only use the lower 32 bits and thus the question of overflow is not an issue.

23.4 Convert Infix to Suffix

In the example in Figure 86 we use a simplified algorithm to convert fully parenthesized infix notation to suffix notation. In infix notation, the operators appear between the operands. In suffix notation, the operands appear after the operands.

The algorithm uses a stack. When we place a new item on a stack, the existing items are *pushed down.* When we remove an item, the remaining items *pop-up.* Stacks are very useful in many algorithms and are an example of a *last in, first out* data structure.

A simplified infix-to-suffix procedure is as follows:

1. Examine the next character in the input.

2. If it is an open parenthesis, ignore it and go to step 1.

3. If it is a dollar sign (terminator character), done. Check results.

4. if it is an operand, copy it to the output string.

5. If it is an operator, push it on the stack.

6. If it is a close parenthesis, *pop* the top element on the stack to the output string.

```
1    SUFFIX   SUBENTRY
2             EQUREGS
3             XPRNT    IN,L'IN
4             MVI      OUT,C' '      * PUT BLANK IN 1ST POSITION
                       OUT+1(19),OU
5             MVC      T             * PROPOGATE BLANK ACROSS FIELD
6             LA       R2,IN         * ADDRESS OF INPUT STRING
7             LA       R3,OUT        * ADDRESS OF OUTPUT STRING
8             LA       R4,STACK      * ADDRESS OF STACK
9    *
10   * LOOP TO EXAMINE AND PROCESS INPUT
11   *
12
13   LOOP     CLI      0(R2),C'('    * IS INPUT CHAR ( ?
14            BNE      L1            * NO
15            LA       R2,1(R0,R2)   * INCREMENT INPUT POINTER
16            B        LOOP          * PROCESS NEXT CHARACTER
17
18   L1       CLI      0(R2),C'$'    * IS INPUT CHAR $ ?
19            BE       FIN           * YES - END OF INPUT
20
21            CLI      0(R2),C'+'    * IS INPUT +. -, * OR / ?
22            BE       OPR           * YES
23            CLI      0(R2),C'-'
24            BE       OPR
25            CLI      0(R2),C'*'
26            BE       OPR
27            CLI      0(R2),C'/'
28            BE       OPR
29            B        L2
30
                       0(1,R4),0(R2
31   OPR      MVC      )             * PUSH OPERATOR ONTO STACK
32            A        R4,=F'1'
33            A        R2,=F'1'      * INCRMENT INPUT POINTER
34            B        LOOP          * PROCESS NEXT CHARACTER
35
36   L2       CLI      0(R2),C')'
37            BNE      L3
38            S        R4,=F'1'
                       0(1,R3),0(R4
39            MVC      )
40            A        R3,=F'1'
41            A        R2,=F'1'
42            B        LOOP
```

215

```
43
                        0(1,R3),0(R2
44   L3     MVC         )
45          A           R3,=F'1'
46          A           R2,=F'1'
47          B           LOOP
48
49   FIN    XPRNT       OUT,L'OUT
50          SUBEXIT
51
                        C'((A+B)*(C/
52   IN     DC          D))$'
53   OUT    DS          CL20
54   STACK  DS          CL20
55          END
```

Output:

`((A+B)*(C/D))$`

`AB+CD/*`

Figure 86 Convert Infix to Suffix

When done, the output should contain the translation to suffix and the stack should be empty. For example:

`((A+B)*(C-D))$` yields `AB+CD-*`

In our example we assume that all operands are a single character, there are no embedded blanks in the input string, and that the input string has a dollar sign at the end as a terminator character.

The program works as follows:

1. On line 3 we print the infix expression to be converted. The figure L'IN in the XPRNT tells the assembler to calculate the implied length of the data declared at label IN and place the number here.

2. In lines 4 and 5 we copy blanks into the output field OUT. The easy way to do this is to place a blank in the first position (line 4) and then propagate it across the remaining 19 positions (line 5). The MVC on line 5 moves this offset by one from its source to its target and the length is 19, not 20. Thus, byte 0 (the blank) is copied to byte 1 then byte 1 is copied to byte 2 and so forth.

3. We initialize our registers in lines 6 through 8. R2 will point to the current byte in the input string, R3 will point to the next available byte in the output string, and R4 will point to the next available byte in the stack. The stack will start empty (R4 points to the start of STACK) and grow to higher addresses in STACK when items are added. The address in R4 will always point at the

---

216

next available position. When items are removed from the stack, the address in R4 will be decremented.

4. The main input character processing loop begins at line 13. This line and several following it examine each character of the input in order to determine how to handle same.
On line 13 itself, we test if the byte of input pointed to by R2 is an open parenthesis. If it is not, we branch to label L1. If it is, we increment R2 (line 15) and branch back to the top of the loop (effectively, we ignore the open parenthesis).
Note the first operand on the CLI instruction on line 13. It means zero displacement past the address in R2. That is, R2 has the address of the operand. In an SI instruction the first operand is addressed by a combination of displacement and base: D1(B1). In this example, the base position is taken by R2.

5. Line 18 tests for the terminating dollar sign and, if it does, branches out of the loop to print the results.

6. Lines 21 through 28 test if the input character is one of the operators. If it is, we branch to the label OPR. If not, on line 29, we branch around the operator handling section to label *L2*.

7. At *OPR* we move the operator character onto the stack. R2 points to the input operator character and R4 points to the next available position in the stack. The MVC on line 31 copies the operator byte from the input string to the stack. Again, the displacements are zero because the registers contain the entire address. The 1 in the first operand is the length. We must provide the length as the assembler cannot calculate an implied length (it needs a label to do this). On lines 32 through 34 we increment the input and stack pointers then branch to the top of the loop for the next input character.

8. On line 36 we test if the input is a close parenthesis. If it is not, we branch to label L3. If it is, we decrement the stack pointer and copy the byte from the stack to the next available byte in the output string (pointed to by R3). Then we increment both the input and output pointers. Note that we needed to decrement the stack pointer first because it always points to the next available position. It needs to be decremented to point to the last used position. After the byte from the stack has been copied to the output, the current position in the stack is no longer in use so the stack pointer (R4) is correct.

9. Finally, beginning at line 44, the only alternative remaining is that the character is an operand which we copy to the output string, increment the input and output pointers and branch to the top of the loop.

10. At line 49 we write out the output string and exit.

```
 1   BUBBLE   SUBENTRY

 2            EQUREGS

 3
 4   OUTER    SR        R8,R8          * FLAG
 5            SR        R2,R2          * COUNTER

 6
 7   LOOP     LR        R4,R2
 8            SLA       R4,2           * MULT by 4
 9            L         R3,TAB(R4)     * GET VALUE
                        R5,4(R0,R4
10            LA        )              * OFFSET OF NEXT VALUE
11            C         R3,TAB(R5)     * COMP VALUES

12            BH        SWAP

13
                        R2,1(R0,R2
14   INC      LA        )              * INCR COUNTER
15            C         R2,=F'9'       * INNER LOOP DONE?

16            BL        LOOP
17            C         R8,=F'0'       * CHECK FLAG
18            BE        DONE           * DONE?
19            B         OUTER          * DO INNER LOOP AGIAN

20
21   SWAP     L         R6,TAB(R4)     * LOWER
22            L         R7,TAB(R5)     * HIGHER
23            ST        R7,TAB(R4)     * HIGHER TO LOWER
24            ST        R6,TAB(R5)     * LOWER TO HIGHER
25            LA        R8,1(0,0)      * SET FLAG

26            B         INC

27
28   DONE     SR        R2,R2          * LOOP AND PRINT RESULTS

29   PLOOP    LR        R4,R2

30            SLA       R4,2

31            L         R3,TAB(R4)

32            XDECO     R3,OUT

33            XPRNT     OUT,L'OUT
```

```
34              LA        R2,1(0,R2)

35              C         R2,=F'10'

36              BL        PLOOP

37              SUBEXIT
38   *
39   * TABLE OF NUMBERS TO SORT
40   *

41   TAB        DC        F'9'

42              DC        F'7'

43              DC        F'3'

44              DC        F'10'

45              DC        F'4'

46              DC        F'1'

47              DC        F'2'

48              DC        F'11'

49              DC        F'5'

50              DC        F'0'

51

52   OUT        DS        CL12

53

54              END
```

Figure 87 Bubble Sort

23.5 Bubble Sort

The program in Figure 87 performs a bubble sort on the table of ten full word binary numbers beginning at label TAB. The program consists of two loops: an outer loop beginning at OUTER and an inner loop beginning at LOOP.

The inner loop examines each entry of the table from positions 0 to 9 and compares each with the entry in the position above it. That is, the entry at position 0 is compared with the entry at position 1, entry 1 is compared with entry 2 and so forth until entry 9 is compared with entry 10.

If the value of an entry is greater than the value of the entry above it, their contents are swapped with one another. When a pair of entries are swapped, a flag is set to indicate that a swap has taken place.

After all entries have been compared, the flag is examined. If the flag indicates that a pair of entries were swapped, the process is repeated. If the flag indicates that no swap took place, the sort is finished and the results are printed.

In the program R2 is the counter from 0 to 9 and R8 is the swap flag. At the beginning of the outer loop these are both set to zero (lines 4 and 5).

Inside the inner loop we convert the counter contained in R2 to an offset relative to the table start and store it in R4. That is, the value of the counter is 0, 1, 2, ..., but we need the actual offset into the table in order to address the entries. These are of the form 0, 4, 8, 12, ...

To convert the count into an offset, we load the count into R4 and then shift the value left by two bits (lines 7 and 8). A shift left by 2 is the equivalent of multiplying by 4 and thus the value becomes our offset.

We load the value from the table into R3 on line 9. Note that the format of the statement in line 9 causes R4 to be used as the index register. Thus, the value we load is at TAB+R4.

Next we load into R5 the value of R4 incremented by 4 (Line 10). We use the LA instruction which sums the value of R4 and the displacement (4) and places the result in R5. Now R5 is the offset into the table of the element just above the element whose value is in R3.

On line 11 we compare the contents of R3 with the value in the table at offset R5. If the contents of R3 are greater than the value of this element, we branch to the section of code where we swap the contents (SWAP).

If we do not swap, we advance to line 14 and increment R2. We compare the contents of R2 with 9. If the value in R2 is less than 9 we continue and execute another loop cycle (note: the value in R2 will range between 0 and 8 which is nine values - our first offset to be zero). If not, we have completed a full 9 iterations of the inner loop.

Next we check the contents of R8. If the value in R8 is zero, it means that all nine iterations of the inner loop resulted in no swap and the table is now sorted. So we branch to the location where we print the results. If the contents of R8 are not zero, we branch to the top of the outer loop and reset R2 and R8.

In the swap section (lines 21 through 26), we load the values of the two elements that need to be swapped into R6 and R7 and then store the upper element's value (R7) into the lower element slot (R4 offset) then store the lower element's value in the upper element's slot (R5 offset). We place a 1 in R8 indicating a swap has taken place then branch to label *INC* to increment the counter and test as described above.

At DONE we do a very similar loop based on offsets and print the results. As before, R2 is a counter but this time it will range between 0 and 9 rather than 0 to 8. R4 becomes the offset as before by shifting it left by two. We load the value from the table into R3 then convert it to printable characters and print it (lines 31 through 33). We increment R1 by 1, compare it with 10 and iterate if the value is less than 10.

23.6 Search for Prime Numbers

The program in Figure 88 searches for prime numbers in the range of 4 through 999. The program is a loop that tests each number to see if it is divisible by any number between 2 and one-half the number being tested. The program operates as on outer loop whose counter is the number to be tested and an inner loop whose counter iterates between 2 and one-half the outer loop counter.

The outer loop counter is R3 and it is initialized to the value 3 on line 4. The outer loop begins on line 6 where the counter is incremented by one (thus, we begin with the counter having a value of 4).

We compare the counter with 1000 and, if equal, we exit. Consequently, we test the values between 4 and 999. On lines 10 and 11 we set up the limit for the inner loop. We load the counter (R3) into R4 then shift the value in R4 right by one. In effect, this divides the value in R4 by 2 and this gives us the upper limit for the inner loop counter. On Line 13 we initialize the inner loop counter to 1.

The inner loop begins on line 15 and extends to line 24. First we increment the counter (we begin our testing with 2, not 1). The loop will iterate testing all the values between 2 and one-half the value being tested to see if they divide evenly.

If we find a case where some counter value from the inner loop divides evenly (remainder of zero), we exit the inner loop and try the next outer loop value (number not prime). If on the other hand, we make it through the entire inner loop finding no value that divides evenly into our candidate value, the value must be prime so we print it and continue to the next.

At line 16 we compare the value in R2, our inner loop counter, with the limit value in R4. If the value in R2 is greater than or equal to the value in R4, we branch to label PRIME and print the number. We have tried all the alternatives.

```
1  PRIME    SUBENTRY
2           EQUREGS
3
4           L        R3,=F'3'
5
6  LOOP     A        R3,=F'1'      * CANDIDATE NUMBER TO TEST
7           C        R3,=F'1000'   * DONE?
8           BE       DONE
9
10          LR       R4,R3         * CALCULATE INNER LOOP LIMIT
11          SRA      R4,1          * DIVIDE BY 2
12
13          L        R2,=F'1'      * INNER LOOP COUNTER
14
15 INNER    A        R2,=F'1'
16          CR       R2,R4         * INNER LOOP LIMIT TEST
17          BNL      PRNT
18
19          LR       R6,R3
20          SRDA     R6,32         * PREPARE EVEN/ODD REGISTER PAIR
21          DR       R6,R2
22          C        R6,=F'0'      * CHECK THE REMAINDER
23          BE       LOOP          * NOT PRIME
24          B        INNER
25
26 PRNT     XDECO    R3,OUT
                     OUT,L'OUT+L
27          XPRNT    'OUT1
28          B        LOOP
29
30 DONE     SUBEXIT
31
32 OUT      DS       CL12
                     C' IS
33 OUT1     DC       PRIME'
34
35          END
```

Figure 88 Search for Prime Numbers

Otherwise, we load the candidate outer loop counter into R6 and double shift it 32 bits to the right into R7. This places the candidate into R7 and (since we are only using positive numbers) zeros out R6. Note: when doing a right arithmetic shift, bits like the sign bit are supplied at the high end. Since our numbers are all positive, the sign bit is zero.

Next we divide the candidate by the inner loop counter on line 21. The quotient will be in R7 and the remainder in R6. If the remainder is zero (line 22), the number is not prime and we branch back to the outer loop. If the remainder is not zero, we test the next inner loop counter value.

If a number is prime, we print it at line 26 then branch back to the outer loop for the next candidate to test.

23.7 XDECI/XDECO Replacement Code

The Assist macro/pseudo-instructions XDECI and XDECO simplify the process of converting from zoned decimal to binary and from binary to zoned decimal. The program in Figure 89 gives an example of reading signed zoned decimal integers, converting them to binary, summing them and, finally, converting to zoned decimal and printing the total without the use of XDECI/XDECO.

Initially, we zero R8 which will be the accumulator (line 5). Lines 6 through 8 read a line and echo it. At end of input, a branch is made to ATEND.

On line 9 a character zero is stored at NEGFLG. This byte will be used to determine if the number we are converting from zoned to packed is positive or negative. Initially, we assume the number is positive (NEGFLG is zero). NEGFLG will be set to one if a minus sign is encountered.

Lines 11 through 17 scan for the first non-blank byte on the line. If none is found, a branch to ERR1 is made. If one is found, a branch is made to L1 and R1 contains its address.

On lines 19 through 25 we copy the address of the first non-blank byte from R1 to R2 and test to determine if the non-blank byte is a minus sign. If it is not a minus sign, we branch to PLUS. If it is, we set NEGFLG to one, increment R1 to point to the next byte, copy this value to R2 (it is now the first digit) and branch to L5.

If the number was not a minus sign, we execute lines 27 through 30 where we test if the first non-blank byte is a plus sign. If it is, we increment R1 past it, copy R1 to R2, and drop to label L5. If not, we branch to L5 with no increment to R1.

Lines 32 through 42 test the character pointed to by R1. If it is in the range character 0 through character 9, we increment R1, test that we are not at end on line and, if not, test the next character. If we are at limit, we branch to L4. If we encounter a non-numeric character, we branch to L3 and test if it is a blank.

If it is not a blank, we branch to ERR2, print an error message and halt.

Lines 44 through 50 pack the number and make it negative if necessary. On line 44, R1 becomes the length of the number (R1 is the address of the last byte of input number and R2 is the address of the first byte). We decrement the length by one since it will be used in the EX instruction as a length in the PACK instruction. When we write assembly language code, we use the correct length, but in the machine language code the length field is coded as one less which is what the EX will execute. The BCTR decrements the first register but can never branch since the second operand is R0. This is a very fast decrement. The EX on line 46 executes the PACK instruction at label PL with the length from R1 substituted. The packed result is in NBR. If NEGFLG is one, the sign is made negative.

Lines 52 and 55 convert the packed decimal to binary, sum the value into R8 then branch to read the next line.

The remainder of the program converts the packed decimal to zoned decimal placing *(NEG)* at the end of negative numbers (blanks otherwise), then shifting the non-blank portion of the number to be left justified.

Line 60 converts the signed fixed point value in R8 to packed decimal and stores the result in the 8 byte field SUM. Line 61 copies the Edit pattern from PAT to RSLT. The Edit pattern, on line 102, has a fill character of blank (40_{16}) and is also coded to insert commas ($6B_{16}$) as appropriate. In the position next to last, the selector byte is 21_{16} so as to insure that if the number is all zeros, a zero will be printed in the rightmost position and not the fill character.

The ED instruction on line 62 performs the conversion from packed decimal to zoned decimal. Note that the target of the ED, the first argument, begins at RSLT and has a length (L'RSLT+L'SIGN) which includes RSLT and the immediately following SIGN field. SIGN is, therefore, part of the target. Thus, if the number is positive, the SIGN portion will be changed to the fill character (blanks) but if the number is negative, the value in SIGN will be retained this placing *(NEG)* after the number. A format similar to this can be seen in many financial statements for this reason.

Next we search the result for the first non-blank. Line 63 loads the starting address of the RSLT field into R5. Line 64 prints the current contents of RSLT for illustration only. Lines 65 through 68 search for the first non-blank and branch to L7 when found. At L7, R5 contains the address of the first non-blank digit in RSLT (there must be one because of the 21_{16} selector).

Line 72 loads into R6 the address of the last byte of the RSLT/SIGN fields (address of RSLT plus the lengths of each). Line 73 subtracts R5 (the address of the first non-blank) from the address of the last byte yielding in R6 the length in bytes of the number and any attached sign indicator. In line 74 the non-branching BCTR decrements R6. R6 needs to be decremented because it will become the machine language length in the MVC at MVC1 which is executed by the EX in line 75. This MVC shifts the number and any attached sign indicator to the start of RSLT. The XPRNT on line 76 illustrates the contents of RSLT after this has been done.

Line 77 loads into R7 the address of the last byte of the number and attached sign indicator. This is the address of RSLT plus the contents of R6 plus one. This is to undo the BCTR decrement.

The byte pointed to by R7, the first byte after the meaningful text, is set to blank by line 78 and the result is shown with the XPRNT in line 79. The LA in line 80 loads into R6 the address of the last byte of the combined RSLT/SIGN fields. The subtraction on line 81 leaves the length of the area after the text (difference between the address of the last byte and the byte after the last byte of text). The BCTR decrements the length and the EX ripple moves the blank (from line 78) across the end of the combined RSLT/SIGN fields thus blanking out the text residue which remained after the shifting. The final answer is then printed.

```
1               PRINT    NOGEN
2               EQUREGS
                SUBENTR
3    ADD        Y
4
5               SR       R8,R8            zero accumulator
6    LOOP       XREAD    REC,L'REC        read a record
7               BC       B'0100',ATEND    EOF?
8               XPRNT    REC,L'REC        write the record
9               MVI      NEGFLG,C'0'      set flag to 0
10
11              LA       R1,REC           addr 1st byte of REC
12   L2         CLI      0(R1),C' '       scan for 1st non-blank
13              BNE      L1               found one
14              LA       R1,1(0,R1)       increment ptr
15              C        R1,LIM           at limit?
16              BNL      ERR1             line is all blanks
17              B        L2               again
18
19   L1         LR       R2,R1            R2 addr 1st non-blank
20              CLI      0(R1),C'-'       is is a minus sign?
```

```
21          BNE     PLUS                    no
22          MVI     NEGFLG,C'1'             nbr is negative
23          LA      R1,1(0,R1)              incr ptr byte after -
24          LR      R2,R1                   remember start of nbr
25          B       L5
26
27 PLUS     CLI     0(R1),C'+'              plus sign found?
28          BNE     L5                      no
29          LA      R1,1(0,R1)              yes incr ptr past it
30          LR      R2,R1                   remember start
31
32 L5       CLI     0(R1),C'0'              scan for digits
33          BL      L3                      could be a blank
34          CLI     0(R1),C'9'
35          BH      ERR2                    char not a digit
36          LA      R1,1(0,R1)              incr ptr
37          C       R1,LIM                  limit?
38          BNL     L4                      yes
39          B       L5                      no
40
41 L3       CLI     0(R1),C' '              blank after number?
42          BNE     ERR2                    no
43
44 L4       SR      R1,R2                   R1 is length of number
45          BCTR    R1,R0                   adjust for EX - 1 less
46          EX      R1,PK                   pack the number into NBR
47          CLI     NEGFLG,C'1'             is this number neg?
48          BNE     ADD                     no
49
50          NI      NBR+7,X'FB'             yes make sign neg
51
52 ADD      CVB     R7,NBR                  convert to binary
53          AR      R8,R7                   add to accumulator
54
55          B       LOOP                    read next line
56 *
57 *           EOF processing
58 *
59
60 ATEND    CVD     R8,SUM                  convert ans to decimal
61          MVC     RSLT,PAT                copy pattern to target
                    RSLT(L'RSLT+L'SIGN),
62          ED      SUM                     edit to RSLT + SIGN
63          LA      R5,RSLT                 start addr RSLT
```

```
64              XPRNT   RSLT,L'RSLT              after ED example
65  L6          CLI     0(R5),C' '              find 1st digit in output
66              BNE     L7                      find 1st non blank
67              LA      R5,1(0,R5)              incr R5
68              B       L6
69
70  *           Load address of last byte of string into R6
71
                        R6,RSLT+L'RSLT+L'SIG
72  L7          LA      N                       addr last byte
73              SR      R6,R5                   lngth string to print
74              BCTR    R6,R0                   decr for EX
75              EX      R6,MVC1                 shift nbr to beginning
76              XPRNT   RSLT,L'RSLT             after text shifted
77              LA      R7,RSLT+1(R6)           address end of txt
78              MVI     0(R7),C' '              blank out end
79              XPRNT   RSLT,L'RSLT             after blank placed
                        R6,RSLT+L'RSLT+L'SIG
80              LA      N                       end
81              SR      R6,R7                   R6 is length to end
82              BCTR    R6,R0                   subtract 1
83              EX      R6,MVC2                 ripple the blank
84              XPRNT   MSG,L'MSG+L'RSLT+6      answer is ...
85  RET         SUBEXIT
86
87  ERR1        XPRNT   ERRMSG1,L'ERRMSG1       all blanks
88              B       RET
89  ERR2        XPRNT   ERRMSG2,L'ERRMSG2       must be bad data
90              B       RET
91
92              LTORG
93
94  REC         DS      CL40                    actual input record
95  LIM         DC      A(*)                    addr of byte after rec
96  PK          PACK    NBR,0(0,R2)
97  MVC1        MVC     RSLT(0),0(R5)           for EX
98  MVC2        MVC     1(0,R7),0(R7)           for EX
99  NBR         DC      PL8'0'
10
0   NEGFLG  DC      C'0'
10
1   SUM     DS      PL8
10
2   PAT     DC      X'402020206B2020206B2020206B2020206B202120'
10
3   MSG     DC      C'ANS = '
10  RSLT    DS      CL20
```

```
4
10
5  SIGN    DC      C' (NEG)'             blanks if nbr positive
10 ERRMSG
6  1       DC      C'LINE ALL BLANK'
10 ERRMSG
7  2       DC      C'ERROR - BAD DATA'
10
8          END     ADD
```

Example output

```
 1234
-23456
+33244
-10000000
23456

9,965,522
9,965,522
(NEG)5,522
9,965,522 (NEG) ,
522
ANS = 9,965,522 (NEG)
```

Figure 89 XDECI/XDECO Replacement

23.8 Print a String in Hexadecimal

The program in Figure 90 prints a string of bytes in hexadecimal notation. For example, for the character string *ABC123*, the equivalent hexadecimal is: *C1C2C3F1F2F3*

The program in Figure 90 advances through the input string byte by byte. For each byte, it first extracts the high order four bits and uses these as indices (between 0 and 15) into a table of printable characters which correspond to the value of the four bit field. For example, if the four bit field has 1010_2 (10_{10}), this indexes to the eleventh position in the table where the character A is located. Note: the table begins at zero. Hence, offset 10 into the table is to the eleventh entry.

```
1                 PRINT    NOGEN
2                 EQUREGS
3    HEX          SUBENTRY
4
5                 WTO      'HEXADECIMAL'
6
7                 L        R2,STRLEN       * LENGTH OF STRING
8                 SR       R4,R4           * OFFSET INTO INPUT STRING
9                 SR       R5,R5           * REGISTER TO RCV STRING CHARS
10               SR       R6,R6           * OFFSET INTO OUTPUT STRING
11
12   LOOP         IC       R5,STRING(R4)   * LOAD NEXT INPUT CHAR
                                           * MAKE 4 HIGH BITS the 4 LOW
13               SRA      R5,4            BITS
14               IC       R5,TABLE(R5)    * LOAD CHAR FROM HEX TABLE
15               STC      R5,OUT(R6)      * STORE CHAR in OUTPUT STRING
16               LA       R6,1(R0,R6)     * INCREMENT OUTPUT OFFSET
17
18               IC       R5,STRING(R4)   * LOAD INPUT CHAR AGAIN
19               N        R5,MASK         * ZERO HIGH 4 bits
20               IC       R5,TABLE(R5)    * LOAD FROM HEX TABLE
21               STC      R5,OUT(R6)      * STORE TO OUTPUT
22               LA       R6,1(R0,R6)     * INCREMENT OUTPUT OFFSET
23               LA       R4,1(R0,R4)     * INCREMENT INPUT OFFSET
24
25               BCT      R2,LOOP         * DECR R2, BRANCH IF > 0
26
27               XPRNT    OUT,STRX*2      * PRINT RESULTS
28               SUBEXIT
29
30   STRING       DC       C'THIS IS A TEST STRING 0123456789'
31   STRX         EQU      *-STRING
32   STRLEN       DC       A(STRX)
33   OUT          DS       CL(STRX*2)
34   MASK         DC       X'0000000F'
35   TABLE        DC       C'0123456789ABCDEF'
36
37               END      HEX
```

Figure 90 Print Hex Equivalent

The program proceeds as follows:

1. The length of the input string is loaded into R2 (line 7). The length is derived from the value stored at label STRLEN on line 32. This value is declared as an A-type address constant which contains the value of the label STRX. The value of STRX is

calculated by the EQU on line 31. This is the difference between the value of the current location counter at STRX and the location counter at the beginning of STRING. STRX could not be loaded directly because it does not exist at run time, it is only an equate symbol. While STRX is not really an address, A-type address constants are often used for this purpose since they permit initialization of their run time content by computed values as is the case here.

2. Registers R4 through R6 are set to zero (lines 8,9, and 10). R4 will be an offset into the input string pointing to the next character to be converted to hexadecimal, R5 will be a register into which we load the individual input characters for conversion to hexadecimal, and R6 will be an offset into the output string where we will write the results.

3. Beginning on line 12 we loop through the input until done. The loop control is the BCT instruction on line 25. Each time the BCT is executed, it decrements the value in R2 (the string length) by one. If the contents of R2 are still greater than zero, branch is made to LOOP. When R2 is zero, no branch is made and the loop ends.

4. On line 12 we use the Insert Character instruction to load a byte from the string into the low order 8 bits of R5 (we zeroed all the bits of R5 - this instruction only modifies the low order 8 bits so the high bits remain zero). The address of the byte to be loaded is computed with the displacement, index, and base format. The assembler computes the base and displacement for STRING and R4, our offset into the string, is the index register. As the loop progresses, the value in R4 will increment by one for each passage through the loop (line 23) thus progressing through the input.

5. We now have an input character in the low order 8 bits of R5. We need to (1) extract the high order four bits, (2) do a lookup, (3) copy a result to the output, (4) do the same for the low order four bits. The SRA on line 13 shifts the contents of R5 to the right by four. This removes the low order 4 bits and causes what were the high order four bits to now be in the low order position. R5 now consists of 28 bits of zeros in the high order bits positions followed by the four bits that were in the high bits of the input character. R5 is now a number between 0 and 15 and the offset into our lookup table.

6. On line 14 we use the Insert Character instruction indexed by the value in R5 to load a character from TABLE. TABLE is a string containing the characters 0 through A used to represent hexadecimal numbers. Thus, if the value in R5 is 10_{10}, we will load A into the low byte of R5 and likewise for any value in R5

between 0 and 15. The previous contents of the low byte of R5 are lost in this operation. The high 3 bytes remain zeros.

7. On line 15 we store the low order byte from R5 into the output string, indexed by the contents of R6, and increment the R6 on line 16.

8. Lines 18 through 23 process the low order four bits from the original character. To process the low bits, we only need to eliminate the high four bits. We do this by an And instruction with a mask. The mask is a memory resident 32 bit value zeros in all but the last four bits. These are ones. When this mask is and'ed with another 32 bit value, only the low order four bits will remain. This is done on line 19. Lines 20 through 22 do the lookup and store the result as before. As we have now processed all 8 bits of the input character, line 23 increments the offset into the input. Line 25 determines if we should process any more characters as noted above.

9. Line 27 writes to output. Note that the length of the output is twice the length of the input (there are two characters of hexadecimal for each input character).

23.9 Word Count Program

The next program builds a dictionary of words that stores up to 1000 words up to 8 characters in length along with a count of the number of times each word occurs. Word counts are useful to identify words that may make poor indexing terms in an indexing application. Historically, many indexing systems used a limited number of characters in an indexing word because the stem of a word in English is mainly in the first part of the word. The Salton SMART System (see Salton, G., *The SMART Retrieval System— Experiments in Automatic Document Processing* (Prentice-Hall, Upper Saddle River, NJ, 1971)), for example, was originally based on six character words because the early mainframe word size could hold six characters (characters were six bits).

In this program the data structure for each word consists of eight characters of text followed by a four byte of fixed point binary integer giving the number of times the word has occurred in the document. Thus, each entry requires 12 bytes.

The word count program is given in Figure 91 where the data structure for words and counts is contained in a table whose declaration is on line 121. This is a 12,000 byte table which allows for 1,000 12 byte entries. The first eight bytes of each word is the word text and the last four bytes are the count.

Because our data structure uses full word fixed point binary counts and because these must be on full word aligned memory addresses if they are to be accessed by Load and Store instructions, the initial byte of the table must, therefore, be on a full word boundary. As the table one line 121 is declared with a C data type code, there is no guarantee that the first byte will on a full word boundary. The data type code C has no alignment requirement.

However, we are assured that the table does, in fact, begin on a full word boundary because of the declaration on line 116. The notation 0F in a DS statement causes the assembler to allocate zero instances of a full word binary. That is, nothing. But this has the side effect of forcing the location counter to advance to the next full word boundary (an address value evenly divisible by 4). Since there is nothing allocated by the DS on line 116, this is the byte on which the table begins. Thus the table TAB begins on a full word boundary.

In our program, entries in the table will be accessed as offsets from a register. The word entry will be at zero bytes from the register and the count at eight bytes from the register. The next entry will be at 12 bytes from the register.

Note that the table TAB on line 121 is the last declared field in the program and that the LTORG appears prior to TAB. The LTORG causes any literals, such as =F'100', to be placed in memory beginning at the point where the LTORG appears. Thus, all literals will appear prior to our definition of TAB.

Why is it important to place the literals prior to the TAB declaration? Since the extent of TAB is much larger than 4095, the largest displacement allowed in ordinary RX, RS, SS, and SI instructions, anything placed after TAB would be *out of using* in a program with a single base register. We could have more than one base register, but it is unnecessary. We only need that the first byte of TAB be within using so that we can load the address of this initial byte into a register. After that, all table addressing will be relative to this register.

The program works as follows:

1. Input consists of lines of text up to 80 characters long. Input lines are processed in a loop beginning at line 7 and extending through line 62. Input is read into the field IN on line 7 and a branch is made to EOF when there is no more data (line 8).

2. Each input line is processed by a Translate (TR) instruction to remove punctuation (except the hyphen and single quote characters) and numerics. The TR converts all alphabetics to upper case (a common case for indexing terms is normally used in retrieval applications).

3. The TR uses the table declared on lines 91 through 112. The table is built as follows. We declare an area of memory 256 bytes long (as is normally the case with a TR table) and we initialize each byte to blank - the default (line 91). At this point, every character looked up will return a blank.

Next, we backup into the table by means of the ORG directive and change some of the blanks. The ORG directive resets the assembler's location counter back into the address space of the table. Once repositioned, the DC statements replace the blanks.

The first set of changes to TAB are lines 92 through 105. In these lines, we replace the blanks in the table at the offsets associated with the upper and lower case characters with their upper case equivalents. That is, at the offset into the table associated with the letters *a* and *A* we replace the blanks with a capital A. Thus, when the TR looks up an upper or lower case *A*, it will return (and substitute) a capital A. We do this for all the alphas. The net effect is that input containing upper or lower case letters will be converted to upper case letters. Since the alphabetics in EBCDIC are discontinuous, several statements are required to make all the table entries. Note that we must include the upper case letters otherwise they would be converted to blanks.

Next we modify the TR table at the offsets for the hyphen and single quote which will likewise be retained in the resulting input image.

The final ORG with no operand causes the location counter to spring back to the highest value it has had so far which, in this case, is the address of the first byte just beyond the TR table.

4. After the TR instruction on line 9, the input image consists only of blanks, upper case alphabetics, hyphens and single quote marks. Retention of hyphens and single quote marks was due to the test input used, Dryden's translation of the Aeneid, in which these characters are important.

5. Next, we scan each line of input and extract each word thereon. On Line 11 we load the address of the input line into R3 and the address of the end of the line into R4. On line 14 we test if the byte being pointed to by the contents of R3 is a blank. If it is not, we branch to label L2. If it is, we fall through to line 17 where we increment the pointer in R3 and compare it with the limit value in R4. If we have reached the end of the input, we branch to LOOP and read a new line of input. If not, we branch to L1 to process the next character. Thus, we ignore blanks in the input.

6. Reaching line 22 we know we are at the start of a word whose address we copy into R5 in order to preserve the origin of the word. Lines 24 through 28 locate the end of the word by incrementing the input pointer (R3), testing it against the end in line limit. If we reach the end of the input image, we branch to label L4. We then (line 27) test if the character pointed to by the contents of R3 is a blank. If yes, we advance to line 30. If not, we loop and look at the next character

When we get to line 30, R5 has the address of the starting point of the word and R3 has the address of the byte just beyond the end of the word. We copy R3 to R6 and subtract R5 from R6 leaving in R6 the length of the word that begins on at the address contained in R5. This is decremented in line 32 as we will use this length in an EX instruction. Lines 33 and 34 perform an overlapped move of a blank across the field OUT (this program assumes no word will be longer that 30 characters, the length of OUT).

7. In line 35 we use the EX (Execute) instruction to move R6 bytes from the input beginning at the address contained in R5 to OUT. The EX uses the data area MVC at the label MVC. This is the image of the MVC that the EX will execute after ORing the low byte of R6 (contains the length) with the second byte of the MVC at MVC. Since the second byte of the MVC at label MVC is a zero, this effectively substitutes the low byte of R6 into the length portion of the MVC instruction and exactly R6 bytes are moved to OUT. The remaining bytes of OUT remain blanks.

8. Now we need to do a lookup on the table to see if we have this word. The words in the table are no longer than 8 bytes. Thus, we truncate long input words. Each table word field is followed by a four byte binary integer giving the number of times the word has appeared. If we do not find the word in the table, we add it with a count of one.

9. On line 36 we load the count of the number existing entries in the table into R5. Initially, COUNT is 0. On line 37 we load the address of the table of words TAB into R6. Even though most of TAB is beyond the reach of *using* (base register + 4095), the start of the table is within *using*. Thus, we can load its address. Once we have its location in a register, we can address its contents without need for large displacements as will be seen.

10. The loop to search the table to see if the word in OUT is already in the table extends from lines 38 through 46. Lines 38 and 39 test if we have examined the entire table. Each time we examine an entry, we decrement the count in R5. When the contents of R5 become zero, we have examined all entries and

we branch to L6 where we add our word from OUT as a new entry.

11. Lines 41 and 42 compare the first 8 bytes of the word in OUT with the word in the table. The CLC (Compare Logical Character) on line 41 specifies an 8 byte length. The first operand begins at label OUT and the second operand begins at the address contained in R6. Note that there is no displacement. R6 has the address. If the words match, we branch to L7 to increment the count for this word. If they do not, we increment the contents of R6 by 12 (line 44), decrement the count in R5 and branch to look at the next entry, if any.

12. If we find the word, lines 48 through 51 increment its count. We load into R5 the 4 bytes at offset 8 bytes from the word in the table, that is, the 4 byte binary count entry. To this we add 1 and then store the result back in the table. Then we branch to the top to process the next word (label L1A).

13. If we have looked at every entry in the table and did not find the word, we arrive at label L6. At label L6 we know that R6 will be pointing at the first byte of the next available 12 byte slot in the table. We simply copy the first 8 bytes from OUT to the first 8 bytes of the new entry we are creating (line 53), load a 1 into R7 (line 54) and store the 4 byte binary 1 in the last 4 bytes of the 12 byte entry (line 55). We load the original value of COUNT, increment it, test it against the table limit, and store it (lines 56 through 60). The we return to the top to process the next word.

14. Lines 64 through 77 print the table of words and counts using a similar loop to that used to search the table above.

```
1              PRINT    NOGEN
2              EQUREGS
3      WORDS SUBENTRY
4
5              WTO      'WORDS'
6
7      LOOP  XREAD    IN,80
8              BC       B'0100',EOF
9              TR       IN,TRTAB      * CVT TO UPPER & REM NON-ALPHAS
10
11             LA       R3,IN
12             LA       R4,80(R0,R3)  * ADDRESS OF END OF INPUT
13
14     L1    CLI      0(R3),C' '    * BLANK?
15             BNE      L2            * BRANCH IF NOT BLANK
16
17     L1A   LA       R3,1(R0,R3)   * INCR PTR INTO INPUT
18             CR       R3,R4         * AT END?
19             BNL      LOOP          * YES - END OF INPUT STRING
20             B        L1            * NO - PROCESS NEXT CHARACTER
21
22     L2    LR       R5,R3         * COPY WORD START ADDR TO R5
23
24     L3    LA       R3,1(R0,R3)   * INCR INPUT POINTER
25             CR       R3,R4         * END?
26             BNL      L4            * YES
27             CLI      0(R3),C' '    * BLANK?
28             BNE      L3            * NO - CONTINUE
29
30     L4    LR       R6,R3         * COPY WORD END ADDR TO R6
31             SR       R6,R5         * LENGTH OF WORD IN R6
32             BCTR     R6,R0
33             MVC      OUT(1),BLANK  * COPY BLANK TO POSITION 1
34             MVC      OUT+1(29),OUT * PROPOGATE BLANK
35             EX       R6,MVC        * COPY WORD TO OUT
36             L        R5,COUNT      * NUMBER OF ENTRIES IN TABLE
37             LA       R6,TAB        * START OF ARRAY OF ENTRIES
38     L5    C        R5,=F'0'      * NO MORE ENTRIES IN TABLE?
39             BE       L6            * YES
40                                    * COMPARE NEW WORD WITH TABLE
41             CLC      OUT(8),0(R6)  ENTRY
42             BE       L7            * FOUND WORD IN TABLE
43
```

```
44          LA       R6,12(R0,R6)    * INCREMENT PTR TO NEXT ENTRY
45          S        R5,=F'1'        * DECREMENT LOOP COUNTER
46          B        L5              * CONTINUE
47
48  L7      L        R5,8(R0,R6)     * WORD FOUND - LOAD COUNT
49          A        R5,=F'1'        * INCR COUNT
50          ST       R5,8(R0,R6)     * STORE COUNT
51          B        L1A             * LOOK FOR NEXT WORD IN INPUT
52
53  L6      MVC      0(8,R6),OUT     * COPY WORD TO TABLE
54          LA       R7,1(R0,R0)     * LOAD 1 INTO R7
55          ST       R7,8(R0,R6)     * STORE IN COUNT FIELD
56          L        R5,COUNT        * MAIN COUNT OF ENTRIES
57          LA       R5,1(R0,R5)     * INCR
58          C        R5,=F'1000'     * TEST LIMIT
59          BNL      ERROR           * OVER LIMIT
60          ST       R5,COUNT        * STORE UPDATED COUNT
61
62          B        L1A             * PROCESS NEXT INPUT WORD
63
64  EOF     LA       R5,TAB          * TABLE ADDRESS
65          L        R6,COUNT        * COUNT OF ENTRIES
66          C        R6,=F'0'        * EMPTY?
67          BE       BYE             * DONE
68  L8      MVC      OUT(8),0(R5)    * COPY WORD TO OUTPUT STRING
69          L        R7,8(R0,R5)     * LOAD WORD COUNT
70          XDECO    R7,OUT+8        * CVT WORD COUNT TO CHARS
71          XPRNT    OUT,20          * WRITE WORD AND COUNT
72          LA       R5,12(R0,R5)    * INCR TO NEXT ENTRY
73          BCT      R6,L8           * DECR R6 AND REPEAT IF > 0
74
75  BYE     L        R5,COUNT        * TOTAL NUMBER OF ENTRIES
76          XDECO    R5,OUT          * CVT TO PRINTABLE
77          XPRNT    OUT,12          * PRINT TOTAL
78          SUBEXIT
79
80  ERROR   WTO      'ERROR - TABLE OVERFLOW'
81          SUBEXIT
82
83  BLANK   DC       C' '
84  OUT     DS       CL30            * OUTPUT STRING & TEMP STORE
85  MVC     MVC      OUT(0),0(R5)    * FOR EX INSTRUCTION
86  IN      DS       CL80            * INPUT STRING
87  COUNT   DC       F'0'            * NBR ENTRIES COUNT
```

```
88   *
89   * TRT TABLE TO CONVERT TO UPPER CASE AND REMOVE NON-ALPHAS
90   *
91   TRTAB  DC       256C' '
92          ORG      TRTAB+C'a'
93          DC       C'ABCDEFGHI'
94          ORG      TRTAB+C'A'
95          DC       C'ABCDEFGHI'
96
97          ORG      TRTAB+C'j'
98          DC       C'JKLMNOPQR'
99          ORG      TRTAB+C'J'
100         DC       C'JKLMNOPQR'
101
102         ORG      TRTAB+C's'
103         DC       C'STUVWXYZ'
104         ORG      TRTAB+C'S'
105         DC       C'STUVWXYZ'
106
107         ORG      TRTAB+C'-'     * RETAIN HYPHENS
108         DC       C'-'
109
110         ORG      TRTAB+C''''    * RETAIN SINGLE QUOTES
111         DC       C''''
112         ORG
113
114         LTORG    * LTERALS NEED TO BE PRIOR TO TABLE
115
116         DS       0F             * FULL WORD ALIGN
117  *
118  * TABLE IS 1000 ENTRIES. EACH ENTRY IS 8 CHARS FOR WORD
119  * AND 4 BYTES COUNT.
120  *
121  TAB    DS       12000C
122         END      HEX
```

Figure 91 Word Count Program

23.10 Word Count Program with DSECT

The previous program works but it doesn't deal with the word/count data structure very intelligently. Instead, it handles these as numeric displacements relative to a register as in lines 68 through 72. Line 68 copies the word from a node pointed to by R5 to an output field and then lines 69 and 70 load the count (8 bytes displaced from the word) into R7, convert it to printable decimal, and store it in the last 12 bytes of the output field. Even for a simple two element data structure, this is not very readable code.

So, in Figure 92 we add a DSECT. The DSECT is declared on lines 85 through 88. When we enter the DSECT declaration, we exit the CSECT. Line 90 rejoins the CSECT. Everything between the DSECT statement on line 85 and the resumption of the CSECT belongs to the DSECT. Note that since a program may have multiple CSECTs, the label on the CSECT is needed to tell the assembler which CSECT we are continuing. CSECTs may be intermingled.

The DSECT sets up a two part node. One part is the eight byte character string labeled WRD and the second is the full word fixed binary labeled FREQ. Together, they constitute our simple data structure.

The labels in a DSECT are addressed relative to a base register for the DSECT. We declare the DSECT base register in the normal manner with a USING as seen in line 7. This tells the assembler that any reference to a label in the DSECT NODE should be calculated using R6 as the base register.

While the DSECT is used in several places in the code, we can see an example of it used in lines 66 through 75. This is the section that prints the words and counts. On line 66, we load the DSECT base register with the address of the first element in the table TAB and the count of the total number of entries is loaded into R5 on line 67. Line 70 copies the word from the table using the DSECT label WRD to the output area and line 71 loads the count for the word into R7. Both of these are coded into machine language using R6 as the base and the appropriate displacements. On line 74, the value in R6 is incremented by the length of the DSECT which is the value of the symbol NODELEN calculated on line 88 as the difference between the location counter at NODE and just after FREQ. The * normally refers to the current value of the location counter.

```
1              PRINT    NOGEN
2              EQUREGS
3    WORDS     SUBENTRY
4
5              WTO      'WORDS'
6
7              USING    NODE,R6
8
9    LOOP      XREAD    IN,80
10             BC       B'0100',EOF
11             TR       IN,TRTAB         * CVT UPR CASE REM NON-ALPHAS
12
13             LA       R3,IN
14             LA       R4,80(R0,R3)     * ADDRESS OF END OF INPUT
15
16   L1        CLI      0(R3),C' '       * BLANK?
                                         * BRANCH NOT BLANK TO PROCESS
17             BNE      L2               WORD
18
19   L1A       LA       R3,1(R0,R3)      * INCR PTR INTO INPUT
20             CR       R3,R4            * AT END?
21             BNL      LOOP             * YES - END OF INPUT STRING
22             B        L1               * NO - PROCESS NEXT CHARACTER
23
24   L2        LR       R5,R3            * COPY WORD START ADDR TO R5
25
26   L3        LA       R3,1(R0,R3)      * INCR INPUT POINTER
27             CR       R3,R4            * END?
28             BNL      L4               * YES
29             CLI      0(R3),C' '        * BLANK?
30             BNE      L3               * NO - CONTINUE
31
32   L4        LR       R6,R3            * COPY WORD END ADDR TO R6
33             SR       R6,R5            * LENGTH OF WORD IN R6
34             BCTR     R6,R0            * decrement R6
35             MVC      OUT(1),BLANK     * COPY BLANK TO POSITION 1
36             MVC      OUT+1(29),OUT    * PROPOGATE BLANK
37             EX       R6,MVC           * COPY WORD TO OUT
38             L        R5,COUNT         * NUMBER OF ENTRIES IN TABLE
39             LA       R6,TAB           * START OF ARRAY OF ENTRIES
40   L5        C        R5,=F'0'         * NO MORE ENTRIES TO LOOK AT?
41             BE       L6               * YES
42
                                         * COMPARE NEW WORD WITH TABLE
43             CLC      OUT(8),WRD       ENTRY
```

```
44            BE      L7              * FOUND WORD IN TABLE
45
                      R6,NODELEN(R0,R
46            LA      6)              * INCREMENT PTR TO NEXT ENTRY
47            S       R5,=F'1'        * DECREMENT LOOP COUNTER
48            B       L5              * CONTINUE
49
50   L7       L       R5,FREQ         * WORD FOUND - LOAD COUNT
51            A       R5,=F'1'        * INCR COUNT
52            ST      R5,FREQ         * STORE COUNT
53            B       L1A             * LOOK FOR NEXT WORD IN INPUT
54
55   L6       MVC     WRD,OUT         * COPY WORD TO TABLE
56            LA      R7,1(R0,R0)     * LOAD 1 INTO R7
57            ST      R7,FREQ         * STORE IN COUNT FIELD
58            L       R5,COUNT        * MAIN COUNT OF ENTRIES
59            LA      R5,1(R0,R5)     * INCR
60            C       R5,=F'1000'     * TEST LIMIT
61            BNL     ERROR            * OVER LIMIT
62            ST      R5,COUNT        * STORE UPDATED COUNT
63
64            B       L1A             * PROCESS NEXT INPUT WORD
65
66   EOF      LA      R6,TAB          * TABLE ADDRESS
67            L       R5,COUNT        * COUNT OF ENTRIES
68            C       R5,=F'0'        * EMPTY?
69            BE      BYE             * DONE
70   L8       MVC     OUT(8),WRD      * COPY WORD TO OUTPUT STRING
71            L       R7,FREQ         * LOAD WORD COUNT
72            XDECO   R7,OUT+8         * CVT WORD COUNT TO CHARS
73            XPRNT   OUT,20          * WRITE WORD AND COUNT
                      R6,NODELEN(R0,R
74            LA      6)              * INCR TO NEXT ENTRY
75            BCT     R5,L8           * DECR R6 AND REPEAT IF > 0
76
77   BYE      L       R5,COUNT        * TOTAL NUMBER OF ENTRIES
78            XDECO   R5,OUT          * CVT TO PRINTABLE
79            XPRNT   OUT,12          * PRINT TOTAL
80            SUBEXIT
81
                      'ERROR - TABLE
82   ERROR    WTO     OVERFLOW'
83            SUBEXIT
84
85   NODE     DSECT
```

```
86   WRD      DS        CL8
87   FREQ     DS        F
88   NODELEN EQU        *-NODE
89
90   WORDS    CSECT
91
92   BLANK    DC        C' '
93   OUT      DS        CL30          * OUTPUT STRING & TEMP STORE
94   MVC      MVC       OUT(0),0(R5)  * FOR EX INSTRUCTION
95   IN       DS        CL80          * INPUT STRING
96   COUNT    DC        F'0'          * NBR ENTRIES COUNT
97   *
98   * TRT TABLE TO CONVERT TO UPPER CASE AND REMOVE NON-ALPHAS
99   *
100  TRTAB    DC        256C' '
101           ORG       TRTAB+C'a'
102           DC        C'ABCDEFGHI'
103           ORG       TRTAB+C'A'
104           DC        C'ABCDEFGHI'
105
106           ORG       TRTAB+C'j'
107           DC        C'JKLMNOPQR'
108           ORG       TRTAB+C'J'
109           DC        C'JKLMNOPQR'
110
111           ORG       TRTAB+C's'
112           DC        C'STUVWXYZ'
113           ORG       TRTAB+C'S'
114           DC        C'STUVWXYZ'
115
116           ORG       TRTAB+C'-'     * RETAIN HYPHENS
117           DC        C'-'
118
119           ORG       TRTAB+C''''    * RETAIN SINGLE QUOTES
120           DC        C''''
121           ORG
122
                                       * LTERALS NEED TO BE AHEAD OF
123           LTORG                    TABLE
124
125           DS        0F             * FULL WORD ALIGN
126  *
127  * TABLE IS 1000 ENTRIES. EACH ENTRY IS 8 CHARS FOR WORD
128  * AND 4 BYTES COUNT.
```

```
129   *
130   TAB    DS        12000C
131
132          END       WORDS
```
Figure 92 Word Count with DSECT

23.11 Word Count Program with List

Next we modify the word count program to change the data base of words from an array to a list structure. The program is shown in Figure 93. The DSECT for this is:

```
NODE     DSECT
WRD      DS  CL8
FREQ     DS  F
NEXT     DS  A
```

As you can see, we've added one more item: a pointer named NEXT which is a four byte address. Each node now has a pointer to the next node and the last node will have a NULL pointer (0). The first node will be pointed to by a START pointer, which is initially NULL. Nodes will be allocated from the same large data array although dynamic memory allocation using system macros is also possible.

The initial part of the program is the same as the previous example.

Changes occur in lines 43 through 55 where we search the list for each newly read word. On line 43 the address of the first node is loaded into R6. It is checked for NULL and, if it is, we branch to the section that creates a new node. Otherwise, we compare the input word with the table entry WRD and branch to L6 is they are the same. If they are not equal, we load R6, the DSECT base, with the contents of the current node's NEXT pointer thus advancing the base register R6 to point the next node. We check that the new value of R6 is not NULL on line 44. If it is, there are no more nodes to test and our word is not in the list.

If we found the word in the list, we increment its count (FREQ) on lines 57 through 59 and proceed to process the next input word.

If we did not find the word, we allocate a new node. This is done in lines 62 through 73. First, we load R6 with the pointer (CRNT) to the next available byte in our data array. The field CRNT is an address stored in memory which points to the next available byte in the data area TAB.

We add the contents of R6 with the length of a node and the result is placed in R5 on line 63. We compare value in R5 with LIMIT which is the address of the first byte beyond the data array and generate an error message if we have exceeded it.

Next we copy the word to the node and store one in FREQ. We load the address of the current START node into R7 and store it in NEXT and then store in START the address of this node. Thus the new node becomes the first node and the previous first node becomes second.

The output section (lines 75 through 89) uses a technique very similar to the search loop described above.

```
1                PRINT    NOGEN
2                EQUREGS
                 SUBENTR
3    WORDS       Y
4
5                WTO      'WORDS'
6
7                USING    NODE,R6        * DSECT BASE
8
9    LOOP        XREAD    IN,80
10               BC       B'0100',EOF
11
12   *
13   *           EXTRACT WORDS FROM INPUT LINE
14   *
15
                                         * CVT UPPER CASE & REMOVE NON-
16               TR       IN,TRTAB       ALPHAS
17
18               LA       R3,IN
19               LA       R4,80(R0,R3)   * ADDRESS OF END OF INPUT
20
21   L1          CLI      0(R3),C' '     * BLANK?
                                         * BRANCH IF NOT BLANK TO PROCESS
22               BNE      L2             WORD
23
24   L1A         LA       R3,1(R0,R3)    * INCR PTR INTO INPUT
25               CR       R3,R4          * AT END?
26               BNL      LOOP           * YES - END OF INPUT STRING
27               B        L1             * NO - PROCESS NEXT CHARACTER
28
29   L2          LR       R5,R3          * COPY WORD START ADDR TO R5
30
31   L3          LA       R3,1(R0,R3)    * INCR INPUT POINTER
```

```
32          CR      R3,R4           * END?
33          BNL     L4              * YES
34          CLI     0(R3),C' '      * BLANK?
35          BNE     L3              * NO - CONTINUE
36
37  L4      LR      R6,R3           * COPY WORD END ADDR TO R6
38          SR      R6,R5           * LENGTH OF WORD IN R6
39          MVC     OUT(1),BLANK    * COPY BLANK TO POSITION 1
40          MVC     OUT+1(29),OUT   * PROPOGATE BLANK
41          EX      R6,MVC          * COPY WORD TO OUT
42
43          L       R6,START        * START ADDR OF ENTRIES
44  L5      C       R6,=F'0'        * NO MORE ENTRIES TO LOOK AT?
45          BE      L6              * YES
46
47  *
48  *       SEARCH SECTION
49  *
50
51          CLC     OUT(L'WRD),WRD  * COMP NEW WORD WITH TABLE ENTRY
52          BE      L7              * FOUND WORD IN TABLE
53
54          L       R6,NEXT
55          B       L5              * CONTINUE
56
57  L7      L       R5,FREQ         * WORD FOUND - LOAD COUNT
58          A       R5,=F'1'        * INCR COUNT
59          ST      R5,FREQ         * STORE COUNT
60          B       L1A             * LOOK FOR NEXT WORD IN INPUT
61
62  L6      L       R6,CRNT
            R5,NODELEN(0,R
63          LA      6)
64          C       R5,LIMIT
65          BNL     ERROR
66          ST      R5,CRNT
67          MVC     WRD,OUT         * COPY WORD TO TABLE
68          LA      R7,1(R0,R0)     * LOAD 1 INTO R7
69          ST      R7,FREQ         * STORE IN COUNT FIELD
70          L       R7,START
71          ST      R7,NEXT
72          ST      R6,START
73          B       L1A             * PROCESS NEXT INPUT WORD
74
```

```
75  *
76  *           OUTPUT SECTION
77  *
78
79  EOF      L        R6,START        * FIRST NODE ADDRESS
80           SR       R8,R8           * COUNT WORDS
81  L8A      C        R6,=F'0'        * NO NODE?
82           BE       BYE             * DONE
83  L8       MVC      OUT(L'WRD),WRD  * COPY WORD TO OUTPUT STRING
84           L        R7,FREQ         * LOAD WORD COUNT
85           XDECO    R7,OUT+8        * CVT WORD COUNT TO CHARS
86           XPRNT    OUT,20          * WRITE WORD AND COUNT
87           L        R6,NEXT         * INCR TO NEXT ENTRY
88           LA       R8,1(0,R8)      * INCR WORD COUNT
89           B        L8A
90
91  BYE      XDECO    R8,OUT          * CVT TO PRINTABLE
92           XPRNT    OUT,12          * PRINT TOTAL
93           SUBEXIT
94
95  ERROR    WTO      'ERROR - TABLE OVERFLOW'
96           SUBEXIT
97
98  NODE     DSECT
99  WRD      DS       CL8
100 FREQ     DS       F
101 NEXT     DS       A
102 NODELEN  EQU      *-NODE
103
104 WORDS    CSECT
105
106 START    DC       A(0)
107 BLANK    DC       C' '
108 OUT      DS       CL30            * OUTPUT STRING & TEMP STORE
109 MVC      MVC      OUT(0),0(R5)    * FOR EX INSTRUCTION
110 IN       DS       CL80            * INPUT STRING
111 COUNT    DC       F'0'            * NBR ENTRIES COUNT
112 *
```

```
113   * TRT TABLE TO CONVERT TO UPPER CASE AND REMOVE NON-ALPHAS

114   *

115   TRTAB     DC      256C' '

116             ORG     TRTAB+C'a'

117             DC      C'ABCDEFGHI'

118             ORG     TRTAB+C'A'

119             DC      C'ABCDEFGHI'

120

121             ORG     TRTAB+C'j'

122             DC      C'JKLMNOPQR'

123             ORG     TRTAB+C'J'

124             DC      C'JKLMNOPQR'

125

126             ORG     TRTAB+C's'

127             DC      C'STUVWXYZ'

128             ORG     TRTAB+C'S'

129             DC      C'STUVWXYZ'

130

131             ORG     TRTAB+C'-'     * RETAIN HYPHENS

132             DC      C'-'

133

134             ORG     TRTAB+C''''    * RETAIN SINGLE QUOTES

135             DC      C''''

136             ORG

137

138             LTORG                  * LTERALS AHEAD OF TABLE

139

140             DS      0F             * FULL WORD ALIGN

141   *

142   * TABLE IS 1000 ENTRIES. EACH IS 8 CHARS FOR WORD
```

```
14
3   * AND 4 BYTES COUNT.
14
4   *
14
5   CRNT      DC       A(TAB)
14
6   LIMIT     DC       A(TAB+16000)
14
7   TAB       DS       16000C
14
8
14
9             END      WORDS
```

Figure 93 Word Count with List

23.12 Iterative Calculation of PI

To calculate PI we need fractions. To this point, we have only discussed fixed point integers and floating point calculations are beyond the scope of this book as they are very specialized and not often done in assembly language. If floating point is needed, a FORTRAN subroutine is often written and called. But fixed point numbers can be used to calculate fractions. It is not required that we assume the binary or decimal point is to the right of all the digits. The assumed point could be elsewhere.

Anyone who has used an old mechanical calculator or who remembers some of the early primitive electronic calculators will be familiar with the concept of fixed point calculations where the point was fixed but not necessarily at the right end of the number. When using devices such as these, each number entered had an assumed decimal point, usually two digits to the left of the final digit. All numbers entered had to include a full set of digits to the right of the decimal point. On modern calculators, however, only the significant numbers are entered. For example, on a modern calculator to add 2.3, 3, 5.63, and 100, you would enter the numbers as shown. The calculator understands the significance of the decimal point and aligns the values correctly for addition.

However, on a fixed point calculator there is no decimal point key on the keyboard although there would be a fixed decimal point illuminated on the display ordinarily two positions from the right end of the display. Instead, in a fixed point calculator, you would enter the numbers above with the keystrokes 230, 300, 563, and 10000 and the calculator would perceive the numbers aligned as:

```
  2 30
  3 00
  5 63
100 00
```

Now, addition could proceed correctly by summing the columns in the usual manner and this would yield the same answer if you envision the fixed decimal point two positions to the left of the last digit. By assuming the presence of a decimal point at a fixed location in each number, it is possible to perform arithmetic that is similar to floating point. The same principle involved with fixed point calculations on calculators can be extended to packed decimal calculations as we show next.

Figure 94 gives a program which is an example of using fixed point packed decimals to calculate PI. It is based on the Gregory-Leibniz method which can be summarized as the series: PI/4 = 1 − 1/3 + 1/5 − 1/7 + 1/9 ...

the right hand side of which, in decimal, is:

$$1 - 0.3333 + 0.2000 - 0.1428 + 0.1111 \ldots$$

```
1 #include <stdio.h>
2
3 int main() {
4
5 int i,j=3;
6 double pi = 1.0;
7
8 for (i=0;i<500000; i++) {
9         if (i%2!=0) pi=pi+1.0/j;
10              else pi=pi-1.0/j;
11         j=j+2;
12        }
13 printf("iterations=%d pi=%f\n",i,4*pi);
14 return 0;
15 }
```

Figure 94 Calculation of PI in C

A C program to accomplish this is shown in Figure 94. The final value of i is multiplied by 4 to give PI. The formula converges very slowly so many iterations are needed to obtain even a modest number of digits of accuracy.

When using floating point (**double** in C), the PI program is simple because the divisions on lines 9 and 10 result in numbers with fractional parts. Thus, the calculation of 1.0/3.0 yields 0.333333333333333 when converted to decimal and printed.

However, a packed decimal division (DP instruction) of the same values yields 0 with a remainder of 1 which is not exactly what the formula requires. So, the question becomes, how can you get a series of numbers such as: 0.3333, 0.2000, 0.1428, 0.1111 and so forth?

The answer is quite simple. First, initialize PI as a large integer packed decimal number such as 10 000 000 000.

Next, take a large integer packed decimal number such as

```
10 000 000 000
```

and divide it by 3, 5, 7, 9 and so on. The results will be

```
3 333 333 333
2 000 000 000
1 428 571 428
1 111 111 111
```

and so forth (remainders ignored).

Add or subtract, as appropriate in the series, the results of the division to the candidate PI. If you print out PI at each step with a decimal point inserted after the first digit the results will be:

```
0.6666666667
0.8666666667
0.7238095239
0.8349206350
```

Which, when multiplied by 4, converges to PI.

The program in Figure 95 (output in Figure 96) follows the same pattern as the program in Figure 94.

On lines 5 and 6 we use the pre-processor to set the number of iterations (&ITER) of the series we will run. This is substituted into the Compare Packed instruction on line 40 during pre-processing (note: many iterations are required to begin to get a usable value for PI).

Register R3 is zeroed on line 3. This register will toggle between 0 and 1 to indicate if the next term of the equation is to be added or subtracted, respectively, from the approximation. The toggle is done by the Exclusive Or on line 23 which also sets the condition code to indicate the result in R3 thus saving a Compare instruction. If R3 is 1, and Exclusive OR with 1 results in 0. If R3 is 0, an Exclusive or with 1 results in 1. The Condition Code indicates if the result is or is not zero and this informs the Branch Conditional (BNE).

The denominator B is initially set to 1 in line 10. This is incremented by 2 in line 13 at the top of the main loop.

The numerator A for each term is set on line 14 to a very large power of 10. The denominator B is divided into it on line 16. The results of the DP are in are in A. The first 6 bytes of A are the quotient and the last 4 are the remainder. The quotient values will be 3 333 333 333, 2 000 000 000, 1 428 571 428, 1 111 111 111 and so forth. These are converted to printable decimal with

in line 18. The pattern PAT2 contains a decimal point so the numbers will display as

```
.333333333
.200000000
.142857142
.111111111
```

R3 is toggled and, depending on the new value, the quotient from A is added or subtracted to or from PI. Note the length of 6 in the AP and SP instructions. The quotient resides in the first 6 bytes of A while the remainder is in the final 4 bytes.

For display purposes the current value of PI is copied to P_CRNT, multiplied by 4 and printed. The loop continues if the result of the Compare Packed instruction on line 41 indicates we have not reached the required number of iterations.

```
1               PRINT      NOGEN
2               TITLE      'Gregory-Leibniz series calculation of PI'
3               EQUREGS
4
5               LCLA       &ITER
6   &ITER       SETA       100                    * NUMBER OF ITERATIONS
7
8   PICALC      SUBENTRY
9               SR         R3,R3
10              ZAP        B,=P'1'
11              XPRNT      HDR,L'HDR
12
13  LOOP        AP         B,=P'2'                * INCR DENOM: 3, 5, 7
14              ZAP        A,=P'10000000000'      * INIT numerator
15
16              DP         A,B                    * 1/3, 1/5, 1/7 ...
17              MVC        DEC_FRAC,PAT2
18              ED         DEC_FRAC,A             * AMOUNT TO ADD/SUB
19
20              MVC        DENOM,PAT1
21              ED         DENOM,B                * 3, 5, 7 ...
22
23              X          R3,=F'1'               * TOGGLE R3
24              BNE        SUB                    * NOT ZERO -> SUBTRACT
25
26              MVI        SGN,C'+'
27              AP         PI,A(6)                * ADD
28              B          L1
29
```

```
30 SUB      SP      PI,A(6)                 * SUBTRACT
31          MVI     SGN,C'-'
32
33 L1       ZAP     P_CRNT,PI
34
35          MP      P_CRNT,=P'4'            * MULT BY 4
36          MVC     P4,PAT2
37          ED      P4,P_CRNT
38
39          XPRNT   DENOM,OUT_END-DENOM     * LEN IS DIFF OF ADDRS
40          CP      B,=P'&ITER'             * AGAIN?
41          BNH     LOOP
42          XPRNT   DENOM,OUT_END-DENOM     * LEN IS DIFF OF ADDRS
43          SUBEXIT
44
45 A        DS      PL10
46 B        DS      PL4
47
                    C'  DENOM    S
48 HDR      DC      AMOUNT          PI'
49
50 DENOM    DS      CL8
51          DC      C' '
52 SGN      DS      C                       * ADD OR SUBTRACT TERM
53 DEC_FRAC DS      CL12
54          DC      C' '
55 P4       DS      CL13
56 OUT_END  EQU     *
57
58 PAT1     DC      X'F0212020202020202020202020202020'
59 PAT2     DC      X'40214B2020202020202020202020'
60 PI       DC      PL6'10000000000'
61 P_CRNT   DS      PL6
62          LTORG
63          END
```

Figure 95 Iterative Calculation of PI

```
00009977 +  .000100230   3.1417930932
00009979 -  .000100210   3.1413922516
00009981 +  .000100190   3.1417930128
00009983 -  .000100170   3.1413923320
00009985 +  .000100150   3.1417929328
00009987 -  .000100130   3.1413924124
00009989 +  .000100110   3.1417928528
00009991 -  .000100090   3.1413924928
```

```
00009993 +   .000100070   3.1417927728
00009995 -   .000100050   3.1413925728
00009997 +   .000100030   3.1417926928
00009999 -   .000100010   3.1413926528
00010001 +   .000099990   3.1417926128
00010001 +   .000099990   3.1417926128

              Figure 96 PI Iterations
```

Figure 96 shows the final 14 lines of output for an execution of 10,001 iterations.

23.13 Matrix Multiplication

Figure 97 is a program in C to multiply two matrices. Figure 98 gives an example of this program written in assembly language interspersed with comments from the C program. The assembly code corresponds to the C code with some exceptions.

At the beginning of the program (lines 16 through 30), are a number of pointers and integer counts to correspond to the C program declarations. These are branched around by the Branch instruction on line 12.

Basically, the program reads a line of input which contains the number of rows and columns of the first (A) matrix and second (B) matrix (lines 38 through 47). These values are stored in memory.

The number columns in the A matrix is compared with the number of rows in the B matrix. If they are unequal, the program halts (lines 54 through 59).

The dimensions of the result C matrix are calculated (lines 67 through 70).

The total memory requirements for the A matrix, the B matrix and the C matrix are calculated as the sum of number of rows times the number of columns times 4 (each element is a 4 byte fixed point binary integer) for each of the three matrices (lines 72 through 94). The final result, in R7, is passed to the GETMAIN macro on line 96. GETMAIN requests memory from the system. The result, the address of the area allocated by GETMAIN, is returned in R1. The length and address of the allocated area are stored in GLEN and GADDR.

The matrices are to be stored in the allocated area in row major order. That is, the first row followed by the second row and so forth. Lines 101 through 107 determine, based on lengths previously calculated, the addresses in the allocated area (APTR, BPTR and CPTR) of the first elements of each of the matrices and store the pointers to same in memory.

```c
#include <stdio.h>
#include <stdlib.h>

int main() {

        int arows, acols, brows, bcols;
        int *a, *b, *c;
         int i, j, k, m;

        // read dimensions

        scanf("%d %d %d %d",&arows, &acols, &brows, &bcols);

        if (acols != brows) {
                printf("Incompatible matrices\n");
                return 16;
                }

        // allocate matrices

        a =  (int *) malloc (arows * acols * 4);
        b =  (int *) malloc (brows * bcols * 4);
        c =  (int *) malloc (arows * bcols * 4);

        // initialize result matrix

        for (i = 0; i< arows * bcols; i++) * (c + i) = 0;

        // read a and b matrices

        for (i = 0; i < arows * acols; i++) scanf("%d", a + i);
        for (i = 0; i < brows * bcols; i++) scanf("%d", b + i);

        printf("Matrix A\n");
        for (i = 0; i < arows; i++) {
                for (j = 0; j < acols; j++) {
                        printf("%3d ",*(a + i * acols + j));
                        }
                printf("\n");
                }
        printf("\n");

        printf("Matrix B\n");
        for (i = 0; i < brows; i++) {
                for (j = 0; j < bcols; j++) {
                        printf("%3d ", * ( b + i * bcols + j));
                        }
                printf("\n");
                }
        printf("\n");

        // calculate product of a and b

        for (i = 0; i < arows; i++) { // for each a row
         for (j = 0; j < bcols; j++) { // for each b column
          for (k = 0; k < acols; k++) { // sum ( a[i][k] * b[k][j] )
           *(c+ i * bcols +j) = *(c+ i * bcols +j) + * (a + i *
acols
                                + k) * *(b+ k * bcols + j);
```

```
            }
        }
    }

    printf("Matrix C\n");
    for (i = 0; i < arows; i++) {
            for (j = 0; j < bcols; j++) {
                    printf("%3d ",* (c + i * bcols + j));
                    }
            printf("\n");
            }

    return 0;
    }
```

Lines 112 through 119 initialize the C matrix to zeros. It does this by calculating the number of elements (AROWS times BCOLS), then loading the starting address of the C matrix (CPTR) into R4 and, in a BCT loop (lines 117 through 119), storing zero at the address pointed to by R4. For each iteration, the address in R4 in incremented by four so as to point to the next element. This technique, initializing a two dimensional array as though it were a one dimensional vector, is the same as done in the C code shown on line 110.

Lines 124 through 146 read the A and B matrices. They assume that each matrix is on one input line whereas the C code (lines 122 and 135) will read multiple input lines. The input is assumed to be in row major order and the elements are scanned, converted to binary, and stored in sequential array locations in a manner similar to that done to initialize the C matrix. Note: at the time of this writing, the XDECI macro was not correctly processing negative numbers so all examples are shown only with positive input values.

Lines 158 through 198 print the A and B matrices using a nested loop technique similar to the C code shown on lines 150 through 156.

Initially the address of the array (APTR or BPTR) is loaded into R3 and the number of rows (AROWS or BROWS) loaded into R5. The output line is blanked with a ripple move and the number of columns and the address of the output print row (ROWOUT) are loaded.

For each element in a row, the Edit pattern is copied to NUM, the value pointed to by R3 is loaded and converted to packed decimal then Edited to zoned decimal (lines 168 to 171). The result is copied to the output row. The pointers to the output row (R7) and the input matrix (R3) are incremented by four. The process repeats for each element on a row. When all elements of a row have been converted to zoned decimal and placed in the output, the line is printed. The entire process repeats for each row by means of the BCTs.

The actual matrix multiplication takes place on lines 212 through 273. It follows the example in the C code on lines 202 through 210.

Registers R2, R3 and R4 correspond to C variables i, j, and k. The code consists of a three nested loop as in the C code. The outermost (for C variable I) reenters at label L8 for each iteration which promptly initializes j and k. The loop for variable j reenters at label L9 for each iteration and initializes k. Label L10 is the iteration entry point for the innermost loop, that involving k.

The looping mechanism is in lines 262 to 272. Lines 262 through 264 increment R4 (C program variable k) and test if it is still less than the limit AROWS. If so, it reiterates.

Likewise lines 266 through 268 and lines 270 through 272 test if R3 (C variable j) and R2 (C variable I) have reached their limits. The innermost loop iterates the most and the outermost the least, as in the C program.

Lines 222 through 260 calculate and sum the values that contribute to each element of the C matrix. Lines 222 through 229 calculate the address of which element of matrix C we are working on and store it. Likewise lines 231 through 238 and lines 240 through 247 calculate the addresses in the A and B matrices, respectively. The addresses are calculated in the same manner as the C program except for the multiplications by 4. In C, address arithmetic is done in units of the underlying data type which in this case has a length of 4. In assembly language, we must adjust the values by 4 as address arithmetic is always in units of one.

Once the addresses of the components have been calculated, lines 249 through 260 multiply the A matrix element by the B matrix element and add the result to the C matrix element and store the result.

Once the result C matrix has been calculated, it is printed (lines 284 through 305) in the same manner as used earlier to print the A and B matrices.

Example input and output are shown.

```
1    * #include <stdio.h>
2    * #include <stdlib.h>
3
4              PRINT    NOGEN
5              EQUREGS
6
7    * int main()
8    * {
9
10   MAIN     SUBENTRY
11
12             B        L1
13
14   *    int arows, acols,brows, bcols;
15
16   AROWS    DS       F  * NBR ROWS A MATRIX
17   ACOLS    DS       F  * NBR COLS A MATRIX
18   BROWS    DS       F  * NBR ROWS B MATRIX
19   BCOLS    DS       F  * NBR COLS B MATRIX
20   CROWS    DS       F  * NBR ROWS C MATRIX
21   CCOLS    DS       F  * NBR COLS A MATRIX
22
23   *    int *a, *b, *c;
24
25   APTR     DS       A  * A ARRAY START
26   BPTR     DS       A  * B ARRAY START
27   CPTR     DS       A  * C ARRAY START
28   AADDR    DS       A  * TEMP
29   BADDR    DS       A  * TEMP
30   CADDR    DS       A  * TEMP
31
32   *    int i, j, k;
33
34   *    // read dimensions
35
36   *    scanf("%d %d %d %d",&arows, &acols, &brows, &bcols);
37
38   L1       XREAD    IN,L'IN
39            LA       R1,IN
40            XDECI    R2,0(0,R1)
41            ST       R2,AROWS     * A ROWS
42            XDECI    R2,0(0,R1)
43            ST       R2,ACOLS     * A COLS
44            XDECI    R2,0(0,R1)
```

```
45          ST      R2,BROWS    * B ROWS
46          XDECI   R2,0(0,R1)
47          ST      R2,BCOLS    * B COLS
48
49  *   if (acols != brows) {
50  *       printf("Incompatible matrices\n");
51  *       return 16;
52  *   }
53
54          L       R2,ACOLS
55          C       R2,BROWS
56          BE      L2
57          XPRNT   ERR1,L'ERR1
58          SUBEXIT
59  ERR1    DC      C'Incompatible matrices'
60
61  *   // allocate matrices
62
63  *   a = (int *) malloc (arows * acols * 4);
64  *   b = (int *) malloc (brows * bcols * 4);
65  *   c = (int *) malloc (arows * bcols * 4);
66
67  L2      L       R2,AROWS
68          ST      R2,CROWS    * C ROWS
69          L       R2,BCOLS
70          ST      R2,CCOLS    * C COLS
71
72  *       CALCULATE MEMORY NEEDS
73
74          SR      R2,R2
75          L       R3,AROWS
76          M       R2,ACOLS    * AROWS * ACOLS
77          SLA     R3,2        * TIMES 4
78          LR      R4,R3       * NBR BYTES A MATRIX
79
80          SR      R2,R2
81          L       R3,BROWS
82          M       R2,BCOLS
83          SLA     R3,2
84          LR      R5,R3       * NBR BYTES B MATRIX
85
86          SR      R2,R2
87          L       R3,AROWS
88          M       R2,BCOLS
```

```
89            SLA     R3,2        * NBR BYTES C MATRIX
90            LR      R6,R3
91
92            LR      R7,R6
93            AR      R7,R5
94            AR      R7,R4       * TOT NBR BYTES NEEDED
95
96            GETMAIN RU,LV=(R7)  * ALLOCATE MEM - RSLT in R1
97
98            ST      R1,GADDR    * ADDR ALLOC MEM
99            ST      R7,GLEN     * LEN ALLOC MEM
100
101 *      CALCULATE ADDRS OF MATRICES IN ALLOC MEM
102
103           ST      R1,APTR     * ADDR A MATRIX
104           AR      R1,R4       * ADD SIZE OF A MATRIX
105           ST      R1,BPTR     * ADDR B MATRIX
106           AR      R1,R5       * ADD SIZE OF B MATRIX
107           ST      R1,CPTR     * ADDR C MATRIX
108
109 *   // initialize result matrix
110 *   for (i = 0; i< arows * bcols; i++) * (c + i) = 0;
111
112           L       R3,AROWS    * NBR A ROWS
113           SR      R2,R2       * ZERO
114           M       R2,BCOLS    * TIMES NBR B COLS. ANS IN R3
115           L       R4,CPTR     * START OF C MATRIX
116
117 L3        ST      R2,0(0,R4)  * R2 IS ZERO
118           LA      R4,4(0,R4)  * INCR TO NXT C WORD
119           BCT     R3,L3       * MORE?
120
121 *   // read a and b matrices
122 *   for (i = 0; i < arows * acols; i++) scanf("%d", a + i);
123
124           SR      R4,R4
125           L       R5,AROWS    * NBR A ROWS
126           M       R4,ACOLS    * TIMES NBR A COLS
127           L       R6,APTR     * ADDR OF A MATRIX
128           XREAD   IN,L'IN     * READ LINE
129           LA      R1,IN       * ADDR OF INPUT REC
130 L4        XDECI   R3,0(0,R1)  * SCAN INPUT
131           ST      R3,0(0,R6)
132           LA      R6,4(0,R6)
```

```
133           BCT      R5,L4        * R5 IS COUNT NBR VALS TO READ
134
135 *   for (i = 0; i < brows * bcols; i++) scanf("%d", b + i);
136
137           SR       R4,R4
138           L        R5,BROWS     * NBR B ROWS
139           M        R4,BCOLS     * TIMES NBR B COLS
140           L        R6,BPTR      * ADDR OF B
141           XREAD    IN,L'IN      * READ LINE
142           LA       R1,IN        * ADDR OF INPUT REC
143 L5        XDECI    R3,0(0,R1)   * SCAN INPUT
144           ST       R3,0(0,R6)
145           LA       R6,4(0,R6)
146           BCT      R5,L5        * R5 IS COUNT NBR VALS TO READ
147
148 ************************************************************
149
150 *   printf("Matrix A\n");
151 *   for (i = 0; i < arows; i++) {
152 *      for (j = 0; j < acols; j++) {
153 *        printf("%3d ",*(a + i * acols + j));
154 *      printf("\n");
155 *      }
156 *   printf("\n");
157
158           XPRNT    MSG1,L'MSG1
159
160           L        R3,APTR
161           L        R5,AROWS
162
163 L7        MVI      ROWOUT,C' '
164           MVC      ROWOUT+1(L'ROWOUT-1),ROWOUT
165           L        R6,ACOLS
166           LA       R7,ROWOUT
167
168 L6        MVC      NUM,NUMPAT    * ED PATTERN
169           L        R8,0(0,R3)    * MATRIX VALUE
170           CVD      R8,OUT        * CVT TO DECIMAL
171           ED       NUM,OUT+6     * CVT TO ZONED
172           MVC      0(4,R7),NUM   * ADD TO ROW
173           LA       R7,4(0,R7)    * ROW PTR
174           LA       R3,4(R3)      * MATRIX PTR
175           BCT      R6,L6         * FOR EACH ROW
176           XPRNT    ROWOUT,L'ROWOUT
```

```
177              BCT      R5,L7          * FOR EACH COL
178
179              XPRNT    MSG2,L'MSG2
180
181              L        R3,BPTR        * PRINT B - AS ABOVE
182              L        R5,BROWS
183
184 L7A          MVI      ROWOUT,C' '
185              MVC      ROWOUT+1(L'ROWOUT-1),ROWOUT
186              L        R6,BCOLS
187              LA       R7,ROWOUT
188
189 L6A          MVC      NUM,NUMPAT
190              L        R8,0(0,R3)
191              CVD      R8,OUT
192              ED       NUM,OUT+6
193              MVC      0(4,R7),NUM
194              LA       R7,4(0,R7)
195              LA       R3,4(R3)
196              BCT      R6,L6A
197              XPRNT    ROWOUT,L'ROWOUT
198              BCT      R5,L7A
199
200 *********************************************************
201
202 *    // calculate product of a and b
203 *    for (i = 0; i < arows; i++) { // for each a row
204 *     for (j = 0; j < bcols; j++) { // for each b col
205 *      for (k = 0; k < acols; k++) { // sum ( a[i][k] * b[k][j] )
206 *       *(c+ i * bcols +j) =
    *           *(c+ i * bcols + j) + * (a + i * acols + k) * *(b+ k *
207 bcols + j);
208 *             }
209 *           }
210 *       }
211
212              SR       R2,R2    * i
213              SR       R3,R3    * j
214              SR       R4,R4    * k
215
216 *        LOOP ENTRY PTS
217
218 L8          SR       R3,R3    * re-init j
219 L9          SR       R4,R4    * re-init k
```

261

```
220 L10      NOPR      R0

221

222          L         R6,CPTR     * c
223          SR        R8,R8       * ready for mult
224          LR        R9,R2       * i
225          M         R8,BCOLS    * i * bcols
226          AR        R9,R3       * add j
227          SLA       R9,2        * mult by 4.
228          AR        R6,R9       * *(c + i * bcols +j)
229          ST        R6,CADDR

230

231          L         R6,APTR     * a
232          SR        R8,R8       * ready for mult
233          LR        R9,R2       * i
234          M         R8,ACOLS    * i * acols
235          AR        R9,R4       * add k
236          SLA       R9,2        * mult by 4.
237          AR        R6,R9       * *(a + i * acols + k)
238          ST        R6,AADDR

239

240          L         R6,BPTR     * b
241          SR        R8,R8       * ready for mult
242          LR        R9,R4       * k
243          M         R8,BCOLS    * k * bcols
244          AR        R9,R3       * add j
245          SLA       R9,2        * mult by 4.
246          AR        R6,R9       * *(b + k * bcols + j)
247          ST        R6,BADDR

248

249          L         R7,CADDR
250          L         R5,0(0,R7)  * LOAD C VALUE
251          SR         R8,R8
252          L         R9,AADDR
253          L         R9,0(0,R9)  * LOAD A VALUE

254

255          L         R6,BADDR
256          M         R8,0(0,R6)   * MULT B VALUE BY A VALUE

257

258          AR        R5,R9        * ADD TO C

259

260          ST        R5,0(0,R7)   * STORE TO C

261

262          LA        R4,1(0,R4)
263          C         R4,ACOLS    * k < ACOLS ?
```

```
264           BL        L10         * NO - ITERATE
265
266           LA        R3,1(0,R3)
267           C         R3,BCOLS    * j < BCOLS
268           BL        L9          * NO - ITERATE
269
270           LA        R2,1(0,R2)
271           C         R2,AROWS    * i < AROWS ?
272           BL        L8          * NO - ITERATE
273
274   ************************************************************
275
276   *   printf("Matrix C\n");
277   *   for (i = 0; i < arows; i++) {
278   *       for (j = 0; j < bcols; j++) {
279   *           printf("%3d ",* (c + i * bcols + j));
280   *           }
281   *       printf("\n");
282   *       }
283
284           XPRNT     LINE,L'LINE
285
286   *       PRINT RESULT - SAME TECHNIQUE USED ABOVE
287
288           L         R3,CPTR
289           L         R5,CROWS
290
291 L11       MVI       ROWOUT,C' '
292           MVC       ROWOUT+1(L'ROWOUT-1),ROWOUT
293           L         R6,CCOLS
294           LA        R7,ROWOUT
295
296 L12       MVC       NUM,NUMPAT
297           L         R8,0(0,R3)
298           CVD       R8,OUT
299           ED        NUM,OUT+6
300           MVC       0(4,R7),NUM
301           LA        R7,4(0,R7)
302           LA        R3,4(R3)
303           BCT       R6,L12
304           XPRNT     ROWOUT,L'ROWOUT
305           BCT       R5,L11
306
307   *   return 0;
```

```
308 * }
309         SUBEXIT
310
311 GADDR    DS      A       * ADDR OF GETMAIN AREA
312 GLEN     DS      F       * AMOUNT GOT
313 IN       DS      CL80
314 OUT      DS      D
315 ROWOUT   DS      CL130
316 MSG1     DC      C'A Matrix'
317 MSG2     DC      C'B Matrix'
318 NUMPAT   DC      X'40202120'
319 NUM      DS      CL4
320 LINE     DC      C'-------------------------------------------'

321 TEMP     DS      CL12
322          LTORG
323          END

Input:
2 3 3 2
1 2 3 4 5 6
7 8 9 10 11 1

Output:
A Matrix
    1    2    3
    4    5    6
B Matrix
    7    8
    9   10
   11   12
-------------------------------------------
   58   64
  139  154
```

Figure 98 Matrix Multiplication

24. General Instruction Set

Note: The letter *C* in the format column means that the instruction sets the Condition Code.

Instruction	Mnemonic	Format	OpCode
ADD (extended BFP)	AXBR	RRE C	B34A
ADD (long BFP)	ADBR	RRE C	B31A
ADD (long BFP)	ADB	RXE C	ED1A
ADD (short BFP)	AEBR	RRE C	B30A
ADD (short BFP)	AEB	RXE C	ED0A
ADD (32)	AR	RR C	1A
ADD (32)	A	RX C	5A
ADD (32)	AY	RXY C	E35A
ADD (64<32)	AGFR	RRE C	B918
ADD (64<32)	AGF	RXY C	E318
ADD (64)	AGR	RRE C	B908
ADD (64)	AG	RXY C	E308
ADD DECIMAL	AP	SS C	FA
ADD HALFWORD	AH	RX C	4A
ADD HALFWORD	AHY	RXY C	E37A
ADD HALFWORD IMMEDIATE (32)	AHI	RI C	A7A
ADD HALFWORD IMMEDIATE (64)	AGHI	RI C	A7B
ADD LOGICAL (32)	ALR	RR C	1E
ADD LOGICAL (32)	AL	RX C	5E
ADD LOGICAL (32)	ALY	RXY C	E35E
ADD LOGICAL (64<32)	ALGFR	RRE C	B91A
ADD LOGICAL (64<32)	ALGF	RXY C	E31A
ADD LOGICAL (64)	ALGR	RRE C	B90A
ADD LOGICAL (64)	ALG	RXY C	E30A
ADD LOGICAL WITH CARRY (32)	ALCR	RRE C	B998
ADD LOGICAL WITH CARRY (32)	ALC	RXY C	E398
ADD LOGICAL WITH CARRY (64)	ALCGR	RRE C	B988
ADD LOGICAL WITH CARRY (64)	ALCG	RXY C	E388
ADD NORMALIZED (extended HFP)	AXR	RR C	36
ADD NORMALIZED (long HFP)	ADR	RR C	2A
ADD NORMALIZED (long HFP)	AD	RX C	6A
ADD NORMALIZED (short HFP)	AER	RR C	3A
ADD NORMALIZED (short HFP)	AE	RX C	7A
ADD UNNORMALIZED (long HFP)	AWR	RR C	2E
ADD UNNORMALIZED (long HFP)	AW	RX C	6E
ADD UNNORMALIZED (short HFP)	AUR	RR C	3E
ADD UNNORMALIZED (short HFP)	AU	RX C	7E
AND (character)	NC	SS C	D4
AND (immediate)	NI	SI C	94
AND (immediate)	NIY	SIY C	EB54
AND (32)	NR	RR C	14

Instruction	Mnemonic	Format		OpCode
AND (32)	N	RX	C	54
AND (32)	NY	RXY	C	E354
AND (64)	NGR	RRE	C	B980
AND (64)	NG	RXY	C	E380
AND IMMEDIATE (high high)	NIHH	RI	C	A54
AND IMMEDIATE (high low)	NIHL	RI	C	A55
AND IMMEDIATE (low high)	NILH	RI	C	A56
AND IMMEDIATE (low low)	NILL	RI	C	A57
BRANCH AND LINK	BALR	RR		05
BRANCH AND LINK	BAL	RX		45
BRANCH AND SAVE	BASR	RR		0D
BRANCH AND SAVE	BAS	RX		4D
BRANCH AND SAVE AND SET MODE	BASSM	RR		0C
BRANCH AND SET AUTHORITY	BSA	RRE		B25A
BRANCH AND SET MODE	BSM	RR		0B
BRANCH AND STACK	BAKR	RRE		B240
BRANCH IN SUBSPACE GROUP	BSG	RRE		B258
BRANCH ON CONDITION	BCR	RR		07
BRANCH ON CONDITION	BC	RX		47
BRANCH ON COUNT (32)	BCTR	RR		06
BRANCH ON COUNT (32)	BCT	RX		46
BRANCH ON COUNT (64)	BCTGR	RRE		B946
BRANCH ON COUNT (64)	BCTG	RXY		E346
BRANCH ON INDEX HIGH (32)	BXH	RS		86
BRANCH ON INDEX HIGH (64)	BXHG	RSY		EB44
BRANCH ON INDEX LOW OR EQUAL (32)	BXLE	RS		87
BRANCH ON INDEX LOW OR EQUAL (64)	BXLEG	RSY		EB45
BRANCH RELATIVE AND SAVE	BRAS	RI		A75
BRANCH RELATIVE AND SAVE LONG	BRASL	RIL		C05
BRANCH RELATIVE ON CONDITION	BRC	RI		A74
BRANCH RELATIVE ON CONDITION LONG	BRCL	RIL		C04
BRANCH RELATIVE ON COUNT (32)	BRCT	RI		A76
BRANCH RELATIVE ON COUNT (64)	BRCTG	RI		A77
BRANCH RELATIVE ON INDEX HIGH (32)	BRXH	RSI		84
BRANCH RELATIVE ON INDEX HIGH (64)	BRXHG	RIE		EC44
BRANCH RELATIVE ON INDEX L OR E (32)	BRXLE	RSI		85
BRANCH RELATIVE ON INDEX L OR E (64)	BRXLG	RIE		EC45
CANCEL SUBCHANNEL	XSCH	S	C	B276
CHECKSUM	CKSM	RRE	C	B241
CIPHER MESSAGE	KM	RRE	C	B92E
CIPHER MESSAGE WITH CHAINING	KMC	RRE	C	B92F
CLEAR SUBCHANNEL	CSCH	S	C	B230
COMPARE (extended BFP)	CXBR	RRE	C	B349
COMPARE (extended HFP)	CXR	RRE	C	B369
COMPARE (long BFP)	CDBR	RRE	C	B319

Instruction	Mnemonic	Format		OpCode
COMPARE (long BFP)	CDB	RXE	C	ED19
COMPARE (long HFP)	CDR	RR	C	29
COMPARE (long HFP)	CD	RX	C	69
COMPARE (short BFP)	CEBR	RRE	C	B309
COMPARE (short BFP)	CEB	RXE	C	ED09
COMPARE (short HFP)	CER	RR	C	39
COMPARE (short HFP)	CE	RX	C	79
COMPARE (32)	CR	RR	C	19
COMPARE (32)	C	RX	C	59
COMPARE (32)	CY	RXY	C	E359
COMPARE (64<32)	CGFR	RRE	C	B930
COMPARE (64<32)	CGF	RXY	C	E330
COMPARE (64)	CGR	RRE	C	B920
COMPARE (64)	CG	RXY	C	E320
COMPARE AND FORM CODEWORD	CFC	S	C	B21A
COMPARE AND SIGNAL (extended BFP)	KXBR	RRE	C	B348
COMPARE AND SIGNAL (long BFP)	KDBR	RRE	C	B318
COMPARE AND SIGNAL (long BFP)	KDB	RXE	C	ED18
COMPARE AND SIGNAL (short BFP)	KEBR	RRE	C	B308
COMPARE AND SIGNAL (short BFP)	KEB	RXE	C	ED08
COMPARE AND SWAP (32)	CS	RS	C	BA
COMPARE AND SWAP (32)	CSY	RSY	C	EB14
COMPARE AND SWAP (64)	CSG	RSY	C	EB30
COMPARE AND SWAP AND PURGE	CSP	RRE	C	B250
COMPARE AND SWAP AND PURGE	CSPG	RRE	C	B98A
COMPARE DECIMAL	CP	SS	C	F9
COMPARE DOUBLE AND SWAP (32)	CDS	RS	C	BB
COMPARE DOUBLE AND SWAP (32)	CDSY	RSY	C	EB31
COMPARE DOUBLE AND SWAP (64)	CDSG	RSY	C	EB3E
COMPARE HALFWORD	CH	RX	C	49
COMPARE HALFWORD	CHY	RXY	C	E379
COMPARE HALFWORD IMMEDIATE (32)	CHI	RI	C	A7E
COMPARE HALFWORD IMMEDIATE (64)	CGHI	RI	C	A7F
COMPARE LOGICAL (character)	CLC	SS	C	D5
COMPARE LOGICAL (immediate)	CLI	SI	C	95
COMPARE LOGICAL (immediate)	CLIY	SIY	C	EB55
COMPARE LOGICAL (32)	CLR	RR	C	15
COMPARE LOGICAL (32)	CL	RX	C	55
COMPARE LOGICAL (32)	CLY	RXY	C	E355
COMPARE LOGICAL (64<32)	CLGFR	RRE	C	B931
COMPARE LOGICAL (64<32)	CLGF	RXY	C	E331
COMPARE LOGICAL (64)	CLGR	RRE	C	B921
COMPARE LOGICAL (64)	CLG	RXY	C	E321
COMPARE LOGICAL C. UNDER MASK (high)	CLMH	RSY	C	EB20
COMPARE LOGICAL C. UNDER MASK (low)	CLM	RS	C	BD

Instruction	Mnemonic	Format	OpCode
COMPARE LOGICAL C. UNDER MASK (low)	CLMY	RSY C	EB21
COMPARE LOGICAL LONG	CLCL	RR C	0F
COMPARE LOGICAL LONG EXTENDED	CLCLE	RS C	A9
COMPARE LOGICAL LONG UNICODE	CLCLU	RSY C	EB8F
COMPARE LOGICAL STRING	CLST	RRE C	B25D
COMPARE UNTIL SUBSTRING EQUAL	CUSE	RRE C	B257
COMPRESSION CALL	CMPSC	RRE C	B263
COMPUTE INTERMEDIATE MESSAGE DIGEST	KIMD	RRE C	B93E
COMPUTE LAST MESSAGE DIGEST	KLMD	RRE C	B93F
COMPUTE MESSAGE AUTHENTICATION CODE	KMAC	RRE C	B91E
CONVERT BFP TO HFP (long)	THDR	RRE C	B359
CONVERT BFP TO HFP (short to long)	THDER	RRE C	B358
CONVERT FROM FIXED (32 to ext. BFP)	CXFBR	RRE	B396
CONVERT FROM FIXED (32 to ext. HFP)	CXFR	RRE	B3B6
CONVERT FROM FIXED (32 to long BFP)	CDFBR	RRE	B395
CONVERT FROM FIXED (32 to long HFP)	CDFR	RRE	B3B5
CONVERT FROM FIXED (32 to short BFP)	CEFBR	RRE	B394
CONVERT FROM FIXED (32 to short HFP)	CEFR	RRE	B3B4
CONVERT FROM FIXED (64 to ext. BFP)	CXGBR	RRE	B3A6
CONVERT FROM FIXED (64 to ext. HFP)	CXGR	RRE	B3C6
CONVERT FROM FIXED (64 to long BFP)	CDGBR	RRE	B3A5
CONVERT FROM FIXED (64 to long HFP)	CDGR	RRE	B3C5
CONVERT FROM FIXED (64 to short BFP)	CEGBR	RRE	B3A4
CONVERT FROM FIXED (64 to short HFP)	CEGR	RRE	B3C4
CONVERT HFP TO BFP (long to short)	TBEDR	RRF C	B350
CONVERT HFP TO BFP (long)	TBDR	RRF C	B351
CONVERT TO BINARY (32)	CVB	RX	4F
CONVERT TO BINARY (32)	CVBY	RXY	E306
CONVERT TO BINARY (64)	CVBG	RXY	E30E
CONVERT TO DECIMAL (32)	CVD	RX	4E
CONVERT TO DECIMAL (32)	CVDY	RXY	E326
CONVERT TO DECIMAL (64)	CVDG	RXY	E32E
CONVERT TO FIXED (ext. BFP to 32)	CFXBR	RRF C	B39A
CONVERT TO FIXED (ext. BFP to 64)	CGXBR	RRF C	B3AA
CONVERT TO FIXED (ext. HFP to 32)	CFXR	RRF C	B3BA
CONVERT TO FIXED (ext. HFP to 64)	CGXR	RRF C	B3CA
CONVERT TO FIXED (long BFP to 32)	CFDBR	RRF C	B399
CONVERT TO FIXED (long BFP to 64)	CGDBR	RRF C	B3A9
CONVERT TO FIXED (long HFP to 32)	CFDR	RRF C	B3B9
CONVERT TO FIXED (long HFP to 64)	CGDR	RRF C	B3C9
CONVERT TO FIXED (short BFP to 32)	CFEBR	RRF C	B398
CONVERT TO FIXED (short BFP to 64)	CGEBR	RRF C	B3A8
CONVERT TO FIXED (short HFP to 32)	CFER	RRF C	B3B8
CONVERT TO FIXED (short HFP to 64)	CGER	RRF C	B3C8
CONVERT UNICODE TO UTF-8	CUUTF	RRE C	B2A6

Instruction	Mnemonic	Format	OpCode
CONVERT UTF-16 TO UTF-32	CU24	RRE C	B9B1
CONVERT UTF-16 TO UTF-8	CU21	RRE C	B2A6
CONVERT UTF-32 TO UTF-16	CU42	RRE C	B9B3
CONVERT UTF-32 TO UTF-8	CU41	RRE C	B9B2
CONVERT UTF-8 TO UNICODE	CUTFU	RRE C	B2A7
CONVERT UTF-8 TO UTF-16	CU12	RRE C	B2A7
CONVERT UTF-8 TO UTF-32	CU14	RRE C	B9B0
COPY ACCESS	CPYA	RRE	B24D
DIAGNOSE			83
DIVIDE (extended BFP)	DXBR	RRE	B34D
DIVIDE (extended HFP)	DXR	RRE	B22D
DIVIDE (long BFP)	DDBR	RRE	B31D
DIVIDE (long BFP)	DDB	RXE	ED1D
DIVIDE (long HFP)	DDR	RR	2D
DIVIDE (long HFP)	DD	RX	6D
DIVIDE (short BFP)	DEBR	RRE	B30D
DIVIDE (short BFP)	DEB	RXE	ED0D
DIVIDE (short HFP)	DER	RR	3D
DIVIDE (short HFP)	DE	RX	7D
DIVIDE (32<64)	DR	RR	1D
DIVIDE (32<64)	D	RX	5D
DIVIDE DECIMAL	DP	SS	FD
DIVIDE LOGICAL (32<64)	DLR	RRE	B997
DIVIDE LOGICAL (32<64)	DL	RXY	E397
DIVIDE LOGICAL (64<128)	DLGR	RRE	B987
DIVIDE LOGICAL (64<128)	DLG	RXY	E387
DIVIDE SINGLE (64<32)	DSGFR	RRE	B91D
DIVIDE SINGLE (64<32)	DSGF	RXY	E31D
DIVIDE SINGLE (64)	DSGR	RRE	B90D
DIVIDE SINGLE (64)	DSG	RXY	E30D
DIVIDE TO INTEGER (long BFP)	DIDBR	RRF C	B35B
DIVIDE TO INTEGER (short BFP)	DIEBR	RRF C	B353
EDIT	ED	SS C	DE
EDIT AND MARK	EDMK	SS C	DF
EXCLUSIVE OR (character)	XC	SS C	D7
EXCLUSIVE OR (immediate)	XI	SI C	97
EXCLUSIVE OR (immediate)	XIY	SIY C	EB57
EXCLUSIVE OR (32)	XR	RR C	17
EXCLUSIVE OR (32)	X	RX C	57
EXCLUSIVE OR (32)	XY	RXY C	E357
EXCLUSIVE OR (64)	XGR	RRE C	B982
EXCLUSIVE OR (64)	XG	RXY C	E382
EXECUTE	EX	RX	44
EXTRACT ACCESS	EAR	RRE	B24F
EXTRACT AND SET EXTENDED AUTHORITY	ESEA	RRE	B99D

Instruction	Mnemonic	Format	OpCode
EXTRACT FPC	EFPC	RRE	B38C
EXTRACT PRIMARY ASN	EPAR	RRE	B226
EXTRACT PRIMARY ASN AND INSTANCE	EPAIR	RRE	B99A
EXTRACT PSW	EPSW	RRE	B98D
EXTRACT SECONDARY ASN	ESAR	RRE	B227
EXTRACT SECONDARY ASN AND INSTANCE	ESAIR	RRE	B99B
EXTRACT STACKED REGISTERS (32)	EREG	RRE	B249
EXTRACT STACKED REGISTERS (64)	EREGG	RRE	B90E
EXTRACT STACKED STATE	ESTA	RRE C	B24A
HALT SUBCHANNEL	HSCH	S C	B231
HALVE (long HFP)	HDR	RR	24
HALVE (short HFP)	HER	RR	34
INSERT ADDRESS SPACE CONTROL	IAC	RRE C	B224
INSERT CHARACTER	IC	RX	43
INSERT CHARACTER	ICY	RXY	E373
INSERT CHARACTERS UNDER MASK (high)	ICMH	RSY C	EB80
INSERT CHARACTERS UNDER MASK (low)	ICM	RS C	BF
INSERT CHARACTERS UNDER MASK (low)	ICMY	RSY C	EB81
INSERT IMMEDIATE (high high)	IIHH	RI	A50
INSERT IMMEDIATE (high low)	IIHL	RI	A51
INSERT IMMEDIATE (low high)	IILH	RI	A52
INSERT IMMEDIATE (low low)	IILL	RI	A53
INSERT PROGRAM MASK	IPM	RRE	B222
INSERT PSW KEY	IPK	S	B20B
INSERT STORAGE KEY EXTENDED	ISKE	RRE	B229
INSERT VIRTUAL STORAGE KEY	IVSK	RRE	B223
INVALIDATE DAT TABLE ENTRY	IDTE	RRF	B98E
INVALIDATE PAGE TABLE ENTRY	IPTE	RRE	B221
LOAD (extended)	LXR	RRE	B365
LOAD (long)	LDR	RR	28
LOAD (long)	LD	RX	68
LOAD (long)	LDY	RXY	ED65
LOAD (short)	LER	RR	38
LOAD (short)	LE	RX	78
LOAD (short)	LEY	RXY	ED64
LOAD (32)	LR	RR	18
LOAD (32)	L	RX	58
LOAD (32)	LY	RXY	E358
LOAD (64<32)	LGFR	RRE	B914
LOAD (64<32)	LGF	RXY	E314
LOAD (64)	LGR	RRE	B904
LOAD (64)	LG	RXY	E304
LOAD ACCESS MULTIPLE	LAM	RS	9A
LOAD ACCESS MULTIPLE	LAMY	RSY	EB9A
LOAD ADDRESS	LA	RX	41

Instruction	Mnemonic	Format	OpCode
LOAD ADDRESS	LAY	RXY	E371
LOAD ADDRESS EXTENDED	LAE	RX	51
LOAD ADDRESS RELATIVE LONG	LARL	RIL	C00
LOAD ADDRESS SPACE PARAMETERS	LASP	SSE C	E500
LOAD AND TEST (extended BFP)	LTXBR	RRE C	B342
LOAD AND TEST (extended HFP)	LTXR	RRE C	B362
LOAD AND TEST (long BFP)	LTDBR	RRE C	B312
LOAD AND TEST (long HFP)	LTDR	RR C	22
LOAD AND TEST (short BFP)	LTEBR	RRE C	B302
LOAD AND TEST (short HFP)	LTER	RR C	32
LOAD AND TEST (32)	LTR	RR C	12
LOAD AND TEST (64<32)	LTGFR	RRE C	B912
LOAD AND TEST (64)	LTGR	RRE C	B902
LOAD BYTE (32)	LB	RXY	E376
LOAD BYTE (64)	LGB	RXY	E377
LOAD COMPLEMENT (extended BFP)	LCXBR	RRE C	B343
LOAD COMPLEMENT (extended HFP)	LCXR	RRE C	B363
LOAD COMPLEMENT (long BFP)	LCDBR	RRE C	B313
LOAD COMPLEMENT (long HFP)	LCDR	RR C	23
LOAD COMPLEMENT (short BFP)	LCEBR	RRE C	B303
LOAD COMPLEMENT (short HFP)	LCER	RR C	33
LOAD COMPLEMENT (32)	LCR	RR C	13
LOAD COMPLEMENT (64<32)	LCGFR	RRE C	B913
LOAD COMPLEMENT (64)	LCGR	RRE C	B903
LOAD CONTROL (32)	LCTL	RS	B7
LOAD CONTROL (64)	LCTLG	RSY	EB2F
LOAD FP INTEGER (extended BFP)	FIXBR	RRF	B347
LOAD FP INTEGER (extended HFP)	FIXR	RRE	B367
LOAD FP INTEGER (long BFP)	FIDBR	RRF	B35F
LOAD FP INTEGER (long HFP)	FIDR	RRE	B37F
LOAD FP INTEGER (short BFP)	FIEBR	RRF	B357
LOAD FP INTEGER (short HFP)	FIER	RRE	B377
LOAD FPC	LFPC	S	B29D
LOAD HALFWORD (32)	LH	RX	48
LOAD HALFWORD (32)	LHY	RXY	E378
LOAD HALFWORD (64)	LGH	RXY	E315
LOAD HALFWORD IMMEDIATE (32)	LHI	RI	A78
LOAD HALFWORD IMMEDIATE (64)	LGHI	RI	A79
LOAD LENGTHENED (long to ext. BFP)	LXDBR	RRE	B305
LOAD LENGTHENED (long to ext. BFP)	LXDB	RXE	ED05
LOAD LENGTHENED (long to ext. HFP)	LXDR	RRE	B325
LOAD LENGTHENED (long to ext. HFP)	LXD	RXE	ED25
LOAD LENGTHENED (short to ext. BFP)	LXEBR	RRE	B306
LOAD LENGTHENED (short to ext. BFP)	LXEB	RXE	ED06
LOAD LENGTHENED (short to ext. HFP)	LXER	RRE	B326

Instruction	Mnemonic	Format	OpCode
LOAD LENGTHENED (short to ext. HFP)	LXE	RXE	ED26
LOAD LENGTHENED (short to long BFP)	LDEBR	RRE	B304
LOAD LENGTHENED (short to long BFP)	LDEB	RXE	ED04
LOAD LENGTHENED (short to long HFP)	LDER	RRE	B324
LOAD LENGTHENED (short to long HFP)	LDE	RXE	ED24
LOAD LOGICAL (64<32)	LLGFR	RRE	B916
LOAD LOGICAL (64<32)	LLGF	RXY	E316
LOAD LOGICAL CHARACTER	LLGC	RXY	E390
LOAD LOGICAL HALFWORD	LLGH	RXY	E391
LOAD LOGICAL IMMEDIATE (high high)	LLIHH	RI	A5C
LOAD LOGICAL IMMEDIATE (high low)	LLIHL	RI	A5D
LOAD LOGICAL IMMEDIATE (low high)	LLILH	RI	A5E
LOAD LOGICAL IMMEDIATE (low low)	LLILL	RI	A5F
LOAD LOGICAL THIRTY ONE BITS	LLGTR	RRE	B917
LOAD LOGICAL THIRTY ONE BITS	LLGT	RXY	E317
LOAD MULTIPLE (32)	LM	RS	98
LOAD MULTIPLE (32)	LMY	RSY	EB98
LOAD MULTIPLE (64)	LMG	RSY	EB04
LOAD MULTIPLE DISJOINT	LMD	SS	EF
LOAD MULTIPLE HIGH	LMH	RSY	EB96
LOAD NEGATIVE (extended BFP)	LNXBR	RRE C	B341
LOAD NEGATIVE (extended HFP)	LNXR	RRE C	B361
LOAD NEGATIVE (long BFP)	LNDBR	RRE C	B311
LOAD NEGATIVE (long HFP)	LNDR	RR C	21
LOAD NEGATIVE (short BFP)	LNEBR	RRE C	B301
LOAD NEGATIVE (short HFP)	LNER	RR C	31
LOAD NEGATIVE (32)	LNR	RR C	11
LOAD NEGATIVE (64<32)	LNGFR	RRE C	B911
LOAD NEGATIVE (64)	LNGR	RRE C	B901
LOAD PAIR FROM QUADWORD	LPQ	RXY	E38F
LOAD POSITIVE (extended BFP)	LPXBR	RRE C	B340
LOAD POSITIVE (extended HFP)	LPXR	RRE C	B360
LOAD POSITIVE (long BFP)	LPDBR	RRE C	B310
LOAD POSITIVE (long HFP)	LPDR	RR C	20
LOAD POSITIVE (short BFP)	LPEBR	RRE C	B300
LOAD POSITIVE (short HFP)	LPER	RR C	30
LOAD POSITIVE (32)	LPR	RR C	10
LOAD POSITIVE (64<32)	LPGFR	RRE C	B910
LOAD POSITIVE (64)	LPGR	RRE C	B900
LOAD PSW	LPSW	S	82
LOAD PSW EXTENDED	LPSWE	S	B2B2
LOAD REAL ADDRESS (32)	LRA	RX C	B1
LOAD REAL ADDRESS (32)	LRAY	RXY C	E313
LOAD REAL ADDRESS (64)	LRAG	RXY C	E303
LOAD REVERSED (16)	LRVH	RXY	E31F

Instruction	Mnemonic	Format	OpCode
LOAD REVERSED (32)	LRVR	RRE	B91F
LOAD REVERSED (32)	LRV	RXY	E31E
LOAD REVERSED (64)	LRVGR	RRE	B90F
LOAD REVERSED (64)	LRVG	RXY	E30F
LOAD ROUNDED (extended to long BFP)	LDXBR	RRE	B345
LOAD ROUNDED (extended to long HFP)	LDXR	RR	25
LOAD ROUNDED (extended to long HFP)	LRDR	RR	25
LOAD ROUNDED (extended to short BFP)	LEXBR	RRE	B346
LOAD ROUNDED (extended to short HFP)	LEXR	RRE	B366
LOAD ROUNDED (long to short BFP)	LEDBR	RRE	B344
LOAD ROUNDED (long to short HFP)	LEDR	RR	35
LOAD ROUNDED (long to short HFP)	LRER	RR	35
LOAD USING REAL ADDRESS (32)	LURA	RRE	B24B
LOAD USING REAL ADDRESS (64)	LURAG	RRE	B905
LOAD ZERO (extended)	LZXR	RRE	B376
LOAD ZERO (long)	LZDR	RRE	B375
LOAD ZERO (short)	LZER	RRE	B374
MODIFY STACKED STATE	MSTA	RRE	B247
MODIFY SUBCHANNEL	MSCH	S C	B232
MONITOR CALL	MC	SI	AF
MOVE (character)	MVC	SS	D2
MOVE (immediate)	MVI	SI	92
MOVE (immediate)	MVIY	SIY	EB52
MOVE INVERSE	MVCIN	SS	E8
MOVE LONG	MVCL	RR C	0E
MOVE LONG EXTENDED	MVCLE	RS C	A8
MOVE LONG UNICODE	MVCLU	RSY C	EB8E
MOVE NUMERICS	MVN	SS	D1
MOVE PAGE	MVPG	RRE C	B254
MOVE STRING	MVST	RRE C	B255
MOVE TO PRIMARY	MVCP	SS C	DA
MOVE TO SECONDARY	MVCS	SS C	DB
MOVE WITH DESTINATION KEY	MVCDK	SSE	E50F
MOVE WITH KEY	MVCK	SS C	D9
MOVE WITH OFFSET	MVO	SS	F1
MOVE WITH SOURCE KEY	MVCSK	SSE	E50E
MOVE ZONES	MVZ	SS	D3
MULTIPLY (extended BFP)	MXBR	RRE	B34C
MULTIPLY (extended HFP)	MXR	RR	26
MULTIPLY (long to extended BFP)	MXDBR	RRE	B307
MULTIPLY (long to extended BFP)	MXDB	RXE	ED07
MULTIPLY (long to extended HFP)	MXDR	RR	27
MULTIPLY (long to extended HFP)	MXD	RX	67
MULTIPLY (long BFP)	MDBR	RRE	B31C
MULTIPLY (long BFP)	MDB	RXE	ED1C

Instruction	Mnemonic	Format	OpCode
MULTIPLY (long HFP)	MDR	RR	2C
MULTIPLY (long HFP)	MD	RX	6C
MULTIPLY (short to long BFP)	MDEBR	RRE	B30C
MULTIPLY (short to long BFP)	MDEB	RXE	ED0C
MULTIPLY (short to long HFP)	MDER	RR	3C
MULTIPLY (short to long HFP)	MER	RR	3C
MULTIPLY (short to long HFP)	MDE	RX	7C
MULTIPLY (short to long HFP)	ME	RX	7C
MULTIPLY (short BFP)	MEEBR	RRE	B317
MULTIPLY (short BFP)	MEEB	RXE	ED17
MULTIPLY (short HFP)	MEER	RRE	B337
MULTIPLY (short HFP)	MEE	RXE	ED37
MULTIPLY (64<32)	MR	RR	1C
MULTIPLY (64<32)	M	RX	5C
MULTIPLY AND ADD (long BFP)	MADBR	RRF	B31E
MULTIPLY AND ADD (long BFP)	MADB	RXF	ED1E
MULTIPLY AND ADD (long HFP)	MADR	RRF	B33E
MULTIPLY AND ADD (long HFP)	MAD	RXF	ED3E
MULTIPLY AND ADD (short BFP)	MAEBR	RRF	B30E
MULTIPLY AND ADD (short BFP)	MAEB	RXF	ED0E
MULTIPLY AND ADD (short HFP)	MAER	RRF	B32E
MULTIPLY AND ADD (short HFP)	MAE	RXF	ED2E
MULTIPLY AND SUBTRACT (long BFP)	MSDBR	RRF	B31F
MULTIPLY AND SUBTRACT (long BFP)	MSDB	RXF	ED1F
MULTIPLY AND SUBTRACT (long HFP)	MSDR	RRF	B33F
MULTIPLY AND SUBTRACT (long HFP)	MSD	RXF	ED3F
MULTIPLY AND SUBTRACT (short BFP)	MSEBR	RRF	B30F
MULTIPLY AND SUBTRACT (short BFP)	MSEB	RXF	ED0F
MULTIPLY AND SUBTRACT (short HFP)	MSER	RRF	B32F
MULTIPLY AND SUBTRACT (short HFP)	MSE	RXF	ED2F
MULTIPLY DECIMAL	MP	SS	FC
MULTIPLY HALFWORD (32)	MH	RX	4C
MULTIPLY HALFWORD IMMEDIATE (32)	MHI	RI	A7C
MULTIPLY HALFWORD IMMEDIATE (64)	MGHI	RI	A7D
MULTIPLY LOGICAL (128<64)	MLGR	RRE	B986
MULTIPLY LOGICAL (128<64)	MLG	RXY	E386
MULTIPLY LOGICAL (64<32)	MLR	RRE	B996
MULTIPLY LOGICAL (64<32)	ML	RXY	E396
MULTIPLY SINGLE (32)	MSR	RRE	B252
MULTIPLY SINGLE (32)	MS	RX	71
MULTIPLY SINGLE (32)	MSY	RXY	E351
MULTIPLY SINGLE (64<32)	MSGFR	RRE	B91C
MULTIPLY SINGLE (64<32)	MSGF	RXY	E31C
MULTIPLY SINGLE (64)	MSGR	RRE	B90C
MULTIPLY SINGLE (64)	MSG	RXY	E30C

Instruction	Mnemonic	Format		OpCode
OR (character)	OC	SS	C	D6
OR (immediate)	OI	SI	C	96
OR (immediate)	OIY	SIY	C	EB56
OR (32)	OR	RR	C	16
OR (32)	O	RX	C	56
OR (32)	OY	RXY	C	E356
OR (64)	OGR	RRE	C	B981
OR (64)	OG	RXY	C	E381
OR IMMEDIATE (high high)	OIHH	RI	C	A58
OR IMMEDIATE (high low)	OIHL	RI	C	A59
OR IMMEDIATE (low high)	OILH	RI	C	A5A
OR IMMEDIATE (low low)	OILL	RI	C	A5B
PACK	PACK	SS		F2
PACK ASCII	PKA	SS		E9
PACK UNICODE	PKU	SS		E1
PAGE IN	PGIN	RRE	C	B22E
PAGE OUT	PGOUT	RRE	C	B22F
PERFORM LOCKED OPERATION	PLO	SS	C	EE
PROGRAM CALL	PC	S		B218
PROGRAM RETURN	PR	E		0101
PROGRAM TRANSFER	PT	RRE		B228
PROGRAM TRANSFER WITH INSTANCE	PTI	RRE		B99E
PURGE ALB	PALB	RRE		B248
PURGE TLB	PTLB	S		B20D
RESET CHANNEL PATH	RCHP	S	C	B23B
RESET REFERENCE BIT EXTENDED	RRBE	RRE	C	B22A
RESUME PROGRAM	RP	S		B277
RESUME SUBCHANNEL	RSCH	S	C	B238
ROTATE LEFT SINGLE LOGICAL (32)	RLL	RSY		EB1D
ROTATE LEFT SINGLE LOGICAL (64)	RLLG	RSY		EB1C
SEARCH STRING	SRST	RRE	C	B25E
SEARCH STRING UNICODE	SRSTU	RRE	C	B9BE
SET ACCESS	SAR	RRE		B24E
SET ADDRESS LIMIT	SAL	S		B237
SET ADDRESS SPACE CONTROL	SAC	S		B219
SET ADDRESS SPACE CONTROL FAST	SACF	S		B279
SET ADDRESSING MODE (24)	SAM24	E		010C
SET ADDRESSING MODE (31)	SAM31	E		010D
SET ADDRESSING MODE (64)	SAM64	E		010E
SET CHANNEL MONITOR	SCHM	S		B23C
SET CLOCK	SCK	S	C	B204
SET CLOCK COMPARATOR	SCKC	S		B206
SET CLOCK PROGRAMMABLE FIELD	SCKPF	E		0107
SET CPU TIMER	SPT	S		B208
SET FPC	SFPC	RRE		B384

Instruction	Mnemonic	Format		OpCode
SET PREFIX	SPX	S		B210
SET PROGRAM MASK	SPM	RR		04
SET PSW KEY FROM ADDRESS	SPKA	S		B20A
SET ROUNDING MODE	SRNM	S		B299
SET SECONDARY ASN	SSAR	RRE		B225
SET SECONDARY ASN WITH INSTANCE	SSAIR	RRE		B99F
SET STORAGE KEY EXTENDED	SSKE	RRE		B22B
SET SYSTEM MASK	SSM	S		80
SHIFT AND ROUND DECIMAL	SRP	SS	C	F0
SHIFT LEFT DOUBLE	SLDA	RS	C	8F
SHIFT LEFT DOUBLE LOGICAL	SLDL	RS		8D
SHIFT LEFT SINGLE (32)	SLA	RS	C	8B
SHIFT LEFT SINGLE (64)	SLAG	RSY	C	EB0B
SHIFT LEFT SINGLE LOGICAL (32)	SLL	RS		89
SHIFT LEFT SINGLE LOGICAL (64)	SLLG	RSY		EB0D
SHIFT RIGHT DOUBLE	SRDA	RS	C	8E
SHIFT RIGHT DOUBLE LOGICAL	SRDL	RS		8C
SHIFT RIGHT SINGLE (32)	SRA	RS	C	8A
SHIFT RIGHT SINGLE (64)	SRAG	RSY	C	EB0A
SHIFT RIGHT SINGLE LOGICAL (32)	SRL	RS		88
SHIFT RIGHT SINGLE LOGICAL (64)	SRLG	RSY		EB0C
SIGNAL PROCESSOR	SIGP	RS	C	AE
SQUARE ROOT (extended BFP)	SQXBR	RRE		B316
SQUARE ROOT (extended HFP)	SQXR	RRE		B336
SQUARE ROOT (long BFP)	SQDBR	RRE		B315
SQUARE ROOT (long BFP)	SQDB	RXE		ED15
SQUARE ROOT (long HFP)	SQDR	RRE		B244
SQUARE ROOT (long HFP)	SQD	RXE		ED35
SQUARE ROOT (short BFP)	SQEBR	RRE		B314
SQUARE ROOT (short BFP)	SQEB	RXE		ED14
SQUARE ROOT (short HFP)	SQER	RRE		B245
SQUARE ROOT (short HFP)	SQE	RXE		ED34
START SUBCHANNEL	SSCH	S	C	B233
STORE (long)	STD	RX		60
STORE (long)	STDY	RXY		ED67
STORE (short)	STE	RX		70
STORE (short)	STEY	RXY		ED66
STORE (32)	ST	RX		50
STORE (32)	STY	RXY		E350
STORE (64)	STG	RXY		E324
STORE ACCESS MULTIPLE	STAM	RS		9B
STORE ACCESS MULTIPLE	STAMY	RSY		EB9B
STORE CHANNEL PATH STATUS	STCPS	S		B23A
STORE CHANNEL REPORT WORD	STCRW	S	C	B239
STORE CHARACTER	STC	RX		42

Instruction	Mnemonic	Format	OpCode
STORE CHARACTER	STCY	RXY	E372
STORE CHARACTERS UNDER MASK (high)	STCMH	RSY	EB2C
STORE CHARACTERS UNDER MASK (low)	STCM	RS	BE
STORE CHARACTERS UNDER MASK (low)	STCMY	RSY	EB2D
STORE CLOCK	STCK	S C	B205
STORE CLOCK COMPARATOR	STCKC	S	B207
STORE CLOCK EXTENDED	STCKE	S C	B278
STORE CONTROL (32)	STCTL	RS	B6
STORE CONTROL (64)	STCTG	RSY	EB25
STORE CPU ADDRESS	STAP	S	B212
STORE CPU ID	STIDP	S	B202
STORE CPU TIMER	STPT	S	B209
STORE FACILITY LIST	STFL	S	B2B1
STORE FPC	STFPC	S	B29C
STORE HALFWORD	STH	RX	40
STORE HALFWORD	STHY	RXY	E370
STORE MULTIPLE (32)	STM	RS	90
STORE MULTIPLE (32)	STMY	RSY	EB90
STORE MULTIPLE (64)	STMG	RSY	EB24
STORE MULTIPLE HIGH	STMH	RSY	EB26
STORE PAIR TO QUADWORD	STPQ	RXY	E38E
STORE PREFIX	STPX	S	B211
STORE REAL ADDRESS	STRAG	SSE	E502
STORE REVERSED (16)	STRVH	RXY	E33F
STORE REVERSED (32)	STRV	RXY	E33E
STORE REVERSED (64)	STRVG	RXY	E32F
STORE SUBCHANNEL	STSCH	S C	B234
STORE SYSTEM INFORMATION	STSI	S C	B27D
STORE THEN AND SYSTEM MASK	STNSM	SI	AC
STORE THEN OR SYSTEM MASK	STOSM	SI	AD
STORE USING REAL ADDRESS (32)	STURA	RRE	B246
STORE USING REAL ADDRESS (64)	STURG	RRE	B925
SUBTRACT (extended BFP)	SXBR	RRE C	B34B
SUBTRACT (long BFP)	SDBR	RRE C	B31B
SUBTRACT (long BFP)	SDB	RXE C	ED1B
SUBTRACT (short BFP)	SEBR	RRE C	B30B
SUBTRACT (short BFP)	SEB	RXE C	ED0B
SUBTRACT (32)	SR	RR C	1B
SUBTRACT (32)	S	RX C	5B
SUBTRACT (32)	SY	RXY C	E35B
SUBTRACT (64<32)	SGFR	RRE C	B919
SUBTRACT (64<32)	SGF	RXY C	E319
SUBTRACT (64)	SGR	RRE C	B909
SUBTRACT (64)	SG	RXY C	E309

Instruction	Mnemonic	Format	OpCode
SUBTRACT DECIMAL	SP	SS C	FB
SUBTRACT HALFWORD	SH	RX C	4B
SUBTRACT HALFWORD	SHY	RXY C	E37B
SUBTRACT LOGICAL (32)	SLR	RR C	1F
SUBTRACT LOGICAL (32)	SL	RX C	5F
SUBTRACT LOGICAL (32)	SLY	RXY C	E35F
SUBTRACT LOGICAL (64<32)	SLGFR	RRE C	B91B
SUBTRACT LOGICAL (64<32)	SLGF	RXY C	E31B
SUBTRACT LOGICAL (64)	SLGR	RRE C	B90B
SUBTRACT LOGICAL (64)	SLG	RXY C	E30B
SUBTRACT LOGICAL WITH BORROW (32)	SLBR	RRE C	B999
SUBTRACT LOGICAL WITH BORROW (32)	SLB	RXY C	E399
SUBTRACT LOGICAL WITH BORROW (64)	SLBGR	RRE C	B989
SUBTRACT LOGICAL WITH BORROW (64)	SLBG	RXY C	E389
SUBTRACT NORMALIZED (extended HFP)	SXR	RR C	37
SUBTRACT NORMALIZED (long HFP)	SDR	RR C	2B
SUBTRACT NORMALIZED (long HFP)	SD	RX C	6B
SUBTRACT NORMALIZED (short HFP)	SER	RR C	3B
SUBTRACT NORMALIZED (short HFP)	SE	RX C	7B
SUBTRACT UNNORMALIZED (long HFP)	SWR	RR C	2F
SUBTRACT UNNORMALIZED (long HFP)	SW	RX C	6F
SUBTRACT UNNORMALIZED (short HFP)	SUR	RR C	3F
SUBTRACT UNNORMALIZED (short HFP)	SU	RX C	7F
SUPERVISOR CALL	SVC	I	0A
TEST ACCESS	TAR	RRE C	B24C
TEST ADDRESSING MODE	TAM	E C	010B
TEST AND SET	TS	S C	93
TEST BLOCK	TB	RRE C	B22C
TEST DATA CLASS (extended BFP)	TCXB	RXE C	ED12
TEST DATA CLASS (long BFP)	TCDB	RXE C	ED11
TEST DATA CLASS (short BFP)	TCEB	RXE C	ED10
TEST DECIMAL	TP	RSL C	EBC0
TEST PENDING INTERRUPTION	TPI	S C	B236
TEST PROTECTION	TPROT	SSE C	E501
TEST SUBCHANNEL	TSCH	S C	B235
TEST UNDER MASK	TM	SI C	91
TEST UNDER MASK	TMY	SIY C	EB51
TEST UNDER MASK (high high)	TMHH	RI C	A72
TEST UNDER MASK (high low)	TMHL	RI C	A73
TEST UNDER MASK (low high)	TMLH	RI C	A70
TEST UNDER MASK (low low)	TMLL	RI C	A71
TEST UNDER MASK HIGH	TMH	RI C	A70

Instruction	Mnemonic	Format		OpCode
TEST UNDER MASK LOW	TML	RI	C	A71
TRACE (32)	TRACE	RS		99
TRACE (64)	TRACG	RSY		EB0F
TRANSLATE	TR	SS		DC
TRANSLATE AND TEST	TRT	SS	C	DD
TRANSLATE AND TEST REVERSED	TRTR	SS	C	D0
TRANSLATE EXTENDED	TRE	RRE	C	B2A5
TRANSLATE ONE TO ONE	TROO	RRE	C	B993
TRANSLATE ONE TO TWO	TROT	RRE	C	B992
TRANSLATE TWO TO ONE	TRTO	RRE	C	B991
TRANSLATE TWO TO TWO	TRTT	RRE	C	B990
TRAP	TRAP2	E		01FF
TRAP	TRAP4	S		B2FF
UNPACK	UNPK	SS		F3
UNPACK ASCII	UNPKA	SS	C	EA
UNPACK UNICODE	UNPKU	SS	C	E2
UPDATE TREE	UPT	E	C	0102
ZERO AND ADD	ZAP	SS	C	F8

Table 40 Instructions

Over the years people have suggested a number of interesting if less practical extensions (humorously, that is) as shown in Figure 99.

```
ARG : Agree to Run Garbage
BDM : Branch and Destroy Memory
CMN : Convert to Mayan Numerals
DDS : Damage Disk and Stop
EMR : Emit Microwave Radiation
ETO : Emulate Toaster Oven
FSE : Fake Serious Error
GSI : Garble Subsequent Instructions
GQS : Go Quarter Speed
HEM : Hide Evidence of Malfunction
IDD : Inhale Dust and Die
IKI : Ignore Keyboard Input
IMU : Irradiate and Mutate User
JPF : Jam Paper Feed
JUM : Jeer at Users Mistake
KFP : Kindle Fire in Printer
LNM : Launch Nuclear Missiles
MAW : Make Aggravating Whine
NNI : Neglect Next Instruction
OBU : Overheat and Burn if Unattended
PNG : Pass Noxious Gas
QWF : Quit Working Forever
QVC : Question Valid Command
RWD : Read Wrong Device
SCE : Simulate Correct Execution
SDJ : Send Data to Japan
TTC : Tangle Tape and Crash
UBC : Use Bad Chip
```

```
VDP    : Violate Design Parameters
VMB    : Verify and Make Bad
WAF    : Warn After Fact
XID    : eXchange Instruction with Data
YII    : Yield to Irresistible Impulse
ZAM    : Zero All Memory
PI     : Punch Invalid
POPI   : Punch Operator Immediately
RASC   : Read And Shred Card
RPM    : Read Programmers Mind
RSSC   : Reduce Speed, Step Carefully  (for improved accuracy)
RTAB   : Rewind Tape and Break
RWDSK  : ReWind DiSK
SPSW   : Scramble Program Status Word
SRSD   : Seek Record and Scar Disk
WBT    : Water Binary Tree
```

Exhibit 1 Over-Extended Instructions

25. EBCDIC Table

Dec	Hex	Code
0	0	NUL
1	01	SOH
2	02	STX
3	03	ETX
4	04	PF
5	05	HT
6	06	LC
7	07	DEL
8	08	
9	09	
10	0A	SMM
11	0B	VT
12	0C	FF
13	0D	CR
14	0E	SO
15	0F	SI
16	10	DLE
17	11	DC1
18	12	DC2
19	13	TM
20	14	RES
21	15	NL
22	16	BS
23	17	IL
24	18	CAN
25	19	EM
26	1A	CC
27	1B	CU1
28	1C	IFS
29	1D	IGS
30	1E	IRS
31	1F	IUS
32	20	DS

33	21	SOS
34	22	FS
35	23	
36	24	BYP
37	25	LF
38	26	ETB
39	27	ESC
40	28	
41	29	
42	2A	SM
43	2B	CU2
44	2C	
45	2D	ENQ
46	2E	ACK
47	2F	BEL
48	30	
49	31	
50	32	SYN
51	33	
52	34	PN
53	35	RS
54	36	UC
55	37	EOT
56	38	
57	39	
58	3A	
59	3B	CU3
60	3C	DC4
61	3D	NAK
62	3E	
63	3F	SUB

64	40	SP
65	41	
66	42	
67	43	

68	44	
69	45	
70	46	
71	47	
72	48	
73	49	
74	4A	¢
75	4B	.
76	4C	<
77	4D	(
78	4E	+
79	4F	|
80	50	&
81	51	
82	52	
83	53	
84	54	
85	55	
86	56	
87	57	
88	58	
89	59	
90	5A	!
91	5B	$
92	5C	*
93	5D	)
94	5E	;
95	5F	¬

96	60	–
97	61	/
98	62	
99	63	
100	64	
101	65	
102	66	

103	67	
104	68	
105	69	
106	6A	
107	6B	'
108	6C	%
109	6D	_
110	6E	>
111	6F	?
112	70	
113	71	
114	72	
115	73	
116	74	
117	75	
118	76	
119	77	
120	78	
121	79	
122	7A	:
123	7B	#
124	7C	@
125	7D	'
126	7E	=
127	7F	"

128	80	
129	81	a
130	82	b
131	83	c
132	84	d
133	85	e
134	86	f
135	87	g
136	88	h
137	89	i

138	8A	
139	8B	
140	8C	
141	8D	
142	8E	
143	8F	
144	90	
145	91	j
146	92	k
147	93	l
148	94	m
149	95	n
150	96	o
151	97	p
152	98	q
153	99	r
154	9A	
155	9B	
156	9C	
157	9D	
158	9E	
159	9F	

160	A0	
161	A1	
162	A2	s
163	A3	t
164	A4	u
165	A5	v
166	A6	w
167	A7	x
168	A8	y
169	A9	z
170	AA	
171	AB	
172	AC	

173	AD	
174	AE	
175	AF	
176	B0	
177	B1	
178	B2	
179	B3	
180	B4	
181	B5	
182	B6	
183	B7	
184	B8	
185	B9	`
186	BA	
187	BB	
188	BC	
189	BD	
190	BE	
191	BF	

192	C0	
193	C1	A
194	C2	B
195	C3	C
196	C4	D
197	C5	E
198	C6	F
199	C7	G
200	C8	H
201	C9	I
202	CA	
203	CB	
204	CC	
205	CD	
206	CE	
207	CF	

208	D0	
209	D1	J
210	D2	K
211	D3	L
212	D4	M
213	D5	N
214	D6	O
215	D7	P
216	D8	Q
217	D9	R
218	DA	
219	DB	
220	DC	
221	DD	
222	DE	
223	DF	

224	E0	
225	E1	
226	E2	S
227	E3	T
228	E4	U
229	E5	V
230	E6	W
231	E7	X
232	E8	Y
233	E9	Z
234	EA	
235	EB	
236	EC	
237	ED	
238	EE	
239	EF	
240	F0	0
241	F1	1
242	F2	2

243	F3	3
244	F4	4
245	F5	5
246	F6	6
247	F7	7
248	F8	8
249	F9	9
250	FA	
251	FB	
252	FC	
253	FD	
254	FE	
255	FF	

26. Index

www.ingramcontent.com/pod-product-compliance
Lightning Source LLC
Chambersburg PA
CBHW071544080326
40689CB00061B/1809